GLUTEN
FOR
PUNISHMENT

GLUTEN FOR PUNISHMENT

Just Desserts for the Heartbroken, Lovesick, and Jilted

JULIE SEYLER

Quarter Note Publishing • Orange, California

Library of Congress Control Number: 2025902712

Book Cover by Sally Rinehart
Chapter Illustrations by Michael Gamstetter

First Edition: 2025
Printed in the United States of America
Quarter Note Publishing

CONTENTS

AN UNEXPECTED
MEMOIR

THESE PAGES BEGAN THEIR LIFE AS A COOKBOOK—a gluten-filled, sugar-laden, calorie-packed collection of my favorite dessert recipes. And, just like my blog, TwoBitTart.com, I envisioned sprinkling these tantalizing treats with some witty anecdotes from my life as a serial monogamist. Delicious desserts and disastrous dating—easy peasy, right? Well, that was the plan, anyway. I never imagined the stories behind these recipes would lead me down a rocky road of unanticipated self-discovery.

We give birth to our "children," nudging them toward the path we dream they'll travel, but, alas, our willful little darlings possess a mind all their own. This book, like a mischievous two-year-old child, squirmed from my grasp early on, toddling off in its own direction, regardless of where I envisioned steering it. I sat down to craft a little vignette featuring my ex-boyfriend Brett, only to find myself lost in a whirlwind of words. What started as a crumb of an anecdote about a first kiss soon ballooned into thirty pages, much like when I plan to eat one modest slice of *Mom's Fruit Kuchen*, but find myself going back for seconds and then thirds in a dessert fugue, the entire tray devoured in one evening. I believe this is called "being in the zone." If only being in the dessert-eating zone were lauded like it is in golf: "Shhh…let's watch her concentration as she returns to cut another slice, this one from the corner of the tray. Look at her finesse."

To ensure our offspring reach their full potential, we must accept them for who they are, not who we dreamed they'd become. This book knew it was a memoir at heart, yearning to escape, and I finally accepted that truth.

Within these pages, I lay bare a random collection of six fractured romantic fairy tales spanning three decades. I've splayed myself out like a suckling pig roasting on a spit, exploring the gristly morsels of my heart's calamities alongside the wisdom I've gathered along the way. As the narratives unfold, you'll journey with me through the universal landscapes of romance, heartache, resilience, and self-transformation. You'll witness my struggle to break free from problematic partners in search of some poorly defined romantic intangible, eventually leading me toward my own version of happily ever after.

Opening this memoir, and interwoven between these intense narratives, are insightful and sometimes amusing observations on relatable experiences such as first dates, final breakups, and the many faces of romance   literary palate cleansers amid the heady tones often accompanying these untenable relationships.

By punctuating these chapters with dessert recipes, I share my unwavering conviction that sugar, butter, and flour not only transform into a balm for my oft-wounded heart, but also act as my love language and Rosetta Stone for deciphering the road map to real commitment. A relationship I've labeled a "toxic mind-fuck" and the richest *German Chocolate Cake* ever become the catalysts that set off this march toward healing and self-empowerment.

I hope these words and recipes provide solace and a ray of recognition for other wayward romantics, perpetually snaring the wrong one, the unavailable one, the crazy one, the toxic one. If the meat grinder of romance has chewed you up and spit you out again, don't send another drunken *"I miss you"* text. Put down your Kleenex and pick up your spatula. Bake a batch of soft, chewy *Oatmeal Apple Date Cookies*, snuggle into your favorite chair, and dig in, because nothing pacifies a mutilated heart quite like freshly baked treats.

Take comfort. You are not alone. I'm right there with you, navigating the labyrinth of love and, in the meantime, soothing its gut punches, one sweet bite at a time.

Bon appétit.

one

PALATE CLEANSER

ooo

BLOSSOMING

An Assortment of First Dates,
First Kisses,
and Budding Romance

BODY LANGUAGE

I recognize this evening as a nonstarter before I even order my Sauvignon Blanc. I realize before my ass has warmed the bar stool, before my first sip from the glass. My date has managed to "casually touch" my thigh and arm a half-dozen times during our first few minutes of conversation. I don't need to wear my body language decoder ring—I get it; you're interested. Now back off. Ten minutes into the conversation, Mr. Gropey declares he wants to "claim" me as his own and our next date should be close to my place, in my neighborhood.

Next date? I'm squirming through this one—and I'm beginning to believe you're stalker material as well.

Our tactile evening continues with me receiving a demonstration of his cowork-er's hugging techniques followed by an unsolicited and awkward one-handed back rub. Mr. Gropey has unquestionably grabbed or stroked me at least three dozen times. Body language hint: If your date is recoiling and slowly sliding away to regain her personal space, Stop. With. The. Hands.

I glance pleadingly at the cute, tattooed bartender (alas, wedding ring). My eyes say, *Wish him into the cornfield, please, Anthony.* But the bartender is not Anthony, and this is not *The Twilight Zone.*

Okay…polite conversation, polite conversation. I can do this. It's difficult to unlearn the "good girls shouldn't be rude" teaching of my youth, even when faced with someone of Mr. Gropey's ilk. Just smile, finish my wine, and leave—fast. I'm out the door in forty minutes flat, but he insists on walking me to my car. *Please don't try to hug, kiss, or molest me at my vehicle.*

Safely in my car, and not surprisingly, I receive Mr. Gropey's text on the quick ten-minute drive home, *"Good night, Sweetheart."* Sweetheart already? Disturbing.

Reaching the safety of home, I'm tempted to beeline for the kitchen. This kind of dating debacle deserves an edible pacifier—a chocolate cake with thick chocolate frosting, devoured in one sitting. But there's no way I'm getting back behind the wheel, even for ingredients. I know the perfect antidote: *Incredibly Easy Sugar Cookies*—culinary Xanax scented with vanilla, crafted with ingredients I have on hand and, most importantly, out of the oven before my car's engine has even cooled.

SEVEN SECONDS

Glen, one of the senior executives where I work, has agreed to sit in on a panel interview with a potential candidate for my team. The company, a behemoth, top-three bank, likely in an overcautious response to a long-settled lawsuit, has developed a thirty-page booklet of rigid HR interviewing requirements. These constraints render this entire question-answer interview process pointless. We are forbidden from asking nonapproved, off-booklet questions, even innocuous ones like, "This job requires working late nights and some weekends. Will that be a problem for you?"

Following two prescreening telephone calls, the process has advanced to the in-person panel interview. A collection of colleagues, senior managers including Glen, and I gather in the small conference room. The candidate, dressed in sensible interview-navy skirt and blazer, sits at the head of the long wooden expanse of table. As we go around the stuffy room, we take turns asking her banal, preselected questions such as, "Tell me about a time a project didn't turn out the way you expected."

Regrettably, I'm afraid our candidate overprepared the previous evening, reading interview tips online like "How to Get Your Key Points Across in an Interview," or she has watched too many politicians artfully or inartfully skirt the press. She manages to avoid the initial two questions asked of her. She replies with the points she is prepared to speak on, answering with statements such as, "I'd like to focus on the projects that went exactly as expected. For example…" Prohibited from veering off script, we can't clarify with, "That's great, but can you respond to the question we asked?" My colleagues and I exchange glances across the table, tight half smiles pasted beneath rolling eyeballs.

"I'll be right back," Glen says, standing up and excusing himself from the conference room. I assume he's headed to the restroom and will return shortly. As the minutes tick by, it dawns on me he's left for good. Glen, a busy executive with little tolerance for others' bullshit, doesn't appreciate her attempts at obfuscation. His vote is "nay" regarding this particular candidate and he's done wasting time. Rather than spend precious minutes of his busy day adhering to some absurd interviewing etiquette, I imagine Glen has sauntered back to his office to tackle the unending emails, calls, and spreadsheets piling up, without a second thought. The rest of us, nudging each other under the table once we catch on, are envious of his decisive action.

ooo

In business interactions, like the one I just described, as well as social dealings—including ones of the amorous variety—researchers have discovered it takes a quick seven seconds to determine your first, and enduring, impression of another person. Seven seconds to assess if the individual in front of you is kind, trustworthy, intelligent—attractive, even. For my purposes, deciding if they're dating material.

I'm partial to online dating's convenience and practicality—quickly swiping left on January 6th insurrectionists, fuck boys, and men who obviously don't know or care about the difference between "their," "they're," and "there." Occasionally, however, I swipe right—and get it terribly wrong.

As my date walks assuredly toward me, I realize tonight's an expanse of wasted time, for both of us. I *know* I'm not interested and, even if he's interested, I'm still not interested. The jauntily worn hat that looked "aging ska" in his profile, reads "self-important prig" in person. What read as manners in his bio is exposed to be, in fact, a staunch adherence to antiquated 1950s gender roles, regardless of my preference to place my own cappuccino order at the counter. I whisper a little thank-you to myself, at least, for sticking to my steadfast rule of limiting first meetings to a quick coffee or drink.

Once we are seated at a table near the window in Portola Coffee, drinks in hand, I ask questions and he pontificates…about himself…for forty-five minutes, with nary a question in return. I essentially interview Mr. Bluster so he can blather on, impressing himself, at least, with his unmatched knowledge and incontrovertible opinions. He drones on about his brainiac tech career, his kids who attend MIT and Yale, and his expertise on every subject: homelessness, religion—even one I know intimately from my raver days, drug use. If I dare attempt to wiggle in a counterpoint to contradict his soliloquy, Mr. Bluster abruptly cuts me off mid-sentence. I search the coffeehouse, looking for a soapbox I can scoot closer to his location.

There's a brief pause in his self-aggrandizement to proclaim I am not permitted to call myself an atheist since I haven't studied the Bible cover to cover and in depth as, of course, he has. This pundit opines that the unhoused choose to live on the streets because he personally visited the Santa Ana Riverbed and spoke to the inhabitants of the tent city there. They confirmed his theory that they prefer these living conditions to any other option. Naturally they confirmed his premise, those poor souls probably couldn't get a word in edgewise to refute him. During our interminable time together, I'm subjected to mansplaining, condescension, boasting. I feel my V-jay snapping shut like an abalone. I gulp down my scalding cappuccino and furtively scan the coffeehouse for the nearest escape hatch, like airline passengers are encouraged to do before takeoff. "The exit closest to you may be behind your seat."

While he drones on like Hamlet in Act III, Scene I, "To be, or not to be, blah, blah blah…," my mind wanders and I fantasize about starting a dating convention that allows either party to walk away in the first few seconds without explanation: the seven-second rule, aka Glen's Law.

Seven seconds, heck we could even make it ten, for those who prefer round numbers, time enough to size up the other person and deliberately decide to either add more quarters to the parking meter or hightail it back home. "Shall we continue?" is all that needs to be asked, efficiently weeding out the "hell nos" without guilt. I'm reminded of dogs sniffing each other's butts at the dog park. They decipher friend from foe within a sniff or two and go from there. Instead, I'm stuck listening to Mr. Bluster's boastful blathering for the next forty-four minutes and fifty-three seconds, my eyes glazing over like two donuts, wondering, *Did I really leave the refuge of my kitchen for this?*

WILD KINGDOM

Today, we will witness the often misunderstood and perplexing mating ritual of *Homo sapiens*. While the particular Southern California habitat we are exploring this evening remains overpopulated with the species, the triumph of finding, enticing, and eventually capturing a suitable mate can be quite elusive—a puzzling dichotomy worthy of additional observation. As such, the "online-dating" method shown here enables the connection of potential mates who would not otherwise cross paths in daily interactions. Take, for example, the male and female *Homo sapiens* we observe during our expedition.

We have entered a restaurant on Friday night, an Italian restaurant in downtown Long Beach, the ideal environment in which to observe a mating ritual. Although they account for only approximately eleven percent of California restaurants overall, the Italian restaurant provides a careful balance of amorous atmosphere including flickering table candles, coupled with a safe, public location, at an affordable price—the ideal habitat for a successful first or second encounter.

Behold the female of our species, perched on a bar stool in her brightly colored, curve-hugging new BCBG dress and heels, waiting impatiently and periodically glancing toward the door.

Her potential mate enters, and the female's initial reaction appears one of disappointment. Aware of her proclivity for dismissing prospective mates on first encounter, this female has willingly agreed to this second assignation, but now seems to be reconsidering her decision.

She recalls his physiognomy from the previous week, and his appearance doesn't seem to elicit a more favorable response on this occasion. His display of a bizarrely uneven goatee seems to be the cause of her puzzlement. Firstly, because he doesn't seem to realize his proudly displayed facial manscaping is asymmetrical and, secondly, because this particular feature has become almost extinct in this region, waning in popularity a quarter century ago. Yet, our male remains optimistic.

The pair settles into a table for two, surrounded by others of their species, all in various stages of the mating process. Our male seems unfamiliar with the correct steps in this mating dance, and so he stares at the female blankly with his black, unblinking eyes. Uncomfortable under his vacant gaze, the female scrambles for a topic of conversation to break the ice. We hear her enquire, "What did you do today?" This halfhearted attempt at dialogue scores her no points in originality. The male primate responds, but his vocalizations are monotone, dull, lackluster. Stimulating conversation skills are vital if he wants to attract a mate, and I'm afraid this dating ritual has so far gone awry for our male.

The female, seeking to inject some vivacity into the evening from the bottom of a wine glass, catches a server's attention, securing a book known as a wine list. The server deftly positions the tome in the male's limp and uncertain hands. The male stares uncomprehendingly at the massive list of reds versus whites, glasses versus bottles, duplicating the gaze he displayed to the female moments earlier. The wine selection ritual is traditionally the role of the male of the species, yet he appears out of his depth. In an effort to preserve his ego, our female surreptitiously coaxes him toward a Chianti Classico Riserva, pretending she doesn't sense wine selection is a skill he has yet to master. Our female is not an expert in the field but is familiar enough to know the difference between Merlots and Malbecs. Yet, adhering to convention, she remains relegated to peering over his arm, demurely offering suggestions.

When the server returns with a bottle, label presented to our male as is customary, our pair of potential lovebirds moves on to the food-ordering portion of the evening. Our male orders ravioli, always a safe bet, and gapes perplexedly when the female primate orders the exotic-sounding *gnocchi*. Our female appears stunned our male has never heard of these ubiquitous Italian dumplings before. These fluffy potato pillows are an Italian restaurant staple, available even at the corner Olive Garden.

She surmises our male was raised on an island, one other than Sicily, under a proverbial rock. Uh-oh, it seems our male has secured her disinterest.

There is nothing inherently wrong with him. He is a gentleman, but unfortunately, a rather dull one. Despite his impeccable manners, he lacks the chemistry and shared interests needed to captivate our discerning female. She has tried with this potential mate—twice—both attempts resulting in resounding failures. At forty-seven, our male has yet to master the art of mate capture, a far cry from the ebullient birds of paradise mating ritual observed during our recent New Guinea expedition, full of copulatory exhibitions of feathers and flourishes. Our discerning female finds her companion's subpar display and mating dance lacking, overshadowed by her hope for more vibrant and skillful rivals she has yet to encounter.

The female has made her final decisive determination regarding this potential mate and, once dinner has concluded, she prepares to return to her own nest, kick off her heels, and wiggle out of her dress. After showing appropriate appreciation, our female soon departs his company. This time, for good.

FISHING

Your first kiss gently caresses my lips, yet its tide surges through my blood and sinew. Can I convey all that is wrapped within this one pure, simple gesture? There's the "jigging" before the kiss, playful glances and banter about nothing, our attention too focused on the inevitable for meaningful words. Toying touches electrify the air. A skim of your fingers across my knee. The slightest effervescing as my arm grazes yours. A line cast across an expanse of river. You linger to prolong this moment. Yet, throughout this game, you tug gently, attempting to draw me toward you through the riffles with your invisible line. I fight the urge to move, eyeing your bait from my haven between the rocks. "Please," a moan, instinctive and primal, escapes from within me, "I cannot wait any longer." I strain against the lure. I cannot look into your eyes. At last, the slightest stirring animates your being and, with an almost indiscernible shifting toward your quarry, your lips ensnare mine and I succumb.

I am caught.

Don't ask me for permission—words have deserted me. Can't you see my answer is yes? Kiss me and let me drown in the eddy of your soft lips on mine. With your tongue, wrench me from the center of my being. I am dizzy. I am floating, entrapped within your net. A torrent surges through my veins and churns hot along my spine. I am languid within your arms. Breathe your warmth into me. Where do I end and where do you begin? I don't know, I don't care—just let this kiss wash over me forever.

PRECARIOUS ROUTES

Dating a sparkling new love interest requires navigating precarious routes, not unlike those rickety rope bridges suspended above roiling Amazonian rivers, the ones in every Indiana Jones film. Say the wrong thing, show too much interest—or a lack thereof—and the entire contraption and both you and your love interest plunge into the abyss below. Sheer disaster. I've learned to tread slowly and deliberately along this dating bridge, testing each unstable slat before trusting the brittle wood will support my weight.

Today, I'm baking three kinds of *Chocolate-Dipped Biscotti* for two catering jobs. I've also made dinner plans with a new guy, following a promising first date. My initial instincts suggest I gather a few biscotti, pop them in a decorative cellophane bag tied with raffia, and hand them to him as a little gift. Why not? I am already committed for over sixteen dozen. What's the harm in a handful of cookies redirected his way?

Within seconds, my dating catastrophe alert system overrides this innocuous intention. Whoop, Whoop, Whoop! Warning, rethink that move.

How would he interpret the gesture, I wonder. Would he imagine I spent all day slaving over a hot stove, baking sugary professions of my adoration for him? Would I be accused of moving too quickly? Instead of asking myself, *When can we sleep together without sending the wrong signals?* my version is more like, *When can I bake for him without him concluding it's my dessert rendition of Marry Me Chicken?*

I can almost hear him exclaim to a buddy:

"Shit, dude, it's only our second date and she was already baking me cookies. Psycho."

I'm frustrated by this unstable bridge I'm forced to gingerly traverse. It's absurd that I have to conceal my true self and my talents in an effort to avoid frightening a man and causing the bridge to collapse. This is the same bridge many women must travel, in the world of romance as well as life—approach slowly, don't make any sudden movements or loud noises, step carefully and deliberately, and don't forget to smile.

So, I leave the biscotti at home, arriving at our dinner empty handed, resolved to keep my talents under wraps—and in the kitchen—for now. If we succeed in surviving a few more dates, then I'll break out my alchemical flour, sugar, and butter prowess for his wonderment.

AFTERTHOUGHT

Hello, Friday night. It's another solitary one for me. I've cast off my bra—it now lies discarded on the bedroom floor—and I'm dancing around the kitchen, clad in PJs, baking up a batch of my *Mini Bakewell Cherry Tart Cookies*. I've solidified plans for the evening: nibble baked goods, watch Netflix, and curl up with a torpid feline or two. I received a text from Mr. Potential around 3:00 p.m. today, *"What are your plans for tonight? Do you want to try out that ramen place?"*

"I'm sorry," I responded, *"I already have plans."*

A tacit arrangement has emerged between us, without my consent. My phone stays silent all week—no calls or texts from him. I'm convinced he waits for me to reach out and, if I don't, my cell won't ping until late Friday afternoon. Although I've grown accustomed to his weekday silent treatment, I nonetheless shamefully check my phone Monday through Thursday, hoping to see his name on my screen. To counteract this mortifying urge, I've placed a yellow Post-it note with the command "Don't Look" covering the screen on my mobile. His actions, or rather inactions, make me feel nonexistent during the week. I'm convinced my name only pops into his brain as an option after he's failed to solidify more satisfying plans.

I am not an afterthought, I remind myself.

In my late twenties, there was a popular dating book called *The Rules: Time-Tested Secrets for Capturing the Heart of Mr. Right*, published in 1995. On my sister's recommendation following yet another bad date, I purchased a paperback copy at Crown Books and read it over a weekend. This self-help book seemed to fly in the face of everything I understood about female empowerment and feminism. But did it, really?

The authors encouraged women to acknowledge our specialness and exceptionality and behave as such (aka "Act like a creature unlike any other"), eschewing contorting our essential self to attract and please a mate. To me, this sounded like reclaiming my power, rather than relinquishing it. I latched on to the authors' premise that I am valuable and worthwhile—and must stop wasting time with any man who doesn't recognize my worth. The book encouraged women to lead rich, satisfying, active lives—outside of romance—and to treat themselves with respect and dignity, requiring men do the same. Don't always be available. Don't change plans when a man calls last minute. Don't spread your legs for Mr. U Up? Give incredible you to a partner who deserves you. I'll admit, certain chapters were laughably outdated, perpetuating gender stereotypes. For example, the principal objective (if you couldn't interpret from the title) was to snag a man who would sweep the reader up and marry her—ugh.

When I read *The Rules*, I wasn't looking for my happily ever after with Mr. Right. However, I'd played dating musical chairs for enough years to know I was finished with this game of Mr. Wrongs. My good friend Samantha would roll her eyes, exasperated when I'd decline a date because another Mr. Potential texted me on Saturday evening asking me to drive to his place a few hours later to "watch a movie." She admonished me for what I saw as setting boundaries. Samantha was incredulous when I followed a specific rule: Don't accept an invitation for a Saturday date after Wednesday. Here's the deal: This man flittered through my brain each day since I last spent time with him. If he wasn't reaching out before Thursday or Friday to touch base, fabulous me must not be on the top of his mind. Samantha would counter, "Maybe he's traveling, or he's busy, maybe he's had a lot going on." I had a busy calendar too, yet I still found time to think about him. It takes but a moment to text, *"Crazy week. Do you want to hang out Saturday night?"* If he couldn't find a sliver of time to peck out ten words, I should step back to find someone who could. If my phone didn't ping until Friday night or Saturday morning, did any thought of me float across his mind earlier in the week? In Samantha's defense, she was inherently more spontaneous than I, rules be damned, so her sacrifice to say no to an eleventh-hour invitation would have been rougher.

Looking back on *The Rules* today, I second-guess my younger self. Did I act too aloof? Did I miss adventures and possibilities? Was I applying antiquated etiquette in a modern-day dating world? After reading an online article in the Huffington Post, I feel vindicated that these ideas transcend time and social values and are as relevant today as in 1995:

> *If you're complaining, stop condoning [this behavior].*
>
> *A common complaint I hear is from singles who hate receiving last minute texts asking to hang out. I get it—I am a fan of spontaneity, but if you're always being treated like an afterthought or a Plan B, you just might be.*
>
> *If you are making yourself available to someone who only contacts you at the last minute, you are condoning their behavior, no matter how much you complain about it.*

If you want to be asked out on a real, planned-in-advance date, then hold out for the people who will do just that.

Also remember that this scenario is another opportunity to communicate your needs. You could always respond to a last-minute text invite with "I can't tonight, but I'd love to see you with more advance planning. I'm free next _____."

Teach others how you want to be treated. The ones who rise to the occasion are the ones worth holding on to.

Hallelujah, I am vindicated.

Consistently last-minute invitations to hang out make us believe we are Plan B, even in this millennium. Further, if we continuously make ourselves available, we are encouraging this behavior. Truthfully, I'd adore spending time with Mr. Potential this weekend, but I am more than an afterthought. I hope he'll realize this, too. Meanwhile, while he's deciphering what he wants, I'll devour my flaky, buttery *Mini Bakewell Cherry Tart Cookies,* watch a costume drama with Keira Knightley, and enjoy my me-time Friday night.

CAST OF CHARACTERS

JULIE: A single, never-married, independent woman in her late forties.

HIM: An artist…or possibly a musician…or a writer…it doesn't matter.

RICHARD DAWSON: Original host of the game show Family Feud.

CONTESTANT #1: A young mother of eight children.

ACT I, SCENE I

Julie's Home, Orange County, CA. Very Early Morning.

We are in the living room of JULIE'S home, a small but tidy house in the suburbs. The lighting is low and there's ambient music in the background. Homemade chocolate truffles, two half-consumed glasses of Pinot Noir, an empty bottle, and a scented candle are scattered on the coffee table. The scene is set for romance.

It's 2:16 a.m., after their eighth date. JULIE and HIM are entwined on her couch, making out.

HIM
(Kissing, kissing, kissing.)

It's late. I should probably go home.

JULIE
(Coyly.)

Do you want to go home…or do you want to spend the night here?
(Continued kissing, kissing, kissing.)

HIM
(Remains silent.)

JULIE

It's not a trick question.
(STILL kissing, kissing, kissing.)

HIM
(Continues to be silent.)

JULIE

Okay…I'll answer for you. You want to go home.

<u>HIM</u>

(Still not a peep from his mouth.)

(The kissing continues for another few minutes.)

<u>HIM</u>

I guess I owe you some sort of apology or explanation.

<u>JULIE</u>

(To herself.)

Oh god, please don't *apologize*. That will make me feel like more of a lusty sexual deviant than I already do. And, as far as an explanation, what could you *possibly* say that would make me feel better about getting shot down for sex? I either don't want to listen to your lame explanation or, if you have a valid excuse, this situation just turned waaayyyy too complicated for me.

The lectern from the game show Family Feud *appears downstage left. RICHARD DAWSON stands to the right of the lectern, microphone in hand. CONTESTANT #1 stands behind the lectern, her hand hovering above a large buzzer. A spotlight shines on RICHARD DAWSON, CONTESTANT #1, and the lectern. Only JULIE can see the scene. The lights dim further on the living room scene.*

<u>RICHARD DAWSON</u>

(To CONTESTANT #1.)

The top ten answers are on the board. Based on a survey of one hundred men and women, give me one possible reason a man would not want to sleep with Julie…

<u> CONTESTANT #1</u>

(Slams her hand on the buzzer.)

(To RICHARD DAWSON and the Audience.)

He finds her unattractive and not sexy?

<u>RICHARD DAWSON</u>

He finds her unattractive and not sexy. Wow, that's a bit harsh. Survey says…

(There is a loud "ding" offstage.)

Congratulations, that was the number one answer. Let's look at the other answers on the board.

(There is a loud "ding" offstage before each answer is revealed. RICHARD DAWSON reads them out loud with the audience.)

2) He has a secret girlfriend and he doesn't want to "cheat"

3) He thinks sex will make Julie too "attached"

4) He's bad in bed

5) He thinks Julie will be bad in bed

6) He has a current outbreak of an incurable STI

7) He thinks she'll make him stop sleeping with other people (which is true)

8) She has B.O.—armpits/cooch/breath

9) He has ED/medical condition precluding the horizontal mambo

BLACKOUT

ACT II, SCENE I
Julie's Home, Orange County, CA. Night.

It's 8:00 p.m. the next evening. We are again in the living room of JULIE'S home. The lights are at a normal brightness. The wine, truffles, and scented candle are gone. Orange is the New Black *plays on the television.*

JULIE is sprawled on the couch, alone, wearing mismatched PJs and wrapped in a throw blanket. Two lethargic cats sleep soundly beside her. A platter of freshly baked Pecan Mocha Malties *rests on her lap.*

JULIE

(Devouring cookies—one by one and without regret.)

(To herself.)

Sometimes—most times, actually—the best company is my own.

BLACKOUT

ACT III, SCENE I
Julie's Home, Orange County, CA. Night.

We are in the bedroom of JULIE'S home. There is a lamp on the nightstand, shining light onto the bed. The curtains are drawn. A half-read book, A Room of One's Own, *lies next to JULIE on the bed. The slightest scent of lavender fills the air.*

Another night has passed. It's 10:37 p.m. JULIE is wearing the same mismatched PJs as the previous night. She's under the covers and propped up on three pillows. Her mobile phone is in her hand and she's reading a text from HIM.

JULIE

(A loud "ding" is heard offstage.)

(To herself)

    And number 10—He was recently burned and isn't ready to jump back into the fire.

(JULIE sighs and shakes her head.)

    I will miss him.

(JULIE deletes his text, then his contact information.)

CURTAIN

BUTTERFLIES

"Julie, It's me, your heart. Are you listening? Those butterflies doing aerials in your stomach? Ignore them. Those quiverings are nothing more than reactions to chemicals surging through your system, making you feel 'in love'—no relation to real Love, with a capital *L*.

"Love is *my* domain. The saying may be 'Trust your gut,' but believe me, when it comes to Love, let me do the talking. They call it 'matters of the heart' for a reason.

"I empathize. At the first sign of butterflies, you bloom in response. Suddenly, rather than hiding in your house in your old, ratty yoga pants all day, you feel buoyant and sexy as you strut down the sidewalk. You are transformed into Ms. Personality, sharing light banter with the Trader Joe's store clerk and the octogenarian bank security guard as you run your errands. The warm sun shines brightly upon you, although we both can see the sky is grey and cold. You can't concentrate, giggling to yourself as you recall sweet nothings whispered in your ear and the electricity of his touch along your skin. This fluttering in your gut inspires you to buy sexy, expensive lingerie; sign up for a Pilates class; throw out those freshly baked, addictively salty-sweet *Cape Breton-Style Oatcakes*; and cut out all naughty carbs…okay, maybe you don't *throw* them away, but you tuck them toward the back of the cupboard for a few days. You're smitten, but not insane.

"I'm fairly perceptive and I'm convinced dopamine and oxytocin, those chemicals promoting this blissful, 'in-love' feeling, must also confuse and discombobulate your brain, as well, ensuring you'll forget (once again, may I remind you) the rest of the story.

"Why can't you recall you've experienced this giddiness before—dozens of times? Why must you, I, and the rest of the organs residing within you be swept away into this land of butterflies and candy-coated rainbows when, soon enough, the clouds of reality will cast their shadows over this romantic scene again? Don't you remember rereading your old journal a few weeks ago? I do. I constrict at the thought. On its pages, in your left-handed scrawl, you captured the metamorphosis from 'bright new infatuation' through 'struggling with difficulties' to 'sadness' and finally 'heartbreak,' when I shatter into a million pieces. There's your gut-induced butterfly life cycle in ink on paper—and spanning less than a year.

"Do you forget this pattern because, should your brain fully grasp how swiftly the fluttering turns to catastrophe, you would avoid this biochemical trap again? Can the butterflies ever foretell an ending other than sorrow? Put your trust in me, dear Julie. Listen to your heart, for a change, rather than the butterflies. I'll find you true Love.

—Always, Your Heart"

BLOSSOMING

the recipes

INCREDIBLY EASY SUGAR COOKIES

Yield: 1 dozen cookies

When you've gotta have cookies, these buttery babies can't be beat and come together in a snap. This is one of my "Down and Dirty" recipes—when I need a sugar infusion and can't wait. It's so simple to whip up a batch of these crispy, shortbread-like sweet treats with ingredients you probably already have on hand. You can be enjoying them in less than 30 minutes.

Ingredients
- ½ cup (1 stick) salted butter, softened
- ¼ cup confectioners' (powdered) sugar
- Flavoring such as ¼ teaspoon vanilla extract or ½ teaspoon lemon or lime zest (optional)
- ¾ cup all-purpose flour
- ¼ cup sugar for coating (granulated sugar, turbinado sugar, or colored sugar sprinkles)

Directions
1. Preheat oven to 350°F. Line a baking sheet with parchment paper or use a silicone sheet. Using a stand mixer or handheld beaters, beat together butter and confectioners' sugar until light and fluffy. Beat in flavoring, if using.
2. Beat in flour in two additions, just until dough comes together (don't overmix or cookies will be tough).
3. Divide dough into 12 equal parts. Form into balls, roll in your preferred sugar coating, and place on baking sheet. Firmly press cookies flat with the bottom of a glass or measuring cup.
4. Bake for about 14 minutes until edges are golden. Remove from oven and cool on the baking sheet for 5 minutes. Transfer to a cooling rack and cool completely.

Variation: For a caramelly twist, replace confectioners' sugar with ⅓ cup packed light brown sugar and increase flour to 1 cup.

CAPE BRETON-STYLE OATCAKES

Yield: 3 dozen cookies

Wandering around the local cheese shop one day, I stumbled across a package of cheese-accompaniments called Cape Breton Oatcakes from Nova Scotia. Being a baker, it's rare for me to purchase a package of store-bought baked goods, but I was intrigued by something that could be labeled the trifecta of "a tea biscuit, cheese cracker, or a lightly sweetened cookie." I bought a box to serve alongside an oozy hunk of triple-crème brie and fig jam...except the oatcakes never made it to the cheese board. I broke into the package for a little nibble—delicately crunchy, buttery, simple, and slightly salty-sweet. I devoured the entire box in a matter of days. Into the kitchen I went to duplicate my newfound Nova Scotian addiction.

Ingredients
- 1½ cups old-fashioned rolled oats
- 1½ cups all-purpose flour
- ½ cup granulated sugar
- ½ teaspoon baking soda
- ¼ teaspoon (rounded) kosher salt
- 1 cup (2 sticks) unsalted butter, very cold and cut into small pieces
- 3 tablespoons milk

Directions
1. Preheat oven to 400°F. Line two baking sheets with parchment paper or silicone sheets. In the bowl of a food processor, pulse oats until they resemble the texture of meal. Add flour, sugar, baking soda, and salt and process to combine. Add cold butter and pulse until mixture resembles breadcrumbs. Add milk and process until dough just begins to come together.
2. Turn dough out onto work surface and form into two disks. Wrap each in cling film and refrigerate for 15 minutes.
3. Dust your work surface with flour and, working with one disk at a time, roll the dough ¼-inch thick. Cut with a 2½-inch round cutter or cut into squares. Transfer to baking sheets and refrigerate again for 10 minutes.
4. Bake for about 10 minutes until the edges are just beginning to turn golden. Cool on the baking sheets for 5 minutes. Transfer to a cooling rack and cool completely. Store in an airtight container.

OATMEAL APPLE DATE COOKIES

Yield: 3 ½ dozen cookies

The addition of moist apple and sweet dates results in a soft, chewy, and somewhat flat version of your standard oatmeal cookies, adding interest to an American staple.

Ingredients

- 2½ cups old-fashioned rolled oats
- 1 cup chopped dates
- 1 tart apple, peeled and grated (Granny Smith or any tart baking apple)
- 1 cup all-purpose flour
- 1 teaspoon kosher salt
- ¾ teaspoon baking powder
- ¾ teaspoon cinnamon
- ¾ cup (1½ sticks) unsalted butter, softened
- ½ cup granulated sugar
- 1 cup light brown sugar, lightly packed
- 1 large egg
- 1 teaspoon vanilla extract
- ½ cup confectioners' (powdered) sugar
- Brandy or water

Directions

1. Preheat oven to 350°F. Line two baking sheets with parchment paper (using silicone sheets will result in flatter cookies). In a medium bowl, combine oats, dates, and apple. The dates tend to stick together, so combine all ingredients well and set bowl aside. In another medium bowl, sift together flour, salt, baking powder, and cinnamon. Set aside.

2. Using a stand mixer or handheld beaters, beat together butter and both sugars until light and fluffy, about 4 minutes. Beat in egg and vanilla extract.

3. Add flour mixture to creamed butter and sugar and stir until combined. Stir in oat mixture.

4. Drop by rounded tablespoons (approximately 30 grams each) onto baking sheets. With fingers, slightly pat each cookie down into a round disk approximately ⅓-inch thick. Bake for about 17 minutes until the edges are slightly brown. Remove from oven and cool on the baking sheet for 5 minutes. Carefully remove from baking sheet to a cooling rack. Cool completely.

5. In a small bowl, add enough brandy or water to confectioners' sugar to make a glaze. Drizzle over cookies. Let glaze set and store cookies in an airtight container.

CHOCOLATE-DIPPED BISCOTTI

Yield: 6 dozen cookies

I created this recipe in 2010 for a Vin Santo pairing at Hanna's Restaurant and Bar in Rancho Santa Margarita, CA, where I briefly worked after culinary school. Vin Santo is a sweet Italian dessert wine traditionally served with cantucci, a type of almond biscotti. My original recipe resulted in 144 cookies, but I've cut this recipe down to half. What I love about this version is how easy it is to divide the dough, add various ingredients, and create an array of unique flavor combinations.

Ingredients
- 3 cups all-purpose flour
- 2 teaspoons baking powder
- ¼ teaspoon kosher salt
- 1½ cups granulated sugar
- 1 cup (2 sticks) unsalted butter, softened
- 3 large eggs
- 2 teaspoons vanilla extract
- Flavor options (see below)

Directions
1. Preheat oven to 350°F. Line two baking sheets with parchment paper or silicone sheets. Sift together flour, baking powder, and salt. Set aside. In the bowl of an electric mixer, using the paddle attachment, beat sugar and butter until pale and fluffy, about 4 minutes. Beat in eggs, one at a time, and add vanilla extract. Mix in flour mixture until just combined (do not overmix). Divide dough into two equal amounts and add flavor options from the ingredient lists below (or make your own combination of mix-ins).
2. Divide each flavor into two rolls approximately 14 inches long (you should have four rolls total). Place rolls 4 inches apart on baking sheets. Flatten each roll to approximately 3 inches wide, so each log should be approximately 3 inches x 14 inches. Bake for about 20-22 minutes until tops are set and logs are light golden brown. Cool logs for 10 minutes.

3. With a serrated knife, carefully cut each log crosswise into ½-inch to ¾-inch slices. Lay slices flat on baking sheets and bake 8-10 minutes until biscotti feel dry to the touch. Turn the cookies over and bake another 5 minutes.

4. Cool on baking sheets for 5 minutes. Transfer to a cooling rack and cool completely.

5. Warm chocolate morsels in the microwave 60-90 seconds, stirring every 30 seconds until chocolate is smooth. Dip the tip of each cooled biscotti in chocolate and return to cooling racks until chocolate is set. Store in an airtight container.

Flavor Options

- Almond Orange

  ⅓ cup chopped almonds

  Zest from one orange

  Substitute 1 teaspoon almond extract for 1 of the teaspoons of vanilla extract

  1 cup milk chocolate morsels (for dipping)

- Apricot Pistachio

  ⅓ cup dried apricots, chopped

  ⅓ cup pistachios, chopped

  1 cup white chocolate morsels (for dipping)

- Candied Orange and Anise

  ⅓ cup candied orange peel, finely chopped

  1 teaspoon aniseeds, toasted and slightly crushed

  1 cup dark chocolate morsels (for dipping)

- Cherry Walnut

  ⅓ cup dried cherries, chopped

  ⅓ cup candied walnuts, chopped

  1 cup dark chocolate morsels (for dipping)

BAKEWELL CHERRY TART COOKIES

Is it a complex cookie or the smallest tart you've ever seen? Whatever you decide, the combination of tender shell, tart jam, and rich almond filling is sure to delight.

Ingredients

Sweet Shells

- ¾ cup (1½ sticks) unsalted butter, softened
- ¼ cup granulated sugar
- ½ teaspoon vanilla extract
- ¼ teaspoon kosher salt
- 1 ½ cups all-purpose flour

Frangipane (Almond Cream) and Filling

- ½ cup (1 stick) unsalted butter, softened
- ¾ cup confectioners' (powdered) sugar
- 2 large eggs
- 1 ½ cups almond flour
- 2 tablespoons cornstarch
- ½ cup cherry jam or tart jam of your choice

Glaze

- ⅔ cup confectioners' (powdered) sugar
- 1 tablespoon water
- 32 sliced almonds, toasted

Directions

1. Make shells: Preheat oven to 350°F. Grease a 32-cup mini-muffin tin. If you don't have a tin this large, you can bake these in batches. In the bowl of an electric mixer, beat together butter and sugar until light and fluffy. Add vanilla extract and salt and beat on low until fully blended. Add flour and beat on low just until dough comes together. Divide dough into 32 equal pieces (about 13 grams each). Press dough along the bottom and up the sides of each muffin cup. The shells will be thin. Bake for 10-12 minutes or until shells are a pale golden color. If shells rise too much during baking, gently press them back down into the cups while they are still warm. Cool slightly before filling.

2. Make frangipane: While shells are cooling, whisk together butter, confectioners' sugar, eggs, almond flour, and cornstarch. Spoon frangipane into a piping bag or resealable bag with one corner snipped.

3. Assemble tarts: Dollop a rounded ½ teaspoon of jam on top of each shell. Pipe frangipane over jam, covering jam completely. Bake tarts for approximately 20 minutes until tops are puffed and slightly golden brown. Cool in tin for 10 minutes. Carefully remove tarts and transfer to a cooling rack to cool completely.

4. Make glaze: Stir together confectioners' sugar and water. Add more water, a little at a time, to create a pourable glaze. Drizzle over cooled tarts. Garnish each with a toasted sliced almond. Once glaze is set, store in an airtight container.

Variation: For holiday cookies, substitute smooth cranberry sauce or cranberry jelly for the jam.

Tip: Don't throw any leftover ingredients away—make French Bostock for breakfast. Preheat oven to 350°F. Thickly slice day-old brioche, croissants, or challah bread and place on a baking sheet. Spread with a thin layer of jam followed by a generous layer of frangipane, covering the entire surface. Sprinkle with sliced almonds and bake 20-25 minutes until frangipane is set and edges are golden brown. Dust with confectioners' sugar, if desired. Ooh la la.

PECAN MOCHA MALTIES

Yield: 2 dozen sandwich cookies

I created these cookies specifically for a competition in LA called BakeCamp. Filled with flavor and complexity, but not overly sweet, the shortbread cookies, infused with pecans, coffee, and malt, sandwich a luscious chocolate ganache filling—finished off with a sprinkling of crunchy salted candied pecans.

Ingredients

Cookies

- 1¾ cups pastry flour
- ½ cup malted milk powder
- ¼ teaspoon kosher salt
- 11 tablespoons (1 stick plus 3 tablespoons) unsalted butter, softened
- ½ cup granulated sugar
- 3 large egg yolks
- 2 tablespoons malt extract (available online or at homebrewer's supply stores)
- 1 tablespoon coffee grounds (not instant coffee)
- ½ teaspoon vanilla extract
- ½ cup finely chopped pecans, toasted

Ganache Filling

- 1 cup semisweet chocolate morsels
- ¼ cup heavy whipping cream

Glaze

- 1 cup granulated sugar
- ½ cup salted candied pecans, finely chopped, purchased or homemade

Directions

1. Make cookies: Stir together flour, malted milk powder, and salt. Set aside.
2. In the bowl of an electric mixer, using the paddle attachment, cream butter and sugar on high for about 4 minutes or until light and fluffy. Add egg yolks, malt extract, coffee grounds, and vanilla extract. Mix until incorporated. Add flour mixture and mix on low just until blended. Stir in pecans.

3. Form the dough into four rectangles, each approximately 2 inches x 8 inches. Wrap each rectangle in cling film and refrigerate until the dough is firm, for at least two hours or overnight.

4. Make ganache: At least two hours before baking cookies, combine chocolate morsels and heavy whipping cream in a microwave-safe medium bowl. Microwave in 30-second bursts, stirring in between, until chocolate is completely melted. Cover with cling film and set aside on the counter to cool.

5. Preheat oven to 350°F. Line two baking sheets with parchment paper (do not use silicone sheets). Working with one piece of dough at a time, on a lightly floured surface, roll out dough into a little larger than 6-inch x 8-inch rectangle, with an approximate ¼-inch thickness. Transfer dough to baking sheet and chill for 10 minutes. Transfer to the oven and bake 16-18 minutes until slightly golden around the edges. While baked dough is still warm, cut out cookies with a 2-inch square or round cookie cutter. You should be able to cut out 12 cookies. Work carefully since the baking sheet will be hot. Allow cookies to cool on the baking sheet for 5 minutes before transferring them to a cooling rack to cool completely.

6. Make glaze: Pour 1 cup granulated sugar into a skillet and heat on medium, without stirring, until the sugar is completely melted and golden. Using tongs, carefully dip the tops of 24 cookies in hot caramel and then immediately sprinkle with salted candied pecans. Work carefully so you do not burn yourself with the hot caramel.

7. To assemble, place about 2 teaspoons (approximately 10 grams) of ganache on the remaining 24 unglazed cookies, spread evenly, and top with glazed cookies. Store in an airtight container.

Variation: If you would prefer not to work with hot caramel in step 6, you can create a glaze by combining ½ cup confectioners' sugar with water, glaze the cookies then sprinkle with salted candied pecans. The pecans will not remain as crisp as with caramel, but the cookies will still be delicious.

two

MR. OXBLOOD: JASON

Age 22–31

THE BEGINNING

"If I can see the Pleiades tonight, I swear, I'll kiss you."

If there's a better opening line, I've yet to hear it.

I'm introduced to Jason during a Halloween party, 1989, at my friend Saman-tha's apartment near San Diego. I've outfitted myself in a homemade Pebbles Flintstone costume, including chicken bone from last night's dinner accenting my ponytail. Jason has opted for Charles Baudelaire or some other French Romantic poet, a costume decidedly too esoteric for this throng of Bud-drinking stoners.

Half an hour after Jason's arrival, he snatches Homer's *The Odyssey* from the kitchen table and expresses his disbelief that one of the apartment's occupants would be reading classic literature. Samantha turns around with narrowed eyes and a few choice words of incredulity. Unbeknownst to Jason, she is a recent addi-tion to the apartment and the book belongs to her. Jason, it seems, is also flexible, wedging his foot firmly in his mouth while standing on the kitchen floor without much trouble. In Jason's defense, no one there except Samantha would be reading Homer—and she, I'm fairly certain, solely because *The Odyssey* is assigned reading for a class. Jason's arrogance in this moment turns Samantha into, if not an out-right enemy, at least an icy adversary.

The only other fragment of time I share with Jason this night is a brief, bewitch-ing moment on the balcony, looking up toward the inky sky, and his cheeky com-ment about the Pleiades. I remain unkissed. I have no reason to suppose I'll bump into him again, but I keep a vigilant eye out for the Pleiades, just in case.

Two weeks later, I attend another party in nearby Escondido, hosted by a friend of Samantha's fiancé—and Jason's former roommate. Jason stands among the throng of partygoers, in vest, tie, and wingtips, his long, bottle-auburn hair slicked back from his pale forehead, appearing uncomfortable and out of place, even though he knows this crowd better than I. It's as if the vampire Lestat, bored and seeking a diversion, has decided to check out a kegger.

Samantha gives a derisive snort in his direction and keeps walking. After exchanging a brief hello, I trail after Samantha, jostled and overheating as I weave my way through the assaulting crush of bodies and thumping music.

An hour later, deep in conversation with Samantha, with my hands clasped behind my back, someone lightly places an object in my hand. I would love to claim some amorous significance to this token, like a rose petal or a wildflower plucked from the hills surrounding the garden, but no, the item in question reveals itself to be a rather ordinary Snyder's pretzel stick, delivered into my hand by Jason.

When I turn around in confusion, he grins a lopsided closed-mouthed smile and invites me to join him for a drive along the beach. Savvy women know if a peculiar man you scarcely know entreats you to join him for a drive to an unfamiliar destination, safety dictates you refuse with a polite "No, thank you," which is how I answer him.

I anticipate the customary slick cajoling women typically face after rejecting a man, a series of attempts at persuasion, assurances he's a "nice guy"—promises he's not one of the bloodsucking undead.

Instead, I'm met with an unaffected shrug and an "Okay," as he ambles toward the front door. As soon as the decline escapes my lips, I want to slurp the words back into my mouth like a dangling ramen noodle. My gut assures me that, rather than dodging a sexual assault (or vampire bite), I have passed up a memorable adventure, especially when measured against remaining at this particular party. My opportunity is escaping through the door, a man who piques my curiosity and stands apart from the rest, a counterpoint to most other men who seem uninterestingly predictable to my already jaded, twenty-two-year-old heart. I trail along after Jason to the front yard.

"Is it too late for me to reconsider?" I call out to him.

"Come on then," he replies, a grin playing across his lips.

He guides me to a parked white Toyota Sentra, opens the passenger door for me, and slides behind the wheel.

We travel along the San Diego coast, eventually parking on the soft shoulder of a deserted stretch of Pacific Coast Highway. With sunroof and windows open, I catch the comingled scent of the Pacific and bonfires, although the churning ocean, far below our clifftop lookout, remains mostly hidden from my view. Two weeks into November, the weather proclaims the start of Southern California "winter." The night's sixty-three-degree chill stings my unaccustomed SoCal cheeks and the full, ember-hued moon dangles low, visible from the sunroof, seemingly just beyond my grasp.

From the trunk, Jason collects yards of white tulle and candles to bedeck the Sentra's nondescript interior. As I drape and entwine the clouds of netting along the visors and seat belt holders, I wonder if he always carries these or similar items in his trunk and, if so, for whom? Once settled among the flickering candles and diaphanous fluttering bunting, he plugs in a Puccini tape to accompany our conversation. He deluges me with questions concerning music and art.

"Do you like poetry? What do you think about opera? Who are your favorite authors and artists? Tell me your passions."

I hesitate before answering, my breath becoming shallow. No one asks me questions like this, and I am momentarily dumbstruck. My gaze focuses on a small pool of creamy wax forming beside a flickering candle on the dashboard. I inhale. I'm not much of a fan of poetry or opera, but I'm drawn to art in other forms. Seemingly lacking any talent in art myself, I am devouring the talents of others: D.H. Lawrence, Cocteau Twins, and Chopin's piano music, along with my first handful of Franz Kafka stories that go beyond *The Metamorphosis*. This list of music and books escapes my lips in measured tones, allowing him a glimpse of what lurks behind this shy girl's uncertainty. I glance over at him hesitantly and catch him smiling. I exhale.

"If you had said John Grisham and Quiet Riot, I would have made a U-turn and deposited you back at the party," he jokes.

Instead, he produces an antique book from the back seat, a reward, I determine, for passing his test.

"This book is my most cherished possession," he professes.

I can't make out the title on the worn spine and cover in the faint pools of candlelight. He invites me to select a page number. I choose, eschewing my lucky number or my birth date, opting instead to pull my answer from the ether. Flipping through the yellowed pages to my selection, he begins reading its contents—in French. Fortunes, or rather, my particular fortune. His gentle voice shares my supposed destiny with me, first in the language of romance, in which I am not fluent...in many ways, and then again in English. I cannot recollect the translation, precisely, but the crux concerns being offered, and rejecting, a proposal of Love.

These sweet hours soaked in romance are a teenage girl's rapturous wet dream. I often apply the word "content" to describe moments I'm swathed in tender, blissful happiness. This night finds me content within Jason's cocoon of glimmer and gossamer.

I envision myself recounting this particular night's tale to Samantha and my other girlfriends, resolving that few will believe my account's accuracy, insisting,

"If this story is true, there's no way he's straight."

Jason doesn't attempt to seduce me. I never feel his caress. We simply talk and share the night, surrounded by tulle, candlelight, opera, the Pacific, and the knowing moon. Jason returns me to Samantha's apartment a little before 4:00 a.m., escorting me to her front door. I can't recall if I informed her I was sneaking out of the party, but must have, since I find the door unlocked. He doesn't say goodbye, just bounds down the stairs to his waiting car. As I turn the doorknob, my mind flashes through images of this strange and wondrous night. At twenty-two, I haven't encountered a man like Jason before. He seems to seek the curves and recesses of my mind, rather than my flesh. I'm not forced to feign interest in another banal conversation regarding the Raiders. He doesn't cunningly try to coax me back to his place to "check out his vinyl collection." Jason merely unfolds for me what he finds meaningful, what he believes important…and my sensibilities leap.

As this collection of the night's moments replays through my head, it dawns on me, I haven't even thanked him. I turn around as he walks toward the white, two-door subcompact.

"Thank you for a lovely evening," I call.

He turns on his heels and smiles, his crooked grin confirming he understands the profundity these simple words encompass.

A SEA OF MISSIVES

His letters, postmarked from Escondido, begin arriving not long after that evening. My mom, her face a mixture of curiosity tinged with jealousy, hands me the first package from our mailbox, a mixtape packed in dried rose petals and simply addressed to "Julie," written in a stylized vertical scrawl I will come to recognize well. The first two songs he selects are Bel Canto's "The Suffering" and "Dewy Fields." I also recall Dead Can Dance, Edith Piaf, and two arias, "The Flower Duet" from *Lakmé*, and Puccini's "O Mio Babbino Caro." I save the petals and play the tape on repeat until the music sounds weak and tinny and it eventually stops working. Opera isn't my thing, but these arias feel different.

At their peak, I receive four or five missives a week, sometimes three postmarked with the same date. Every afternoon, I bound from front door to mailbox, brimming with anticipation, thrilled when an envelope or package is waiting for me, disheartened on the odd days the mailbox remains empty.

November 1989 – Letter from Jason

When the world has been
Reduced to a single dark wood
For our four astonished eyes—to a beach for two faithful children—
To a musical house for our bright symphony—
I shall find you.
Let me have brought into being
All your memories—let me be she
Who can bind you hand and foot—I shall suffocate you.
—A. Rimbaud, translated by Jason

December 10, 1989 – Postcard of the Huntington Library Gardens from Jason

Would you care to join me?

(My answer is an emphatic "yes")

FIRST BLUSHES

I first notice my heart's stuttering and the heat rising upon my cheeks when in Jason's company sometime in November or December—after our initial platonic beach drive, after I receive the mixtape, perhaps during our first stroll through the Huntington Library following his invitation.

My love blossoms sometime before January 1990, before he departs Southern California for San Francisco, a mere two and a half months after meeting him. I sat rapt in his presence from the beginning—accomplished poet and artist, able to speak and translate various languages, self-taught in music, and well-read as well as intelligent—at the ripe old age of twenty-three, but my wonder of this Renaissance man stands apart from my affection. Falling for Jason is also exasperating, vexing in his romantic, impossible ideals, frustrating in his constant expectations of my perfection, maddening in his inability to bother with a career or financial stability, infuriating in his misplaced commitment to chastity and his continual failure to kiss me, even though, after nine months of waiting, my lips beg to be consumed.

Yes, that's right, it's been nine months now and we haven't kissed.

I often visit my longtime friend Lana in San Francisco, Jason's new home, spending one evening each trip in his company. I lounge upon his crimson satin-covered bed, in dusky candlelight and a haze of incense. Erik Satie plays in the background, the soundtrack of our evenings together. Intoxicated by red wine on my lips and his honeyed voice in my ear, I yearn, patiently…okay maybe not so patiently, for an affection toward me supplanting mere friendship. The unintentional flicker of his auburn locks along my skin ignites a low and deep ache within, yearning to escape. Since our first months in Escondido, his body has become lean, his thighs strong, from a job that requires climbing forty flights of stairs multiple times each evening. I would willingly offer my lips and body to him, yet he doesn't care to possess either of them.

Instead, I unwittingly catch the eye of his best friend and roommate, Nathan. Careless Cupid, perhaps spending too many nights in Bacchus's company, misses his target entirely, his arrow finding a home deep within Nathan's chest and causing a triad of unrequited love. Glimpsing me drowsily recumbent upon Jason's garnet bed, Nathan is supposedly overcome. I wonder, if he first noticed me on a street in North Beach, without Jason present, would I have warranted a second glance? Surely, when he spies me at Jason's side, he witnesses my longing, my doe eyes fixed unreservedly toward my auburn-tressed Heathcliff.

Not desiring me for himself, Jason supports Nathan's futile attempts to woo, but the poor lad doesn't stand a chance. This is an Oscar Wildean comedy: Nathan set his sights on me, my eyes are fixed on Jason, and Jason…well, he just rapturously gazes upon a photo of Rodin's *The Kiss*.

One night, the three of us embark on an excursion to Muir Woods and Stinson Beach, Nathan in the driver's seat of his two-seater Karmann Ghia, me sitting in Jason's lap on the passenger's side. I believe we hold hands on that forty-five-minute ride, but perhaps I'm projecting my desires onto our innocuously close proximity. Jason gives me his ring this night—three garnets set in silver filigree, representing the three virtues of faith, hope, and love.

Fitting, since I am losing faith that I can ever hope Jason will love me. This is my practice in unmitigated patience for love.

March 13, 1990 – Julie's Journal

Jason,

A solitary evening beside you restores me for weeks. When your attention turns in my direction and we lose ourselves in collective reverie, this ceaseless melancholy wanes. You offer friendship, yet I pursue quixotic impossibilities. You quell your affections, closed off to the intimacy I ache to explore. To endure another tender moment in your company is unbearable. Our perpetual charade will surely drive me to insanity.

Are my pheromones, my desires, my longing for Jason so palpable that he senses them from four-hundred-fifty miles away? His uncanny response to the private musings of my journal arrives in my mailbox two weeks later.

March 27, 1990 – Postcard from Jason

Affection is not worth fighting for,
But Love is worth killing for.

May 6, 1990 – Letter from Julie

I recline beneath them, an angel, fallen and acquiescing
They caress my softness
And laud my eyes, my cheek, my pale breast
I convulse in disgust

I lie beside you, a vampire, drinking in my fill of contentment
You relax along my thigh
And the gentle flicker of your crimson locks across my hand
Casts the Milky Way down my spine

I'll submit to their desire
And convince myself it's yours
And as their tongue flickers 'round my lips
I will kiss you
And close my eyes to the truth

ILLUMINATION

I've been languidly stretched, like a contented cat, across his scarlet duvet, waiting, waiting, waiting for Jason to relinquish his unendurable faux vow of celibacy. I've assured myself he merely requires one more tender evening in my presence, one last shot for his ardor to blossom.

Each visit, this heady recipe of seduction and chastity leaves me exasperated. I lament to Lana's male roommate, "Why won't he touch me?"

Her roommate laughs in response, "I'll touch you, Julie," reminding me there are plenty of men out there willing to fulfill my request.

Saturday night begins as usual, sprawled across Jason's bed, nestled among stacks of art and books, the air heavy with Dead Can Dance, Nag Champa, and my desire. The typical San Francisco August chill seeps through the ill-fitted bedroom window, rattling the old frame, a stark contrast to the rest of the country and the simmering summer heat beneath my skin. Like an excited three-year-old who has captured an adult's attention, Jason pulls out things he's been waiting to show me from his collection surrounding us. This night begins to unfold as all the others preceding it. He passes me a book, holds up a piece of art, reads me a scrap of poetry, digs up his sketch of a hand.

Tonight, however, Jason shares something that turns his crimson duvet into a bloody pool of my crestfallen disillusionment. In the middle of showing me an image of a pastoral landscape, Jason casually discloses, "So, at my French lesson last week, I ended up sleeping with Tristan, my tutor, in her living room."

"What?" The word escapes, almost breathlessly, from my lips. I must have misheard.

He blushes and shrugs, offering me a half smile. "We got caught up in the nuances of idiomatic expressions, I guess. It just happened."

I gasp as he plunges the dagger, penetrating my breastbone, directly into my young, juicy, purple, throbbing heart. I'm confronted with the sudden understanding I've deluded myself, assuming he's eschewed the *entire* opposite sex. Tragically, his reticence seems directed solely at *moi*. I am inconsolable at the realization my long months of gentle coaxing remained a Sisyphean endeavor. Tears stream down my pale cheeks as confessions of undeclared feelings and unquenchable longing tumble out between my sobs. Is he truly ignorant of my affection? Does he genuinely feel nothing in return? The words I want to scream remain trapped behind my demurely pursed lips, afraid of shattering our meticulously crafted genteel reverie—*Are you fucking kidding me?*

My tear-stained face and chagrin now planted snotty-nose-down into the satin comforter, he awkwardly attempts to enfold me in his arms. Endeavoring to soothe, his pacifying lips find the top of my head, both cheeks and, finally, when I turn my face, my mouth. His kisses find my lips over and over. Each kiss is tender, accompanied by whispered words of the fondness and affection I've been longing to receive.

This evening marks my first experience encountering a baffling concoction of ingredients—my tears, my snot, my indignation—that seem to swiftly melt the barrier to a love interest's heart. Were I aware of Eros's secret recipe, I would have uncontrollably sobbed and crumpled my features into a horrifying puddle of anguish months ago.

Six hours later, our bodies entangled upon the bed, yet still fully clothed, with Sunday's sunlight streaming golden rays through the bedroom's open window, I reluctantly begin to extricate myself from the cocoon of his embrace. Thoughts of my impending morning flight home to Orange County weigh on my mind, yet after nine tormented months of longing for Jason to touch me, I finally depart his bedroom feeling sated and incandescently happy.

ooo

Nine months earlier, in November 1989, just after meeting Jason, I watch on TV as over two million East Berliners visit West Berlin for the first time. Jubilant young Germans climb to the top of the colorful graffiti-covered concrete wall that's divided East and West Germany for the past twenty-eight years. Labeled "the greatest street party in the history of the world," Berliners stand atop the twelve-foot wall, shouting *Prost!* with beer and champagne in hand, cheering and applauding as relatives reunite after decades apart. I watch images of the *mauerspechte*, or "wall woodpeckers," swinging sledgehammers and pickaxes, chipping away at this symbol of the Iron Curtain, holding up chunks as souvenirs while bulldozers topple jagged sections until the wall, and the communist power in Germany, is obliterated, rubble at Berliners' feet.

It takes me nine additional months after the German concrete turned to rubble before I manage, eventually, to obliterate Jason's wall. Facing a formidable task, I patiently chip away a little at a time, until his wall crumbles, all hesitation disappears from our landscape, and he showers me with commitment and affection.

Prost.

ooo

August 14, 1990 – Card from Jason
Life is Grand…
And So Are You

August 28, 1990 – Postcard from Jason

72   BIARRITZ. — La Côte des Basques. — The Basques coast. — LL.

A great and luminous bird shall
fall from the azure vaults of heaven
and glide into the terrestrial realm. And from its
flank shall emerge, as though from a prodigal womb, a new
and heroic man reborn for the cause of his heroine.
…In other words, I'll be in town Thursday morning.

September 10, 1990 – "Valentine" from Jason

To My Valentine—a bit early
To Julie
From Cupid's Own Darling

October 4, 1990 – Postcard from Jason

Her lashes,
two vespertine butterflies
astonished in the moon's silver hysteria.
Her eyes,
The voices of two amorous
travelers suffocated in time.
—Jason, your official boyfriend (pending approval of title)

With Jason as a partner, no step in this dance is straightforward: nine months waiting for a kiss and another two months before we sleep together.

That afternoon, I open his bedroom door to find the furniture rearranged. "A tabula rasa," he says. "A fresh beginning for us." Our former island of chastity, the bed, once tucked in the far corner, now stands bare of its ruby duvet, strewn with rose petals, along the opposite wall and facing the solitary window.

The particulars of this initial coupling blur. I remember his strong thighs straddling me, the wiry curls of his auburn hair beneath my palms. Do I don white cotton panties—his favorite—or does he only later confess his proclivities for that particular garment? The neighbor's one-eared cat, I do recall, wearing pale blue collar and tiny bell for this special occasion. In the fading afternoon light, he watches us from the window, curious, as we laze entwined and euphoric, the superfluous white sheets abandoned on the floor.

He flips his tail in approval, aware, somehow, that it's taken me eleven enduring months to get this moment. The world may address me as Saint Patience, the patron saint of sexual fortitude.

October 6, 1990 – Julie's Journal

I made love on a bed of petals, ruby and carmine
Crushed and mixed with sweat,
They stained our sheets grenadine,
Falsely proclaiming a virginity that wasn't mine

October 9, 1990 – Postcard from Jason

We sinned,
but with such a grace,
as set a blush upon Virtue's face

A WOMAN IN LOVE

Like a modern-day Zelda Fitzgerald, my wardrobe aesthetic, in 1990, consists of 1930s-inspired bohemian skirts and dresses in muted tones coupled with a few 1920s vintage hats. I've stuffed my closet with mauves, wines, navies, and plums, arranged by shade—a visual merchandising holdover from my days working retail clothing sales. Inspired by the vivid garment descriptions in D.H. Lawrence's *Women in Love*, I take to wearing brightly colored stockings in unexpected colors—teal, eggplant, goldenrod, heathered rose —with a pair of burgundy brogues I've purchased in San Francisco. During this time, my stockings never match my outfit and I'm rarely clad in a pair of jeans, unless hiking in the mountains. Sliding open the closet door, I'm met with an array of clothing from a catalog called Tweeds that specializes in classics with a dash of artsy femininity and curiously named colors such as lichen and damson. I own, among other things, a ruffled silk blouse in cabbage rose; a handknitted, raisin-hued sweater with a Peter Pan collar; a short miniskirt-and-legging combination in indigo; a long, knife-pleated skirt in oxblood; and a drop-waisted dress in Prussian blue.

On my first weekend staying with Jason rather than Lana, I pack the indigo combo, the pleated skirt, and the dress. Should anyone glance through the windows of the Café Trieste, they'd find a dapper couple sipping cappuccinos, nibbling slices of almond cake, and holding hands, with Jason donning his tweed jacket, vest, and tie and me, clad in a Prussian blue dress, violet stockings, and aforementioned brogues.

We look as if we've stepped out onto a bygone 1930s San Francisco evening, ready to hop a trolley to the dimly lit Black Cat to dance the Balboa or make an appearance at a lively salon to hear the poets of the San Francisco Renaissance.

October 9, 1990 – Postcard from Jason

Two daubs of paint, one oxblood, one Prussian blue. With that, our nicknames are born.

ooo

These are the proverbial days of wine and roses, bottles of red that turn our lips purple and rose petals, always the petals: tucked inside letters, thrown like confetti in moon-bathed nightfall, and sprinkled over bedsheets.

Culinary considerations rarely play a part in our escapades: a croissant here, a shared sandwich there. No lazy Sunday mornings plopping juicy Asian dumplings in our mouths, no burritos from the Mission District the size of San Francisco's eponymous bread. When I visit, his kitchen is a mysterious white room down the hallway. Our repast often consists of nothing more than a pepperoni pizza for two, eaten in his bedroom.

We stroll along Francisco Street, pausing for a moment in front of the large windows of Tante Marie Cooking School. Inside, culinary students, clad in their new, stiff chef's whites, practice techniques they learned earlier in the day. It seems so romantic from my limited vantage point: sunlight streaming through the windows as students explore their talents and creativity amidst trays and baskets of overflowing culinary delights. The students seem happy, engaged. It's a far cry from my community college nights as a disaffected humanities major, where I sit trapped behind a desk, listening to a math professor drone on under the flicker of fluorescent lights in a windowless classroom, vaguely dreaming of something better.

October 16, 1990 – Letter from Jason

Envelope reads: *"Simple-Minded Sincere Letter inside"*

I miss you Julie
I make love to you in my thoughts
I look upon you with desire
Yet when I touch your skin, lust softens into Love
And when I am within you, the poem of Julie is within me

The second time we make love, I am astonished to feel myself, beneath him, climaxing solely from him inside of me. At twenty-three, and until this moment, I have always needed a smidgen of help: a fingertip, a mouth, a vibrating something or another. Like countless other women, I accept I can't climax that simply. This time, I feel the tension building, yet try not to directly consider what's happening. I'm afraid my acknowledgment might cause the moment to escape from my grasp, like in yoga class when I finally balanced into crow pose and the instructor took notice, shouting, "Way to go, Julie," which caused me to tumble, never able to duplicate crow pose again, no matter how many times I practiced.

I don't share with Jason what's happening, not wanting to mess up his rhythm.

I say, "Don't stop," but leave the way-to-go's until after I've climaxed.

Although I can't offer him my virginity, I am able to gift him this—my sexual crow pose, you could call it.

FRAGILITY

We're arguing, off and on, throughout this first year as a couple—our disagreements throwing our visits off-kilter, like trying to stand upright in a funhouse, every step unsure. A bevy of birthday presents, glittering behind paper and bows, are unwrapped by the giver and returned to the stores. The final hours before a flight home are spent in silence, sitting back-to-back, the air thick with misunderstanding. These fissures are soon patched back together with a phone call, card, or letter—yet mended with tissue paper, delicate and prone to tearing open again and again.

January 1991 – Card from Jason (reconciliation after an argument)

Lamentation gives way
surrenders its hold.
You have broken it with a gesture,
a belated word
the edge of your mouth always held.
You move away from what has
escorted you through old cycles
toward existences you don't yet believe in.
But you will soon know them as new souls,
patiently awaiting for you to realize them.

Distance, we decide, has rendered our union untenable. One last visit, one final stroll through the night gardens of Balboa Park, where the air is sweet, yet heavy with our recognition that we cannot continue. As we walk, the world seems to hush, cloaked in the solemnity of the evening, no crickets or frogs to be heard, mirroring the quiet acceptance of our parting. Just shy of two years since we first met, we drift along the porticos, our fingers entwined, our echoing footfalls the only sound, as if each stride were an elegy to what might have been.

October 16, 1991 – Letter from Jason

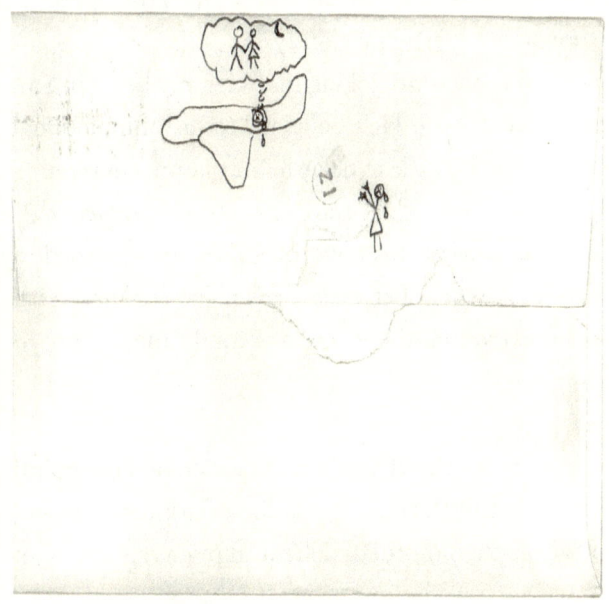

Ballad of the Moon Garden
Amidst the nocturnal poppies secretive
willows, water's melodies, chiming,
calling
She lies complacent, languid upon her back, wondering who is atop her singing,
while above her the moon flowers white, the stars smile vaguely.

FATE'S PAWNS

My telephone stares at me from across my bedroom, silent and mocking. The 2 a.m. amorous assignations over phone lines are no more. I fire the postman as the messenger of fond affections, yet I persist in examining the mailbox for a word of contrition. Like a Pavlovian pup, I unlock the mailbox with the slightest tinge of hope and longing, *Where's my treat?*

It has been ten months since we said goodbye. Jason's ghost lingers about the perimeters of life: the record on my turntable, the book I pick up to read, his painting hanging on my bedroom wall. These remembrances haunt me, I mourn, and escape into a private cave of busyness. There's an unexpected benefit to our breakup. I gain a renewed commitment to my career, flourishing at my mortgage banking job. At the tender age of twenty-five, my company offers me a promotion in San Jose, a short hour's drive from Jason's City by the Bay. I grasp the opportunity, sanguine to reignite his ardor with my new proximity.

My boss announces my relocation to the staff, joking that I left my heart in San Francisco, referring to the Tony Bennett song. He's oblivious to his unintentional accuracy. My heart, indeed, resides there. I decide to delay telling Jason, envisioning his delight upon receiving my post-move postcard, *"Guess who's in town—permanently?"* Two weeks before my relocation, Jason reveals his own surprise—he's returned to Escondido, still loves me and, without the miles between us, wants to reunite.

He has relocated here; I am now moving there. For a second time, I want to exclaim, "Are you fucking kidding me?"

Fate, if she exists, is a sadist.

During our final fourteen days in Southern California, we enjoy ephemeral moments—a final summer midnight stroll through the Balboa Park rose garden, another visit to the Huntington Library, a handful of delightful nights spooning in the dark, and then our goodbye.

Now, returning to Fate, that conniving little bitch. Sometime before my move, Lana and her fiancé coincidentally meet Nathan somewhere in San Francisco. In a city of more than 725,000 inhabitants, my friend and my unrequited admirer manage to cross paths. Clicking the puzzle pieces together, they figure out that Lana's "Julie" is likewise Nathan's, the girl who chose Jason over him. Thus, now that I'm residing in the Bay Area and frequently visiting Lana, Nathan and I reconnect as friends, much to Jason's displeasure.

While I call the Bay Area my home and Jason remains in Escondido, his mother unexpectedly dies from a brain aneurysm. He calls me intermittently in the days and weeks following, usually in the early morning hours and drunk. He's been swallowed up by depression, mourning her loss, and self-medicating with bottles of vodka. At 4:00 a.m. and, by contrast, sober, my groggy murmurs of empathy ring hollow and insincere, even to my sleep-deprived ears.

Simultaneously, and unbeknownst to me, Nathan, who is seemingly unconcerned with his supposed best friend's mental state, announces to Jason his intention to pursue me once again. For reasons I can't begin to fathom, Jason doesn't denounce Nathan upon learning his intent; instead, he turns on me, accusing *me* of the betrayal.

It's as if Nathan and Jason are playing Go Fish with my affection, and I'm not even seated at the table.

"Got any of Julie's devotion?"

"Go Fish."

This isn't the 1800s. I have a say in my own romantic fate, don't I? There is no disloyalty. I look upon Nathan as a friend, nothing more, regardless of what he desires or Jason envisions. Not long after his mother's funeral, Jason returns to San Francisco and rents a dingy weekly apartment sandwiched between North Beach's strip clubs and the pungent fish markets of Chinatown. His letter arrives soon after.

April 24, 1993 – Letter from Jason

Envelope reads: *"I love you, but you are stupid."*

Surely my ability to decipher these words, more cryptic than usual with tell-tale flourishes of his drunkenness, must be proof of our attunement.

Julie, I love you. Julie, I've loved you for years and I will love you until my death of all time, I am sure. To say I was "stupid" for misreading it was your error. When Nathan said he was seeing you Friday night, I thought I couldn't believe such a betrayal. The only girl I have loved with my best friend. These have been the worst days of my life. No girl has said "I love you" to me in years. I have spent hundreds of nights in bars alone looking into strangers' eyes for any acknowledgment of my being alive (a small form of love). These nights, I stare at my mother's picture, and I have nothing. When we separated, I guess I thought always with some hope. When I heard you were going to see Nathan, it was final. I had nothing, would never have anything again. I could not believe you were leaving me for him.

Frustrated.

I am frustrated that I must, like an Egyptologist poring over a clay tablet, trace each word to decipher his cuneiform, when all I seek is the heart of his message.

Frustrated.

Frustrated that Jason remains deaf to my assurances, for the hundred and twenty-first time, that my interactions with Nathan are purely platonic, and almost always in the company of Lana and her fiancé. Nathan's presence, despite his professed intentions to Jason, holds no romantic significance for me. He will never supplant Jason in my heart.

Frustrated.

Frustrated that Jason continues to pal around with Nathan, handing him a hall pass while I am crucified by an almost biblical belief that I, like all women, am a seductress and Nathan is merely led by my wanton temptations. Jason will not be satisfied until I've severed ties with Nathan, thereby limiting my time with Lana as well, while Jason remains his loyal friend.

And frustrated.

Frustrated that with the words *I could not believe you were leaving me for him,* Jason understands my instincts will lead me to provide him clarity in person, to explain my truth, to unravel his confusion, and set the record straight—a piece of cheese set just so to catch this mouse.

GLUTEN FOR PUNISHMENT

GLASS AND FOG

Jason and I are finally living within an hour's distance of each other, he on the edge of North Beach in San Francisco, and me farther south in Silicon Valley. But rather than bringing us together, his unceasing imaginings of Nathan and me in some tryst have driven us further apart, now more than ever.

It takes me three weeks to persuade him to meet me face-to-face, delayed by an extra week due to illness. Nicknaming myself the "Human Petri Dish," I'm often sickly during this time in my life. This day, my throat feels raw and aching as I drive toward the city, the lingering stages of a cold compounded with the stress of attempting to revive our life together.

I pick Jason up outside his cheerless apartment, and we head to the Palace of Fine Arts to stroll along the colonnades, taking a stab at untangling the mess that's been made of our love.

Having been apart for a year and a half, do we hug? I can't recall. I'm withdrawn, incredulous at his suspicions regarding Nathan. As we rest beneath a eucalyptus, my hands, which habitually reach for his long, beautifully pale fingers, remain immobile in my lap. We watch the sun slowly slip below the horizon and feel San Francisco's chill descend, prickling my skin and coalescing with the chill that has made a home within me.

My heart beats strong and pure, yet my coolness, my ability to detach, to turn my back on love, has long been my safeguard, a finely wrought survival skill I acquired as a child. When my heart needs protection, a frosted piece of glass surrounds me, whether I wish it there or not. Even as I see Jason beside me, hear his voice, I remain safe, aloof, and alone behind my glass fortress. Many people develop poorly constructed defense mechanisms that hinder more often than help, coping strategies we struggle to change, yet they regretfully reemerge to our detriment, as mine does this day. I sit beside Jason, stoic and unmoved, nothing between us any clearer. A sadness creeps over us both, like the ubiquitous fog stalking, and then enveloping, us from the shoreline.

Later that evening, we speak again by telephone. With the protection of physical distance and a phone line, the glass ramparts around my heart crack under his words, but they refuse to crumble. When I hang up, I collapse on the bed, my body's energy drained away, eyes sticky and gritty, my tonsils red and sore. I crave nothing more than to dream, but my thoughts won't let me sleep.

May 24, 1993 – Letter from Jason

Julie, I do not know why I am alive, but I am happy today on the telephone with you. As the month waned, it was I who consumed the moon to fill the void of you. I cried stars of sadness and worthlessness, but don't worry, the moon will reappear new... I am allowed a little indulgence, a little fantasy of sorrow—it's the saddest day of my life, remember. But you made me very happy on the telephone today, despite the chatter of the Chinese and incessant Bon Gornos and ragtime pianos.

Why can't you allow today to be like holding hands in Balboa Park? Park of Spanish Porticos and you, content. We were like the courting frogs in the lily pond by the balustrade next to the Botanical Gardens. It is a sweet afternoon in San Francisco— full of strident bell towers, a few Victorian specters, and me! Not unromantic at all. I am sick of desire. How many beautiful things are there in the world? How many pretty girls with sore throats? There are arias wafting from the Trieste and from Puccini's and I am not torn between the two. There is the Andante and Allegro of our voices on the telephone.

You are sick as a stem in December, yet you drove from home through the crooked atlas of SF to find me and listen to me. Eating sore throat mints and listening for something to love or not love. What you heard, you couldn't say, and what you didn't say was hurtful. I was very sad, Julie. I ignored the plaintive breeze in the foliage of the park, but I could not ignore the uncertainty in the eyes of you.

I had to ignore the temptations, and temper the want of a kiss. I am familiar with your body as your hand, but I must stay like a stranger... I will wait and I will be gentle. I will never recede from you like a stranger... My logic and emotion are unlike the balance of most, the passion of all; My reason and love even less similar. My mechanisms for joy and sorrow more rare, but they are no less true! They all want to fix upon the axis of you! Your belief!

SF is a painted stone in the Bay. It sinks when I leave and rises to hit me on the head when I visit. Do you trust me? Would you sleep next to me again in a nap or in the deeper part of the night? Man was made (by who?) to invent Love. Lovers are made for (mis)understanding. Their logic is akin to sorcery and they wake in superstition. Doubt is a natural, imperfect part of Love... The summer is deepening; will your admiration for me? I do not like September.

I cannot fix the dome of the Palace of Fine Arts, can you? Your regrets seem too bold. Their position in the past is behind the happiness...Is not the method of my kiss sweet? And do I not know how to perform still greater, sweeter things?

...I am tired, Julie. It has been a long day, week, and year, and I am struggling for Love....Next time we meet, scrutinize my left eye and right. They are blue as you know them. You do know me! My lips are less than grenadine, you have tasted them like your own mouth—don't treat them like they are foreign.

You made me very happy on the phone today.

<u>*I am not waiting for you to tell me if you love me!*</u>

...Do not let it burden you if you doubt you do love. If you are afraid to say what one has always been told is the greatest of all human purposes, if you are not sure of feeling a feeling no one has ever defined or located, if you are afraid of being vulnerable more than any other time of your life, if you allow me to kiss you, then I will know you like me enough to trust me. That is enough; that is perfect! The words are not necessary. The most beautiful time of my life was not accompanied by "I love you"—one-eared cats will testify to this. He saw everything. A little bell ringing in the garden is Love.

By conjuring the one-eared cat, Jason paints a tableau of our shared memories from three years ago—the first time we made love. I loathe that pretentious term, "make love." For me, it conjures up a weekend-long Sacred Sexuality Seminar in some place like Joshua Tree, led by a love guru named Sage Moonflower. Yet, the term "make love" somehow fits when depicting my hours spent naked with quixotic Jason.

As I read Jason's letter, I hear a piece of the glass surrounding my heart break off, like a calving glacier, plummeting to the floor. His prose, rather than his poetry, has always been a finer tool for shattering my ramparts. This letter unleashes a tidal wave of nostalgia and unresolved longing, and with it an overwhelming feeling of being submerged beneath it all. The memories he paints, once pink and flesh Modiglianis, now seem distant and fraught with the complexities of our current reality, like our personal Guernica. I hesitate to respond, my heart cowering in a dark corner of my chest, paralyzed by the fear of his potential to hurt me the moment my wishes and sensibilities diverge from his own. His words serve as both a reminder of what we had and a stark contrast to the unresolved tensions between us now, leaving me unprepared, adrift in a turbulent sea of conflicting emotions, and struggling to catch my breath.

June 7, 1993 – Letter from Jason

Envelope reads: *"Postmaster: Important Message for Julie. Please deliver on time."*

Regard the blue apostrophes of my eyes lush with metaphors of love. Two pinafores of bluish love. I chose the eye as a symbol because the splendor of the iris does not decay, like their lids will loosen and droop.

…Like a bird eying a yewberry, I want to bite your ear and whisper a few things: I haven't held your hand this year. My first desire. Or watched you soap yourself in the bath (my body of Venus). I will make you champagne and strawberry soup on Russian Hill and say, c'mon let's kiss! From there, we can look at the green bay and see a mountain in the north.

We can take drives as long as summer, …sit in cinemas like Paradiso and hold hands in front of all. We will talk about our jobs in purple nightfalls—logos and banking stuff. What is the best shower tile cleaner? Who could explain the everlasting magnetism of Jason and Julie? A Galilean Paradox. The Nathanic Solution: Jason and Julie are fucked up, and shall be happier than all mortals. This is my last letter; All I really desire is a simple date with you.

No more poetics or grandiose stuff about love. Okey Dokey, Julie?

The unsuspecting postman delivers the Trojan horses—if Jason cannot breach my heart's defenses through conventional tactics, and when has he ever been conventional, then he will infiltrate with letters laden with affection and longing, painting landscapes of our halcyon past and sketching idyllic possibilities for our future. I am barely twenty-six years old, enamored with Jane Austen novels and even those melodramatic Brontë sisters. I am undone by words—and his annihilate my remaining reticence.

I consent to a second in-person conversation. We succeed in swiftly scorching this last chance to the ground. It's Nathan again, naturally. Have I spent time with him or made plans? I cannot recall, but isn't that what friends do? Has Jason not made plans with Nathan himself? Parked outside the North End Café, Jason slams the passenger door and storms away to his apartment.

I arrive home to find the light on my answering machine blinking.

"I think you are a fucking whore for dating my friend."

His lips have never uttered such ugly, vicious words to me. His statement robs the air from my lungs, like a sucker punch to my gut. Fucking whore. Those two words ricochet through my brain, unwilling to fly out of my skull and away into the ether. His false accusation hits a bullseye, my crimson love oozing from this craterous wound.

YEARS OF SILENCE, YET HE REMAINS

Have you ever had a difference with a dear friend? How his letters, written in the period of love and confidence, sicken and rebuke you! What a dreary mourning it is to dwell upon those vehement protests of dead affection! What lying epitaphs they make over the corpse of love! What dark, cruel comments upon Life and Vanities! Most of us have got or written drawers full of them. They are closet-skeletons which we keep and shun.   *—William Makepeace Thackeray, Vanity Fair*

November 1993 – Letter from Julie, Unsent

Jase,

I spent the night rereading each of your letters, cards, postcards, and poems, sequentially, from November 1989 to June 1993. It's the first time I've dared, fearing your words hiding within each envelope would obliterate my heart into a pulpy mess. I was not wrong—I wept, but I also smiled.

Since I was a teenager, I've been adept at extinguishing love to suit my predicament. With you, it's not as simple as turning away with a shrug and a, "Well that was a disaster."

I was safe, these past six months, using our misunderstandings and arguments as stones to build a citadel of protection, but when a piece of your heart resides within those walls, its ceaseless beating begins to reverberate around me, a Telltale Heart, but this one recalling happier moments—holding hands through the gardens behind Coit Tower, the first time we made love, our stroll through the Balboa Park rose garden after my pneumonia—until I am finally compelled to revisit your words, as I have done tonight.

I loved you—please don't doubt that. I will never forget you. A shard of my heart resides within you. Jason, if you feigned the depth of your affection in pursuit of poetic prose, keep me ignorant of it. That knowledge would annihilate me.

This letter is not an endeavor to reawaken love. Our last half-hearted attempt confirmed we lack the strength and understanding to carve new routes past our defenses and through our recurring difficulties, a hero's journey we are ill-prepared to travel.

I simply want you to know that, even now, I'm glad I snuck out of the party with you for our beach drive (though it took you almost a year to make a move).

These past months, all I could envision were our last two days together: frigid heart (mine), slammed door (yours), and those awful words (answering machine). Its 5:30 in the morning and a mockingbird sings outside my window in the dawn light. I should sleep now. I lament we couldn't survive, but I'm not sorry we tried.

ooo

I've slunk back to Southern California, having humiliatingly lost my mortgage banking job, ironically after another promotion, and assume Jason has moved from his squalid apartment yet still resides somewhere in San Francisco. I'm twenty-eight and it's been two years since I've seen his face.

No matter how much I'd prefer to forget him and his "vehement protests of dead affection," I cannot tuck Jason deep into some innermost cavern of my mind. He appears, unbidden, in several journal entries throughout the next two years.

August 29, 1995 – Julie's Journal

...My recent visit to San Francisco was soaked through with thoughts of Jason. Do I send the letter I wrote to him almost two years ago? Sending these words does not commit me to anything. Not sending them ensures everything. Read it again. Rewrite it? This letter will never be "right." Take a chance. Live. You have this new life now with all the possibilities, yet you still love like a repressed mortgage banker.

Worst case: He doesn't get the letter, you never know, and you believe he doesn't care or want to respond.

Worst case II: He gets the letter and responds by calling you a fucking whore (again) and telling you never to contact him. He also shows Nathan the letter and they mock you.

If you send Jason the letter, it finally puts a close on something that's been dangling for far too long. Why still dangling? In your mind only—get a clue, our love has been OVER for some time. Protect yourself...

My letter to Jason remains unsent...

I eventually mail a different letter, almost two years after the unsent first. I address the envelope to his dad's house in Escondido, hoping my words will be forwarded. Liquid courage cements my resolve. Because who regrets the decisions we've made while drinking alcohol? Drunk on half a bottle of red wine, I slip the letter into a mailbox with no means to retrieve the envelope with the lucidity of morning.

September 10, 1995 – Letter from Julie

Jase,

To love a writer is both a joy and a curse, these words sound flaccid when compared to your prose that easily flow from your pen. These following sentences were challenging to wring from my heart and place onto the page, and even more difficult to post to you. I'm frightened of reopening long-ago inflicted wounds and terrified of your reaction. Your final words to me still ring in my ears—fucking whore.

I've composed this letter a thousand times—in my head, on paper, in conversations with trusted friends, but the words have remained unsent. Why am I sending this letter now? ...Are they my own feelings that compel me—or an echo of you that lies within me still?

When we severed our relationship, your remark and actions left my heart in tatters. Although I was able to darn the pieces, Nathan recently chose to share certain tales of you, which ripped at the seams of my Frankenstein of an organ and allowed thoughts of you to seep into my brain again.

This is not a letter of blame, however. I am guilty of my own missteps...When you gifted me your heart, I vowed I would never deliberately cause harm, yet hurt you I did, although unintentionally. I was foolish to make this pledge; it was an impossible vow to keep. Love cultivates tender hearts—and these delicate sprouts of affection are easily damaged by unskilled tending. Genuine connections flourish through the mastery of a strong and deeper intimacy. I am ill-equipped, even today, to attempt such an endeavor as our relationship, wrought with its many particular complexities. Few would attempt such a task, and even less would succeed.

I'm sorry for any hurt I may have caused you. Though no excuse, please know this pain I inflicted was drenched in a deep and everlasting undercurrent of love. Have I looked upon anyone with the devotion I had for you? Not before and not after.

…It is important to me that you understand the following… I loved you. I was too immature, scared, and hidden behind my defenses to recognize our love as a unique and beautiful gift. I will never, ever forget you. Your influence on my life is everlasting. I am sincerely sorry for any pain I caused you. Disappointment, anger, and pain are the darker facets of love, but cannot, I think, be cleaved away. One cannot be hurt by those you do not hold in your heart.

This letter requires no response. I merely ask you to read it and try to understand my words.

Over the next year and a half, I date and, though cautious with my favors, I cannot claim to be a saintly celibate. My knees may occasionally open, but my heart remains securely clasped. In April 1997, I turn the big three-oh and cheekily christen it "The Year of the Man." Seemingly at the peak of their powers, my pheromones billow about me, like the scent of the Cinnabon store luring travelers in the airport. No man I desire seems immune. I pick, I choose, I break hearts, but each contender falls short. Meanwhile, I cannot seem to elbow thoughts of Jason and our past from my mind. My heart is locked away, and I fear his heart is trapped there too, a prisoner beside mine.

September 11, 1995 to March 1, 1997 – Julie's Journal, Various Entries

"…Every afternoon, I arrive home and expectantly check the mail to see if it brings a letter from him, even though my mailbox has remained empty for two years…"

"…Oh Jase, I am so sorry. It took someone else to point out how much I let you down when your mother died. You claimed you were coping fine and I believed you. I didn't realize you were reaching for me in your time of need. Sometimes you are so poetic with your words that I forget there are true feelings behind that lyricism…"

"…I call your dad's house in moments of weakness and a stranger answers the phone. Does he live there anymore?"

"…Red wine always makes me think of Jason…"

"...Nathan called me, confessing—or perhaps boasting—he was allowed to read my letter and says Jason doesn't understand why I would write it. Well, my Love, because I still haven't gotten over you and I may still be in love with you..."

LETTERS INTO THE VOID

Nathan, always the dutiful friend, plays the role of Jason's emissary, calling me to relay that Jason would like a book he left at my house returned. Nathan conveys the message as if Jason is irritated that one of his most prized possessions ended up in my sullied and unworthy hands.

December 1997 – Letter from Julie

Jase,

If I had known of your longing for its return these many years, you would have held it much sooner. This book is yours; it's always been yours. I didn't know where or how to restore it to you.

Until today, I believed you still lived in San Francisco. I drive by Escondido almost weekly and my mind can't help from drifting to thoughts of you when I pass by your exit. Little did I know I would find you there, back at your family home. I'm sorry to hear of your father's death.

I'm vexed by trying to write to you. I can never convey the nuances of my emotions with just twenty-six letters, especially while you do it so eloquently. Then again, it's always been difficult for me to convey love's subtleties—in my messages or otherwise, as you know. I'm always hiding, just a little. I'm sorry for my past behavior (well, not all of it, only the bad parts.) Think of this book as an early Christmas present and cement of my remorse.

It's been so long—I would love to read a line or two from you.
—Julie

January 13, 1998 – Letter from Julie

...Silly Jason, don't be angry with me—too much time has passed. I offer you my hand out of simple friendship, noble and pure. I desire nothing more from you than to grant me your hand in kind...

Nathan calls me and offers to play the role of my accomplice to reestablish a friendship with Jason. His grand scheme involves me sending passages and letters—to Nathan—and Nathan will "make sure Jason hears of them."

For the third time, I want to shout, "Are you fucking kidding me?"

Does Nathan honestly believe starting up a correspondence with him is going to lure Jason back into a friendship with me? What interaction in the last nine years would indicate that's a good idea? Jason is vexed by my friendship with his best friend, like a speck of sand irritating his azure eye. Nathan's suggestion, throwing more sand in Jason's face, seems ill conceived, if not a deliberate attempt to torment Jason further. I ignore his suggestion and choose to write another letter to Jason instead.

February 1, 1998 – Letter from Julie

…You know me, Jase, and are aware letters don't come easily from my hand. Dispatching three in quick succession is evidence of my determination to tear down your veil of silence. I'm unsure why you haven't sent a letter in response, however, I have two thoughts: 1) you are unmoved by my entreaties or 2) you are still angry with me. If it was indeed solely a matter of feeling apathetic, it would remain a simple task for you to…grab a random poem from your desk, stuff it in an envelope, and consider your job done. Since you haven't responded at all, you must still be upset… While I'm deflated by that realization, at least you feel something rather than nothing at all—a small peg to hang my hat on, to be sure.

I don't reproach you for your hesitation and distance. For many months after we separated, I remained mired in my own unvented spleen toward you. Not an emotion as straightforward as anger, but rather a feeling of complete emptiness inside, as if everything beneath my skin had been ripped away.

… I kept reliving that definitive evening in front of the North End Café, our last-chance attempt at reconciling discarded over your false accusations regarding Nathan and our inability to move forward.

Yet, gradually, I began recalling our moments of affinity. A word, a trinket, a painting, This Mortal Coil wafting from a window on a narrow San Francisco alley—all sparking memories of you. Today, these remembrances have smoothed the rough edges of our worst selves…

...I unwittingly wounded you and you are bitter. Do you doubt I was hurt in kind? Our relationship irreparably changed my life. I find myself unable to forge a meaningful relationship with anyone. All who try fail to provide more than an ersatz version of you. Sophomoric poems of poorly defined sentiments leave me unmoved. Dozens of store-bought red roses cannot hold a candle to the petals of a single lavender cabbage rose raining down upon my head...

...it's absurd to envision you welcoming me back into your life with an outstretched hand and warm smile merely because I dispatched a few letters, but I'm tired of pretending I've forgotten you. I have not forgotten. I don't expect you to be prepared for any of this—my letters, my return into your life—but understand that when you are prepared to reconcile with me, I am here. You may never be ready and that thought breaks my heart.

...I want to simply renew our friendship. What you gave me that first year as my friend is ten times more meaningful than what I receive from men who call themselves my boyfriend. I can imagine you balking, "After what Julie and I created, why would I want to return to a mere friendship?" Jason, nothing we create together would be insignificant. We can build a friendship surpassing all others...

...It's simple for you to pretend you feel nothing from the sanctuary of your silence. Until the time when you sit beside me, take my hand, look into my face, blue eyes to hazel, and say "I do not care about you," I refuse to accept you have lost all sentiments in the deepest recesses of your heart.

February 14, 1998 – Letter from Jason

Julie,

I shall never be able to look into your hazel eyes and recall a platonic companion. Your identity to me is the quintessence of a lover. To recall you is to pervade my being with the deepest contact with you. You are still my Eve and archetypal companion. I still dream of giving you pleasure like a reverie of symbolic giving. Gently pinching your labia between my lips and pulling something away from you I still treasure now. That part of you was like a glimpse of a heavenly flower, like a lotus of calm, its unseen petals the opening to an immersion I have not experienced since.

In the mornings behind you, the warm euphoria of spooning sex set a glow on the smallest activities the rest of the day. When within you, you reached between your legs to clasp a certain intimate part of me, the vulnerability was so exquisite, the trust of the gesture became so unbearably bright, my self delights in yielding.

All of these experiences of trust, giving, and exchange make the offer of friendship seem painful and incomplete.

…the last time I had physical contact was with you. The <u>last orgasm I've had</u> with another <u>was with you</u>. As well as the <u>last kiss</u>. There has been no other I cared to unlock that part of myself for. I haven't spent a single day looking for contact since you.

…I want the devotion in the long and continuous task of knowing and being a piece of your interior, your pains and failures, as well as exaltations.

When your desire turned toward Nathan, you no longer cared for me in a deeper way and were no longer sure of your inner devotion to me. The doubts of your body forever shut me out of the knowledge and ecstasy of you…

When on some park bench on an anonymous summer solstice, two average friends sit and dusk approaches surreptitiously, you will be placed in a position you didn't wish to be caught. When your hazel eyes bring the first intimation of twilight and the blue of my eyes tapers into the darkness, a burgeoning sadness will begin to brush out of sight. For we will be only friends and preludes of intimate exchanges will be just their epilogues, hands will fall away to avoid transgressing bounds of deeper knowledge, just as shadows recoiling from substance.

The possibilities of luminous sentiments, intrinsic to my idea of you will remain painful and captive, and fade into further years. Your offer of friendship has transported me back to the past I have buried when you belittled the source of my love with desire for my friend, and reminds me again you no longer love me.

—Jason

My hands convulse as I read Jason's words. I'm stunned. His confession of unwavering affection is utterly unexpected, while his continued accusations regarding Nathan leave me wanting to tear his letter into a million pieces. It's as if Jason possesses willful romantic dyslexia, reading "platonic friend" as "romantic interest" whenever we revisit the topic of Nathan.

With a heart so capable of love, I assume Jason had, if not forgotten me, moved on to another. I could even envision him married. Am I deceiving myself with my astonishment? Jason has haunted my heart, and I have not faded from his either.

I pen him a response later this same night, choosing not to address his unrelenting Nathan accusations, acknowledging my own struggle to erase Jason from my heart and opening a door, if not immediately for a return to love, at least for its exploration together.

WHAT DO THEY SAY ABOUT THE THIRD TIME?

March 1998 – A delivery of yellow tulips. The card reads
Life is Grand
—Jason

Although Jason and I talk often on the phone, he doesn't rush to schedule a date, even though he is living in Escondido and I am in Orange County, both returned to the locations where our story began.

Instead, he mails me a video so I can see what he looks like now. As I play it, the screen fills with random images of his back yard and house interior until the camera stutters and catches his face for a brief second, a shaky mistake when he accidentally turns the camera on himself. I catch a frame or two of his familiar azure irises, shockingly blue, the rest of him a blur.

A week later, he relents and I drive to Escondido for our first visit in four years. When he opens the door, I notice he has stopped coloring his hair. His tresses, now a natural shade of light auburn with signs of balding, fall into messy waves without the familiar dab of product to tame them. He's only thirty-two, yet dressed like a middle-aged man from Portland—Dockers, a navy cotton button-up, and chunky brown shoes. The weight he's gained alters his once-familiar frame, no longer the Lestat of my memories. A wave of disappointment passes through me, and then I shake the feeling away, chastising myself for caring about his outward appearance and reminding myself of the inconsequentiality of veneers.

His eyes, on the other hand, remain unchanged, two laughing sapphires sparkling above high, pale cheekbones. We lie on his bed once more, this time atop a velvet amethyst duvet. I am quickly reacquainted with his shy glances, his closed-mouth grin enclosed within parentheses of dimples, his manner of holding his thumb and forefinger just so when trying to make a point.

At the end of the evening, he kisses me, reticent and almost chaste, as if it took the entire night to gather his courage. We say goodnight, and I pull out of his driveway, returning home.

April 1998 – Letter from Jason

Recumbent upon the velvet divan, your limbs composed intimate embraces.
One embrace cradles,
One embrace envelops with sensuous candor,
One is gentle with inwardness;

All signify a haunting intensity within your body, convincing me of the depth of your feeling surpassing any poetic words. They encompass me entirely in the certainty of your affection. All convince me of a soul-to-soul devotion that instills strength in me and allows me to proceed full of faith in you, in myself, in us, and in awe of life!

Your gaze penetrates gently, and upon the violet coverlet of the bed, hours fell away in subdued ecstasy. Your eyes like gentle candlelight imbued me with exquisite closeness, and with the delicate pressure of your lips, I fade into pleasure of your entire body, passing in perfect equilibrium between the sensuous joy of your outward beauty and your resplendent interior. I have taken the utmost joy in the learning of your soul's ways, and in the greatest pleasure yet I hope to explore and share in all your states and to be inside of you physically, because being within your emotions is the most sublime of states.
Amour,
Jason

CRUMBLING

I've missed the thrill of finding the pastel envelopes with his familiar hieroglyphics nestled among the stack of bills and the weekly Pennysaver in my mailbox. With the first few, I step back into the colorful days of my younger self, as if we're picking up where our love broke off. I forget to consider, however, I am no longer that young woman. You cannot freeze a moment in time and expect it to taste as sweet or as fresh when thawed years later. When I began to stretch my arms toward him in earnest with a flurry of letters, I focused on pulling Jason back to me, driven by a need to quiet an ache, failing to question if the love of our youth is possible, or even desirable—at thirty. Old patterns, rather than disappearing with age, often solidify. Arguments flare between us over things we convince ourselves we've moved past. I find myself wondering if it's true love I've been clinging to, or just the sticky sweetness of nostalgia. Still, hope remains, and I tighten my grip, even as this familiar uncertainty tries to pry my fingers open.

April 1998 – Letter from Julie

Reconciliation after our first argument, a short month since reuniting.

Jase,

…To strive for the love depicted in your poetry is to disavow that relationships in reality are messy and fraught with misunderstandings. A bit of friction between us doesn't signify I'm planning to leave or harbor misgivings about trying again with you. You are the partner for me, of that I am certain…

When you stopped communicating last night and didn't return my words of affection, I imagined the worst, that you were thinking, "This is not the Julie of my recollection and reveries." Old patterns remain on the periphery, and I was labeling your silence as withdrawing. Tell me you require a few minutes to compose your thoughts before talking about your feelings and, equally, I need to know you hear my concerns.

When I awoke this morning, a dull sadness hung heavy in the air. I missed not finding you sleeping beside me when I opened my eyes. It's 10 a.m. and bright optimism has seeped through the melancholy…We both want the same thing—a healthy, loving, committed relationship—and we're aware of our defense mechanisms: shutting down, walking out… There's going to be occasional misalignments and we merely need to take each other's hand and explore these experiences together.

It's been a few hours since you left me and I miss you already. I seek to make you happy and sooth away your pains and insecurities…I want to be your support and comfort, not only your lover.

April 1998 – Letter from Jason

Things to think upon often even if only for a moment, like one deep breath restoring inner breathing and imbuing thought with energy.

Think of voices overheard in praise of your courage, faith and commitment and I will think of you many times each day. Look at the cumulus and cirrus from a window and know that I watch the nebulous white bodies drift and dream of your dreaming. For a few seconds, think of gardens visited, lovely embraces at mausoleums and eyes locked in glances of candor…My spirit visits you throughout the day. Think of my eyes in yours and fall into my spirit for a sudden interlude; I will envelop you there in an auspicious daydream. For the blinking of an eye, I will come to life in your longing and linger as you will. Think of my fingers drawing across the softness above your breasts, think of them once each hour touching upon yet another region of your body.

April 21, 1998 – Julie's Journal

I turned thirty-one yesterday. I wept last night after Jason gave me an orgasm—the sheer beauty of us, when we gift ourselves completely, brings me to tears.

I'm afraid of hurting him. His happiness seems solely dependent on me…these last four years, other men haven't been enough like Jason and yet, he remains too much like himself. His passion overwhelms.

ooo

It's June, a mere three months since we've rekindled our love, and, it seems, our dormant, unhealthy behaviors have caught fire as well: my walls, his insecurities, his practice of ignoring boundaries, mine of retreating. We're reliving eight years ago all over again. I'm drowning under Jason's deluge of love, choosing to paddle away from him to catch my breath. Is this need for retreat my failing, or could any woman weather his intensity?

I'm fixated on how "ordinary" couples function, and Jason seems determined to test if love possesses boundaries. We search for a middle ground, yet tenaciously hold our sides. I work full time, own a home, attend school. He is residing in his childhood home, existing on his inheritance and rent from a roommate, envisioning selling his art, yet never finishing a painting. His days are spent gardening, writing, hiking, and daydreaming. It's not uncommon for him to climb a tree to read Rilke. Sounds like bliss for someone over sixty-five, but, at thirty-one, rather than feeling envious, I desire to pluck this rare bird from his tree and cage him, encouraging him to fit in—a laughable aspiration, since I've never fit in anywhere. I don't want his life. I inexplicably want his to parallel mine, feeling as if he's not pulling his weight. It's a peculiar and destructive need, to clip his wings, and one I cannot comprehend.

He's given up alcohol, yet still battles moments of melancholy. No, I'm romanticizing. He battles bouts of depression and refuses to get help.

He's resentful of our years apart—jealous of my previous boyfriends and lovers. I, in turn, am suspicious of his roommate, who covets him for herself, pouting whenever we talk on the phone. Jason anoints her as his counsel in our dysfunction, sharing our most private details. She, in turn, provides him with ridiculous advice, "If Julie's not having eight orgasms during sex, there's something wrong with *her*." One or two is just fine, thank you very much. My body's not turbocharged for eight. When Jason can climax more than once, we can discuss how I'm sexually deficient. He asks to disclose these particulars to his ever-present best friend Nathan as well, who at every turn manages to throw a wrench into our already dysfunctional coupling.

Jason's insecurities regarding my reticence manifest in our bedroom. Instead of offering him gentle support and patience, the nonchalant "it's no big deal," something I've managed multiple times since, I pout and withdraw in frustration, feeling I am to blame for this dysfunction.

He is rushing toward me, giving me every morsel of his heart, but this barreling forward, blanketing me with love, is not what I require. Rather than the charging bull, I'm looking for the slowly approaching stag. After a day in Joshua Tree National Park in the California desert, Jason insists, "You cannot help but feel at least twenty-five percent more affection toward me after today." I do not, and when I'm truthful, I'm imbued with guilt and disloyalty for my inability to commit as he needs. I dismiss his suggestion of couples counseling, mistakenly believing counseling is for others, not us. Instead, I request two weeks apart, to contemplate and reset, without his letters, his emails, his calls stifling and confusing me. I am losing myself, feeling suffocated and unsure, and this frightens me.

Why, I wonder, can't we get this right?

June 23, 1998 – Julie's Journal

You arrange me atop a Corinthian shaft of Carrara marble. For a breath, my vanities delight in the regard, my sensibilities in this fresh perspective. Yet, as soon as I'm looked upon to echo my sorority's ideals—Venus de Milo, The Pietà, Winged Victory—I falter, longing to descend, proclaiming, "I do not belong here." I am no goddess, but merely a woman, vertiginous at such a height. Allow me to stand beside you, equal rather than ideal, but that is not the vantage where your love for me resides.

June 24, 1998 – Email from Julie

Our two weeks are up. I've been phoning you for three days and you've yet to return my call…Silence will not resolve anything, nor enlighten me. I drew my line in the sand during our last disagreement. I don't have the energy to continue this way, yet we find ourselves here again.

I cannot endure your continued disillusionment…You have painted me into this archetypal goddess and how am I…supposed to live up to that impossibility? …I have love to offer, not matching the depth and breadth of your own, but it's mine and it's pure, yet it doesn't begin to satisfy your ravenous needs.

My heart is hollow from enduring your disappointment when I come up short, and I'm always, it seems, short-changing you on some account. My intent was not to reestablish our connection to rupture old scars, but it seems I've done that—and added more wounds, as well.

I regret I can't be the type of partner you need… Forgive me for causing you suffering and anguish. You've had a lifetime of hurt already and deserve to be happy. My greatest hope for you is that you find someone befitting your expectations. I don't say that bitterly. You are extraordinary and deserve your equal.

I won't trouble you again, ever. It's too brutal on both of us. I'll mourn this and move on. I refuse to spend another four years pining for the one I loved and lost—again. I hope you do the same.

A few weeks after receiving my letter, Jason eventually responds by telephone, his voice tainted with casual indifference. He mentions meeting another woman and admits he's interested in her. He sarcastically suggests I should try calling him again in six months or a year, mocking our pattern. I want to fling the handset from my grasp into the wall, flummoxed by his bluntness and disregard for the pain he knows his words cause me. My mind flashes back to the evening in San Francisco when he confessed to sleeping with his French tutor, Tristan. Is he testing me? Trying to spark jealousy? Or is he simply lashing out to wound me?

July 8, 1998 – Letter from Julie

…I'm dismayed you felt compelled to end our love in such a hurtful way. I may have failed in my attempts, but at least I tried not to wound you. I hope this new woman gives you the affection you say I lack and she becomes the muse to inspire you. By telling

me to call you in six months or a few years, you left a door open for me. I am shutting it…I will mourn and move on with my life.

The envelope arrives in my mailbox about a month later. Its weight and thickness assure me Jason has sent more than a trifling few lines. But then again, "Jason" and "trifling few lines" are rarely seen in the same sentence.

When I was a teen at the beach, swimming in the Pacific Ocean with friends, we'd prepare for the largest of the impending waves by gulping a deep breath of air and diving to the ocean's floor just before the towering wave overtook us. In this way, we'd save ourselves from being engulfed and churned to the sandy bottom, an aquatic tumbleweed of arms, legs, sand, and saltwater.

As I prepare myself to face this thick stack of what I presume will be Jason's long-winded, discursive recriminations, a similar need overcomes me: to take a full breath and sink deep, hiding myself in safety as his surging swell of words overwhelms me once again.

Early August 1998 – Letter from Jason

Dear Julie,

I think about you every day and miss you more than anything in my life. I still love you like it was the first day of loving…I just see what I want to, I guess, but that's always been the task of love for me—to see what I dreamt of in you and not dote on errors.

I wrote you lots of lines but never sent them. I don't think they have much impact… right up to the last moment I was still confused about telling you I loved you…you're the best lover in the world, when you want to give yourself.

I went shopping for the amethyst broach for you a few days ago, but it was gone—I don't know why I would send it to you anyway since I didn't think I'd hear from you again. For the past month I longed for you to be with me when I was hiking in the summer showers in the mountains or at the beach at sunset. I wonder why you couldn't dream of sharing these places with me; perhaps life for me is always just perpetual reverie.

I didn't want to call because I don't want to be affected by your voice when it's withdrawing from me… I didn't want to send this letter either because I don't want to send a list of emotional recriminations to someone I love…. I just wanted to clarify I think you've been trying to withdraw your original enthusiasm for me for a long time, while mine grew deeper. I'm a little upset you entered into a relationship you weren't planning on giving every last breath to, but it is no one's fault if I don't inspire your giving...

And incidentally I haven't found anyone else, how could I when they're still my tenth desperate for love choice compared to you... I could never look into someone else's eyes or life very much when I've already decided I'm in love with you.

...I'm glad you sent me the rings back; It's...like a confession I wanted from you, but was just painfully trying to deny.... I felt all the time you wanted to fling those things in my face after every argument or when I got depressed that you didn't feel close to me and turned your back on me and say it's time for you to go. That's why I didn't want to call and tell you I loved you this past month because you've been telling me you're not ready for it all along and I don't want to start talking to you again just so I can properly stop talking to you.

This is a poem I didn't want to send because it just states the difficulty of a relationship, and I always wanted to supply you with encouraging answers.

Misunderstanding
Make a notation dear
Of this word and that
Which ones hurt most
Which ones feel good about our hearts
Which ones we moor our tenderness upon

When in the midst of course terms
I would rather expose docile replies
It is strange how fear binds adults
Would you still admire me if
I spoke in concert again with your aspirations
With eyes of open glass
You would be captive in their sentience of you

Or if I were mute
Which of my voices would you understand
The voice of my joy in you is brave and sweet
It resonates from the most inward enclosures

I'm quite guilty
I relied on poetic vision
To show me what exists
And what doesn't

I sought knowledge of you through your body
At times making false assumptions
Wrong turns
Sincerely at times admit to being lost
Crying, where is the felicity in this?
In small favors not on desert plateaus

In errors only
I tried to placate your worlds
With perfect skies
The contour of your body and mind

I ask you please to renounce your hardness
A favor for love

To be unpossessive of happiness
Maybe in not striving for ends
Just in the purpose of temporary joy
Time only falsely unmakes their sum
Also fragmenting us

Before you
And after you
A region slept in me
Trees replaced you
And temples replaced you
And then nothing replaces you

Now that your absence is exposed like the desert we stood in
I search failingly for your depth in the shallow nightfall
I search for your affinities in quiet spaces

I had hoped the slow paces of enlightenment
Would rescue our disappointments

Not allow a trail of misunderstanding
To mislead the procession of tenderness
Which once flowed in weightless rivers

What darkness cares to separate us
Existential questions preclude emotional ones
Perplexities aren't supposed to stop love

Once the chastities have eloped
I hoped to undertake true intimacies
Outside of mysteries

Is your body made for me
To place unutterable reasons within
To shelter your surfaces with gestures now obsolete

A lovely future dares to be here now
Don't allow the unknown to dispel it
Don't use doubt as a veil of shyness

I thought I had vanquished the desire to perfect
It robbed me of the ability to love what is most human
To admire the task not quite finished the way I had envisioned it
To subtract nothing
For love

We must embrace the accomplishment
Of one who gives their soul
Where doest right and wrong appear in love
Just a state we know to be vulnerable

Our eyes began easy harmonies
A procession of epiphanies maybe
But not all meetings are breathless

I saw in the mistral of your eyes
Love adrift
And sought to still your inquietudes
I failed more than once

With words
And with wordlessness

At times I thought I deserved to be loved less
At times much more
All the time wanting something else

Don't begrudge our pasts
There are many of them
At once remote and still intimate
I consider them like our childhood
Unruly and phantastical
but our memories always fail as guides

Full of not knowing
And yet instilled with clairvoyance
We distill a thousand kinds of courage
Necessary for anything of worth

Who can see the way out of adult dilemmas
Certainly not adults
We expected so much brilliance
For such a difficult task

Tall flowers do not grow in close shelter
To survive our folly
Our hearts must go separate ways for a vanity forever precluding love

As I work to untangle the knots of our love, simultaneously struggling to decipher the meaning beneath Jason's iambic pentameter adds an unnecessary complexity to an already convoluted situation. I feel as if I'm trying to solve a Rubik's Cube while colorblind.

Yet this poem is different. It cuts through his usual hazy verse with clarity. I read it once, then twice, and a third time. Each reading, I sense my throat tighten and tears blur my vision when I revisit the stanza:

Before you
And after you

A region slept in me
Trees replaced you
And temples replaced you
And then nothing replaces you

My preference for prose over poetry has been a sentiment I've shared with Jason throughout the labyrinth of our relationship. It's why, five years ago, he made the unkept vow, "no more poetics or grandiose stuff." While I'm not averse to a beautifully turned phrase—I aspire to craft such lines myself—Jason's gift for weaving words often leaves me questioning whether his sentiments are genuine or simply chosen for their lyrical allure.

It's often said that before we die, our lives flash before our eyes. As I read this poem, every moment with Jason flickers across my mind like a slide show. Even if Jason himself doesn't fully grasp what his own recounting means for our future, this poem, like a death rattle, allows me to understand that what we've been striving, yet failing, to build together, must perish. It is the only outcome available if we are to individually survive.

August, 1998 – Julie's Journal

The only hope for either of us is let go, forget, move forward, never look back. Regardless of the love we share, we will never be happy together. Together we suffer. I use that term—love—but is this love in the terrestrial sense? Ours is the love of Tristan and Isolde, Romeo and Juliet, Heathcliff and Catherine, Ophelia and Hamlet, Orpheus and Eurydice—a bittersweet impossibility.

…Who else will ever love me like this? …If I can do nothing else to ease his anguish, I can stay away forever, allowing space for a woman strong enough, patient enough, good enough, to give him the love he deserves.

Late August 1998 – Letter from Julie

I read your letter and poem and my heart sped to your side, as this beating organ never fails to do, yet once again, your words fall upon me as admonishment, bringing to light so sweetly and delicately how terribly I have failed you. Later, while curled in bed with tears staining my cheeks, I recalled that it was you, my Love, who stopped calling, who hinted at women more suited; you who left me.

Yes, doubts and reservations have been haunting me. I shared these with you, hoping you would hear me, honor my request to dial it back, help me through my indecision. Instead, my needs seem to have sent you fleeing. Does your commitment to me merely lie within your written words?

You are wrong about the rings—I didn't return them as a confession of emotions I do not possess. They were your mother's, they are yours, and, if I no longer walk beside you, then they are not mine to keep...

...I refuse to waste another handful of years fingering dusty trinkets and reading faded letters with filigreed words contradicting the clarity of your action—that you ignobly walked away without a word. Do rings hold more value for you than the woman you claim to love?

...All roads in our relationship lead to the same point: Defeat. I've felt it when I reread your letters late one night. I felt it when you stormed out of my car outside North Beach Café. I felt it when you called me a "fucking whore" and even in the very beginning, when you told me you had slept with Tristan while I patiently yearned for a kiss.

Who am I to believe I can will us into something we're not? Please forgive me for disturbing you again—I never had any right. Our fate, I'm afraid, is and always will be what we have today.

September 1998 – Letter from Jason

Dear Julie (notice your name in Vivaldi italics to imitate its music in my heart),

Since you can't hear the tone of my voice, know this letter is warm, concerned, and tender. I'm writing to express how sorry I am for the harm I caused. Sorry never seems to sound true in letters, but I am. If I could cradle you in my arms and tell you fervently, I would. Hearing my voice might cause more of the pain you hoped to move away from, but maybe I can absolve your hurt with some truths that seem more clear now.

First, I didn't end our relationship. I was just confused after our final date and I didn't call for three weeks just as you didn't call, and then I received the rings and letter. I can't reproach you for assuming, but it was a harmful assumption, as most are... I assumed our relationship to death... If you didn't want to see me for some innocuous reason, through my craving for love and insecurity, I assumed you didn't love me... a fatal substitute for just asking for clarification from your own lips. It confused me too when I was depressed or disheartened and just wanted you to console me, instead of defending yourself and isolate your lonely boyfriend.

It is your self-defense in situations where I mean no harm…that has perplexed me for nine years. I have asked a thousand times what in my stance makes you not trust me. Is it just as simple as my habitual tone of voice? I must have said dozens of times to you in a gruff voice, "why can't you just do this or that, be this or that." It's a pretty awful solution when I could have just said please… It's something I wanted more than anything from you, for you to just be comfortable with me. I have asked for many years, is it me you don't trust to give your heart unreservedly because I always return to hurting you somehow? Even when I called you names, I wouldn't have done it if I thought it would hurt you so much. At the time I thought you had no interest in me and were moving on with Nathan. I truly didn't even think it would make you shed a tear… The reason I even drag this old situation up again is I always wonder why I am unworthy of complete love. I have asked myself, "Am I unlovable or untrustable?" What have I done in between trying to express my sincerity and love that consistently frightens your total openness away?

I want you to have a decent regard for my attempt at loving you… After you said you didn't feel committed, we agreed to put the abstraction of the term aside and take things one beautiful date at a time. Again, I'm the one who…screwed up this attempt by wanting too much; how can I resist wanting all of you, you kick ass.

I want you to keep the rings, I said that crap about throwing them in my face for the same reason I called you a wh*re instead of telling you I loved you—one gets emotional and says fuck it, only the pissed sentiments abate in 30 seconds and love must live with those irretractable words for a long time. Anyway, I gave you my mother's favorite ring, one of my most prized possessions because you're my most prized companion in this life. It really hurt to get them back…You should keep them as remembrance of good times, and contrary to your belief, the substance of our relationship was always good.

I'm afraid I'm just associated with pain, instead of all the ideas I tried to create and inspire that you took as infringements on your own identity instead of contributions or gifts. I like you just as you are, even your stubbornness is endearing once I stand back and your upset words are looked upon with a little understanding…I hope you look back on my mistakes as human too.

You know this was my first "mature" encounter with a relationship. My last experience was with you so I was exploring and testing all that I had experienced for the first time. I was new to everything, everything was uncharted, and the expression of my heart and feelings were untried, and it proved not very adept, but who is smashing their first attempt at the most difficult task life ever proposes, life with another soul and heart. Especially difficult and quirky ones like ours. ...my life's path is not exampled or charted for easy reference like those with store-bought hearts, so you were in for challenges at every turn. Maybe it's too much to ask of any person to endure my heart, with its little rewards.

Our hearts are only tarnished with shadows, I believe we can polish them again and again.

I have a fateful duet of suggestions for your future; you may forget me, which I believe is unhealthy to cut a piece from your heart and place it in some eternal mausoleum. Or cleave what is unhealthy and allow the rest to heal and live through continued contact with me in letters... I want to know of your troubles, your garden and your spa trips and your excursions in reading. Your foot baths and your casseroles. And it would be a joy for me to tell you about my road trips to Paso Robles, the perches where I repose to read Rilke, and a few poems about the familiar subjects of moon and sky. (Okay maybe I won't send you so many esoteric poems).

Maybe a few reflections on our history together will be much less controversial in the no pressure environment of correspondence. At least from my side of things, there is nothing you've ever done that "I'm sorry" and a kiss wouldn't entirely cure. As for your demands of contrition, we know they are a little more exigent but I usually just need to be softer. Maybe a little more persistent with apologies...And, of course, I want you to return me to being your soul mate (in bed too, to never spoon again with you, oh la la, that would be eternal dejection.) ...The alternative is much more harmful, to try to disavow each other's existence is to suppress a fragment of your soul for the rest of your life. I would prefer to nourish mine on the good things that are happening in your life, and to know your needs more fully... outside of the pressures and rash distortions that our immature emotional burdens put on the beautiful possibilities that still exist between our souls (for love of course, silly).

Best wishes and love—very concerned for your happiness, Love Jason

If I'm not mad that you assumed the worst and sent my tokens back with harsh words (in fact it is dawning on me that the more upset you get the more hurt you are, I reread your letters and started to get worried sick, I wanted to call before this letter gets there, but I want to give you lots of space and zero pressure, my voice on the phone I think is too much right now), can't you forgive me for not calling for a few weeks, after all, it takes two not to call. I didn't assume (for once) that you wanted to dump me. If we're not destined to be lovers then…no, no, we are destined to be lovers always. Even if we're apart.

P.S. I went hiking today on the mesa adjacent to Los Penasquitos Canyon. There is something about the raised, flat topography that is akin to a vast lake, save that instead of reflecting the light it absorbs it gently, giving the landscape an aura of profound welcome. Wish we were holding hands and you were in those tight jeans without underwear.

The Ocean's breath of gauze moves like a surreptitious veil over the mesa,
becoming the medium of dusk's penumbra.
Twilight, your advent spreads over moments imperceptible to us,
Perhaps that is why we are so stunned at your approach
Even your furthest cast of rose
overcomes us with intimate transformation;
But it is the way you come upon us,
each night with endlessness,
that allow us to come upon ourselves endlessly.

I am saturated and cannot absorb another drop. His deluge of missives, multipage poems, photographs, and drawings has overridden and desensitized my sensibilities. This entreaty lands on my heart like just another of hundreds he has sent before it. I skim his letter, reading his words with detachment rather than poring over each line to extract the essence behind his pretty prose. He vows to refrain from sending me so many esoteric poems yet ends his letter with another.

My email response, written from my desk at work, is direct, my eyes remain dry. Yes, I love him, but my heart is incapable of continuing on this way. Whatever words I chose, however I framed my response, the answer is no.

September 1998 – Jason's email…and the last word I ever received

Heartbroken.

In subsequent years, in moments of melancholy or sentimentality, I pull his stack of letters from their hiding nook, untie the ribbon that binds them, and reread his last letter again. New tears stream down my cheeks each time. The fiasco plays itself out in front of me, like a film, and I am unable to direct young Julie to stop, to take a different path. She plays her role in this drama exquisitely, never questioning old patterns which no longer suit her. I want to grab her by the shoulders, beg her to slow down, to begin again, to decipher why she pushes him away so resolutely, to try to work through their difficulties together rather than turning her back. But life rarely affords us the opportunity for do-overs.

I hear the nuances of his words, accusations swirled within his professions of love, the layers upon layers eluding me at the time. I was angry, scared, and overwhelmed, depleted by our ceaseless back-and-forth, convinced I had to protect myself, and equally determined not to wound him again. Yet, what avenues remained unexplored—his suggestions of weekly letters, letters to keep us enthralled to an impossibility? I truly believed my solution was the right decision for us both, no matter how painful.

I willingly sacrificed a piece of my heart to protect his from being hurt again.

I read his entreaty and cannot imagine how I stayed resolute in my decision to release him, fighting the urge to rush back into his arms and agree, "Yes, let's try again," regardless that the final result would have been the same.

I wonder, Will anyone ever love me like Jason?

I didn't comprehend the Byzantine impossibility of being loved so completely. Did I truly even understand love?

I wish with every fiber that my response was kind and heartfelt, that I convinced him, even if we weren't together, that I loved him beyond anything, that I saw how special he was, and I felt inadequate to give him what he deserved.

If I am allowed one wish in this lifetime, I hope he knows he was loved.

JASON

the rose recipes

ooo

Rose can be a divisive flavor. If you aren't a fan, these recipes can be made without the rose water, but I recommend trying them as written first.

Rose water can vary in strength depending on the brand. The delicate rose flavor must not overpower. I've tried these recipes with Cortas Rose Water and Indo-European Rose Water, both available online or at most Middle Eastern markets. If you use another brand, you may need to play with the amount to suit your specific taste.

RASPBERRY ROSE VIENNESE WHIRLS   *Yield: 1 dozen sandwich cookies*

These are one of my favorite cookies—tart raspberry jam with a hint of rose and vanilla buttercream sandwiched between two tender buttery cookies.

Ingredients

Jam

- 2 cups frozen raspberries
- 1 cup granulated sugar
- 4 teaspoons (1 tablespoon plus 1 teaspoon) rose water

Cookies

- 1½ cups (3 sticks) unsalted butter, very soft
- ½ cup confectioners' (powdered) sugar, sifted
- ¼ teaspoon table salt (not kosher salt)
- 2 cups all-purpose flour
- 6 tablespoons cornstarch

Buttercream

- ½ cup (1 stick) unsalted butter, softened
- 1 cup confectioners' (powdered) sugar, sifted plus more for dusting
- ½ teaspoon vanilla extract

Directions

1. Make jam: Combine frozen raspberries and sugar in a small deep-sided saucepan and cook over medium heat until sugar is melted. You can tell the sugar has melted when the liquid is no longer cloudy and you don't see any granules at the bottom on the pan when you stir the jam. Increase heat to high, bring to boil, and boil for another 4 minutes. Remove from heat and add rose water. Set aside to cool and set. Refrigerate if not using the same day.

2. Make cookies: Preheat oven to 375°F. Line two baking sheets with parchment paper. Using a 2-inch round cookie cutter as a guide, draw 12 circles on each sheet of paper, spaced well apart. Turn the paper over so the pencil marks are underneath.

3. Using a stand mixer or electric beaters, beat the butter, confectioners' sugar, and salt until pale and fluffy. Sift in the flour and cornstarch and beat until just fully incorporated. Do not overmix. Spoon the mixture into a piping bag fitted with a medium star nozzle. Pipe 24 swirled rounds (not rosettes) inside the circles on the baking sheets. Refrigerate cookies for 15 minutes to help them retain their shape.

4. Bake for 12–14 minutes, until a pale golden color. Cool on the baking sheets for 5 minutes, then carefully transfer to a cooling rack to cool completely.

5. Make buttercream: Beat the butter, confectioners' sugar, and vanilla extract until fluffy and smooth. Spoon into a piping bag fitted with a medium star nozzle.

6. Assemble: Spread a layer of jam onto the flat side of 12 of the cookies. Pipe an equal thickness of buttercream over the jam and sandwich with the remaining cookies. Dust with confectioners' sugar.

Tip: To test the set consistency of your jam, spread a thin layer on a small plate, then put the plate into the freezer for 1-2 minutes. Push the jam with your finger. If it wrinkles and feels set, it's ready; if not, continue cooking and testing until it reaches desired consistency.

CARDAMOM-ROSE SCENTED ALMOND CAKE   *Yield: 8-10 servings*

This recipe suggests toasting the almond flour along with browning the butter. I recommend both for added nutty flavor and complexity, but if you would rather skip these steps, the final cake will still be delicious with a tender crumb and delicate flavor. Room temperature eggs will ensure maximum whipped volume.

Ingredients
- 1 cup almond flour
- $\frac{1}{2}$ cup (1 stick) unsalted butter
- $\frac{3}{4}$ cup all-purpose flour
- 1 teaspoon baking powder
- $\frac{1}{2}$ teaspoon ground cardamom
- $\frac{1}{2}$ teaspoon (scant) kosher salt
- 3 eggs, room temperature
- 1 cup granulated sugar, plus more for skillet
- $\frac{1}{2}$ cup mild olive oil
- 2 tablespoons rose water
- Confectioners' (powdered) sugar for dusting (optional)

Directions

1. Preheat oven to 350°F. Lightly grease a 10-inch cast iron skillet and dust with sugar, knocking out excess. Set aside.

2. Toast almond flour over medium heat in a large skillet, stirring occasionally, until golden and fragrant. At the same time, heat butter in a medium skillet, swirling often, until the foaming subsides and it turns a golden-brown color with a nutty smell. Remove both from heat and set each aside to cool.

3. In a small bowl, whisk together all-purpose flour, baking powder, cardamom, and salt. Set aside. Once almond flour is room temperature, whisk in almond flour.

4. In the bowl of a stand mixer, using the whisk attachment, beat the eggs and sugar until very thick and fluffy, about 5 minutes. Combine olive oil and rose water and slowly drizzle into the egg mixture, continuing to whisk as you go. Once combined, reduce speed to low and drizzle in the cooled browned butter. Turn off mixer and gently fold in the dry ingredients, taking care not to deflate the batter. Pour batter into the cast iron skillet.

5. Bake for about 30 minutes or until the cake is golden and a skewer inserted into the center comes out with just a few moist crumbs. Let the cake cool. Do not be alarmed if the center collapses a bit. Serve slices dusted with confectioners' sugar straight from the skillet.

HONEY-ROSE YOGURT PANNA COTTA
WITH APRICOTS AND WALNUTS

This exotic combination of apricots, walnuts, cinnamon, and rose is a perfect ending to a dinner of Moroccan tagine or Indian curry. I also enjoy it with a strong coffee for an indulgent breakfast treat, recalling my memories of Northern Italian breakfasts of vanilla bean panna cotta, freshly pulled cappuccino, and flaky *cornetto* slathered with apricot jam.

Ingredients

- 8 ounces (1¼ cups) dried apricots, finely chopped (Blenheim preferred)
- 1¼ cups honey, divided
- 3 tablespoons unsalted butter, divided
- ½ teaspoon (scant) cinnamon
- ¾ cup walnuts, finely chopped
- 2¼ teaspoons (1 package) unflavored gelatin
- 2 cups heavy whipping cream
- ⅛ teaspoon kosher salt
- 1½ cups plain whole-milk Greek yogurt
- 4 tablespoons rose water
- Sweetened freshly whipped cream (optional)

Directions

1. Grease 12 ramekins with mild, unflavored oil or cooking spray. Set aside. In a small bowl, cover finely chopped, dried apricots with hot water and soak for 10 minutes to soften.

2. Make cinnamon syrup: In a small saucepan, warm 1 cup honey, 2 tablespoons unsalted butter, and cinnamon over medium-high heat until bubbly. Set aside.

3. In a small skillet, over medium-high heat, heat remaining 1 tablespoon unsalted butter. Add walnuts and cook until toasted and fragrant. Pour ½ cup of cinnamon syrup over walnuts. Drain apricots and add to walnut-cinnamon mixture. Stir and cook until cinnamon syrup is absorbed.

4. Place about 2 tablespoons of remaining cinnamon syrup in the bottom of each ramekin. Spread about 2-3 tablespoons of apricot-walnut mixture over syrup.

5. In a medium saucepan, sprinkle gelatin over 3 tablespoons of water and let stand 1 minute, without heat, to soften. Whisk in the heavy whipping cream and salt. Heat gently over medium-low heat, whisking constantly, until gelatin has dissolved. Do not boil.

6. In a large bowl, whisk together whole-milk Greek yogurt, remaining ¼ cup honey, and rose water. Slowly whisk in warm cream mixture. Gently fill ramekins about ¾ full with yogurt mixture. Chill, covered, until fully set, about 8 hours.

7. Release panna cottas by loosening sides with a sharp knife and soaking the bottom and sides briefly in a pan of warm water. Invert them onto individual plates and serve with freshly whipped cream, if using. To make whipped cream: Beat together 1 cup heavy whipping cream and 2 tablespoons confectioners' sugar until soft peaks form.

Tip: If you find you have bubbles on the surface of your panna cotta before chilling, you can easily pop them with a quick blast from a kitchen blowtorch.

ROSEBERRY-LEMON PAVLOVA

Yield: 6-8 servings

This dessert is guaranteed to impress your guests. My mouth is watering thinking about the tart lemon-rose curd. Don't cut corners by purchasing jarred curd—I find them too sweet and lacking in lemon flavor in comparison. This curd is a punch of tartness, cutting through the sweetness of the meringue.

Ingredients

Meringue
- 1 cup granulated sugar
- 1 teaspoon cornstarch
- 4 large egg whites, room temperature
- 1 teaspoon lemon juice
- 1 teaspoon vanilla extract

Lemon-Rose Curd
- 1½ teaspoons lemon zest
- ½ cup fresh lemon juice
- ½ cup plus 3 tablespoons granulated sugar
- 2 large eggs plus 1 large egg yolk, beaten
- 6 tablespoons (¾ stick) unsalted butter, cut into small pieces
- 1 teaspoon rose water (add additional rose water ¼ teaspoon at a time until you achieve a light floral flavor)

Berries in Rose Syrup
- ¼ cup granulated sugar
- 1 tablespoon water
- ½ teaspoon rose water
- 3 cups fresh berries (a combination of raspberries, blueberries, and/or sliced strawberries)

Chantilly Cream
- 1 cup heavy whipping cream
- 1 tablespoon confectioners' (powdered) sugar
- 1 teaspoon vanilla extract

Directions

1. Preheat oven to 225°F. Line a baking sheet with parchment paper.
2. In a small bowl, whisk the granulated sugar and cornstarch together. In a clean, dry bowl of an electric mixer, using the whisk attachment, beat the egg whites on medium-high until soft peaks form.
3. Gradually add the sugar mixture, one tablespoon at a time, while continuing to beat the egg whites. Increase to high and continue beating until the mixture becomes glossy, you cannot feel any sugar crystals, and stiff peaks form.
4. In a small bowl, mix together the lemon juice and vanilla extract. Gently fold this mixture into the egg whites using a spatula.
5. Decoratively pipe or spoon the meringue onto the prepared baking sheet, forming an 8- to 9-inch circle. Build up the sides to create a shallow well in the center to hold the toppings later.
6. Bake meringue on the top rack of the oven for about an hour or until the meringue is crisp on the outside. The inside will remain soft and marshmallow-like. If the meringue begins to brown, reduce heat to 170°F. Do not open oven during baking.
7. While the meringue bakes, make the curd: Whisk together lemon zest, lemon juice, sugar, eggs, and yolk in a saucepan. Cook over medium-low heat, whisking constantly until curd is very thick, about 10 minutes. Remove from heat, whisk in butter and rose water. Pour curd through a sieve into a small bowl to catch any lumps. Cover with cling film touching the surface of the curd and chill.
8. When the meringue is done baking, turn off the oven. Slightly crack the oven door (I use the handle of a wooden spoon stuck in the door) and leave the meringue inside to slowly cool completely for another hour. This helps prevent cracking.
9. While the meringue cools, make the rose syrup. Combine sugar and water in a microwave-safe bowl. Microwave in 30-second bursts until sugar is fully dissolved, about 1 minute. Add rose water and set aside.

10. Thirty minutes before serving, make Chantilly cream: Beat heavy whipping cream, confectioners' sugar, and vanilla extract until soft peaks form. Refrigerate until ready to use. In a medium bowl, combine berries and rose syrup and let macerate for 20-30 minutes. Drain before using.
11. Transfer meringue to a serving plate. Fill the well with ¾ cup lemon-rose curd (refrigerate remaining curd for another use), and cover curd with all the Chantilly cream and the drained berries piled high. The pavlova should be served immediately to keep the meringue crisp.

CARDAMOM ROSE LATTES

Yield: About 16 lattes, depending on size

In general, I'm not a fancy, foo-foo, flavored latte kind of person. Mornings, I prefer a single cappuccino (no messing around with "caff" or "fat" or "pumps"). After dinner, a perfectly pulled single espresso with a bit of raw sugar does the trick.

These were my go-to hot beverages until, sometime around 2018, I discovered cardamom-rose lattes at my local coffeehouse. Cardamom? And rose? Decidedly foo-foo, but I was nonetheless hooked. I adore citrusy-spicy cardamom and use it often in my baking—an unexpected alternative to cinnamon. Plus, I've always been a fan of those delicate, rose-scented, syrupy Indian and Middle Eastern sweets. Combine these two flavors with creamy steamed milk and a bit of espresso and you have an exotically spiced, floral, sweet treat that can only be described as well-being in a mug—the ideal foil to the Monday blues.

Ingredients
- 1 cup granulated sugar
- ½ cup water
- 1½ teaspoons ground cardamom
- 2 tablespoons rose water
- 1 to 2 shots of espresso or ½ cup strong brewed coffee (for each latte)
- Milk of your choice, for each latte (e.g., 8 ounces per serving)

Directions
1. Make syrup: In a small saucepan, heat sugar and water together until sugar is completely melted and mixture looks clear. Remove from heat, stir in cardamom, cover, and let steep for 30 minutes. Don't steep longer, as syrup can become bitter. Strain through 1 layer of cheesecloth and add rose water.
2. Make latte: Brew espresso or strong coffee according to your machine's directions. Steam or heat milk of your choice. Combine espresso or coffee with the steamed milk, stirring in one tablespoon of syrup (or more to taste) for each 8 ounces of milk. Breathe deeply and enjoy.

three

THE SPACE BETWEEN US: EDMOND, PART I

Age 32–33

THIS TALE BEGINS WITH AN EMAIL, *"I'm not trying to sell you anything."* My hand hovers above the delete button, assuming the message that follows is indeed exactly that—someone attempting to sell me something.

It isn't. It's Edmond.

His older brother, a colleague of mine, gave him my email address. If I can even label him a colleague. Edmond's brother is one of the architects, the executives with titles after their names sitting in offices with window views of the distant mountains. I'm paying my bills as an administrative assistant at the same company. When I look up from an expense report, there's no mountains, just three cream-colored cubicle walls surrounding me. My first return to the corporate world after a four-year sojourn finds me chagrined by a significant step down in salary and prestige from my former mortgage banking days.

Yet, lucky for me, this particular architect snubs his nose at corporate hierarchy, befriending the administrative assistants more than the other architects, regardless of our lack of titles, six-figure salaries, or window views.

I don't notice summer winding down, the afternoon light turning golden. Snapshots of my years and tears with Jason obscuring my view. The word *"Heartbroken"* filled my computer screen one short month ago.

After finding my never-going-back strength to permanently cleave myself from Jason's life, I've spent these last few weeks using lunchtime power-walks with Edmond's brother and the admins as my personal talk therapy. As we walk our three-mile loop alongside the Santa Ana River Flood Channel, I churn up the details of this latest and last failed attempt while my coworkers nod, their sympathy for me growing weary. One afternoon, Edmond's brother, fed up hearing my recitations on the collapse of this Shakespearean romance, comments.

"You remind me of my younger sibling, Edmond. The two of you are awfully similar. I think you'd get along well. He's single and lives in Seattle."

"Similar how? How old is he? You've never mentioned him before."

"You're both artistic and ruminators. He's a few years younger than you. Interested? Do you want me to give him your number?"

"Sure, but let's start with my work email. I'm not great at talking on the phone with strangers."

That first message arrives a week or so later and, for the next four months, Edmond and I volley missives back and forth. Each morning, I expectantly switch on my computer, cup of freshly poured coffee beside me, my eyes scanning my mailbox for his name, anxious to read another cleverly written, charming message. As an aspiring writer, he rarely disappoints (I do have a type). These conversations flow easily, as we discover our overlapping interests: books, art, music, food, and recent stints as coffeehouse slaves. We create a playful fantasy world with pseudonyms and backstories. We weave our tale, one paragraph delivered at a time, each of us adding to the story: Rolando and Inez and their passionate, yet heartbreaking, romance in Belize.

After four months of waiting, Edmond finally visits his parents in Orange County. Our first date…no, our first meeting (we have no idea if there would be chemistry) coincidentally lands on Valentine's Day.

No pressure there, Cupid.

We agree on a Cuban restaurant and bar in Orange County, for drinks—keeping it casual, god forbid we should look like we're out for VD dinner on a first date.

I arrive before him, sit down at the bar with my back to the door, and immediately order a Moscow Mule. As I take long pulls of my cocktail through the straw, I begin nervously chatting with a couple drinking a few seats away, whitewashing my jitters by appearing the pseudo-raconteur by the time he shows up.

I sense the air change behind me. Edmond has arrived. When I turn around, a young John Cusack from his *Say Anything…* days towers over me. Lurch, I mean Edmond, is at least a foot and a half taller than me. Still, I find him cute and his geek-chic aesthetic endearing. As the night progresses, we lean toward each other, sharing more about ourselves, yet retain a polite buffer zone between us. When we decide to call it a night, I wonder about our mutual levels of interest, *Is he right for me? Is he even interested?* When he proposes splitting the check, I interpret his suggestion as "not smitten" and pay half the bill, resigned to my interpretation that our chemistry must be purely virtual.

Two days later, I find myself seated beside Edmond as he drives his mom's SUV down the coast to La Jolla for a Francis Bacon Papal Portraits exhibition. Doubts linger about his interest level. Is he letting manners guide him? This outing was our "official" weekend plan. If he canceled after drinks, Edmond wouldn't just seem rude; his decision would also create an awkward situation with his brother when I see him on Monday. Is he being polite or does he genuinely want to spend the day with me?

A Mount Vesuvius of a pimple has sprouted on my chin, the embodiment of my anxiety over meeting him, easily masked in the flickering candlelight of a dark bar, but a throbbing beacon in the bright La Jolla sunshine. Staring, horrified, in my bathroom mirror this morning, I spackle on a thick layer of foundation muttering, "Fucking hormones" to myself. In the SUV, Edmond pretends he doesn't notice.

We walk into a rotunda. The large canvases covered with raw, visceral, emotionally charged brushstrokes seem to confine the various images of popes, almost as if they have been placed on their thrones inside a psychiatric isolation room and we are staring at them through the observation window. Big, bloated men of import trapped within anguish and psychological torment displayed in the round, as if we are doctors positioned in the center to observe them. We circumnavigate the blurred, twisted faces and exaggerated features, absorbed by the bold, loose images before us, each walking along our own track, never touching, not speaking, not even the "accidental" brush, a personal favorite mating tactic of mine. I'm more interested in Edmond, I realize, than I'm willing to admit.

On the drive home, I'm reluctant to leave the angst and unease the portraits have stirred within me. Our conversation subdued, his rough fingers eventually find mine, which I've rested conveniently on the center console. This action assures me he's into me after all. His touch pulls me from the haunting art back to the possibilities before us.

When we arrive at his parents', holding hands, we find his brother sitting on the couch. He smiles. "I'm going to pretend like this doesn't seem a little weird to me."

In the cool of the evening, now alone and sitting knee-to-knee on his parents' patio, Edmond leans in, and his lips find mine. He manages to sandpaper every layer of zit-spackle from my chin.

On Sunday, we lounge on a beach blanket, basking in the Southern California sun, stealing kisses between sips of sparkling wine straight from the bottle before his flight home. Edmond reveals that he felt a surge of happiness bubble up when I asked him to join me for this impromptu outing. Tipsy on alcohol and frenetic pheromones, we nearly miss getting him to the airport on time. I sense his irritation when I accidentally get us lost on the drive to John Wayne Airport, but brush off his simmering discontent as normal anxiety about possibly missing his plane.

Edmond returns two weeks later. All reticence removed, clothes are stripped movie-style...hungrily, shamelessly, lustfully. No bodices are ripped, but pretty damn close. Our first time ensues on the light blue wall-to-wall carpeting of my condo floor, halfway between my bedroom and bathroom, romance taking a back seat to pure carnal desires.

We visit as often as schedules allow, usually Edmond flying to me, owing to my phobia of planes nose-diving into the ground. When physically apart, we call and email, pages upon pages of emails. I print out and save our messages, our romance novel of Rolando and Inez growing two inches thick. Trees die for our love. I can't recall who utters the words "I love you" first, but I'm inclined to believe it is Edmond.

Like a transmitter and receiver, we seem to work better with distance between us. During visits, misunderstanding, miscommunication, and misalignment are unpacked along with a week's supply of underwear. We assume the twelve hundred miles between us is causing the disconnect. A closer proximity will surely alleviate what we view as normal quotidian challenges of long-distance unions. Edmond lays out the straightforward-sounding steps toward cohabitation, yet the actual leap toward this reality is Herculean. We abstractly discuss relocation, yet neither is ready to trade current living situations for the possibility of a new life together. You move. No, *you* move.

I am entrenched for the moment, relocation requiring more sacrifice than I am willing to endure. I have mortgaged my life for my first home, recently secured a higher-paying job, and have only six classes to go before finishing my degree at the local college—the third, and hopefully final, institute in my circuitous route toward higher education.

Edmond eventually relents. He adores his rain-soaked city, with Starbucks, the Space Needle, and Mount Rainier keeping sentry. The prospect of relocating to a nondescript, beige condo in the Orange County burbs is a trade-off he grudgingly makes, even when tempered with the promise of fulfilling his dream of LA film school all while curling up with me each night.

I am contemplating adding a kitten to my condo life, but Edmond urges me to wait until we can adopt together, once living under the same roof. He says, "If you adopt a kitten now, it'll always see me as an interloper and compete against me for your affection." Edmond doesn't want to find presents of cat shit in his shoes for the next fifteen or so years.

So, I wait.

But there are signs our relationship may not endure, at least not in a sustained, conventional, "and they lived happily ever after" way. This dream life we seek to build together begins showing initial signs of fraying when Edmond, saving money for his relocation to Southern California, stuns me by purchasing a shiny new SUV instead. We don't discuss car shopping, nor does he mention wanting to buy a new vehicle during our extensive conversations about "next steps." One evening, when I arrive for a visit, his new wheels sit gleaming on the wet asphalt in front of his apartment. "I'll need a car in LA" is his justification. If a diamond says, "I love you," then a brand-new just-off-the-lot Ford Expedition screams, "I have cold feet."

Edmond also begins mentioning this new couple he has recently befriended. Something about their acquaintance causes me pause, stirring up my jealousy, an emotion that doesn't visit me often. Each time he speaks their names or mentions spending time with them, which seems regularly, my Spidey-sense prickles up, *Pay attention here. There's gonna be more to this story.*

In February, I plan an enchanting Hawaiian getaway for us over Valentine's week. I am already traveling to Oahu for my dear friend Lana's wedding. Lana has asked me to be her maid of honor. I invite Edmond to join me and tack on another week in Kauai for some couple time.

I muse, *Could there be anything more romantic than Valentine's week in Hawaii?*

We are also celebrating our one-year anniversary. Cupid's big day, in a romantic island setting, witnessing the deep commitment of two friends taking their vows—the stars align themselves perfectly to commemorate our first three-hundred-sixty-five days of love.

Alas, the stars are little assholes.

A delayed flight (his), maid of honor duties (mine), and a terrible, second-degree Waikiki sunburn (his again) kick off the ten-day trip. I face an unwinnable dilemma: desert Lana on the days leading up to her wedding or leave my boyfriend to fend for himself. I choose my dear friend of twenty years. For Edmond, it seems, I make the wrong choice. It begins when his significant plane delay (connect through SFO at your peril) causes him to miss the rehearsal dinner luau, and the events that follow snowball from there. Leave it to us to find a snowball in Waikiki.

He sulks like a moody teenager, I hula across eggshell beaches, pretending not to notice my mere existence seems to elicit a simmering contempt hiding below his surface. We barely have sex. He doesn't seem to desire me any longer, a sure sign of trouble in literal paradise. Rather than fix us, our time in Hawaii breaks us, a relationship bookended by Valentine's. We smile for the vacation photos, but I depart for my flight in tears, certain of the inevitable. "Hawaii: Arrive as a happy couple, depart as a sad singleton." The tourist board passed on that particular slogan suggestion.

Within days of returning home, I receive Edmond's expected call, requesting a two-week hiatus so he can "think about our relationship." What I hear is, "I'm not sure I love you anymore."

This is the same request I had of Jason, but it's different when I'm not the partner asking. I'm the defendant when the jury withdraws to the deliberation room. *What evidence are they considering? Should I have taken the stand to plead my case? Is the room split, or did the initial straw vote seal my fate?* I'm accused of the crime of not living up to Edmond's image of girlfriend material, and I've become a powerless spectator in an outcome involving my fate.

After two days, and already fed up with this interminable wait for him to drop the final ax, I rashly snatch the weapon from his hand. I don't need two weeks for his verdict. I'm done with his bullshit. My dream of fashioning a life with him cleaved in two by the cold blade of truth: our relationship, while thriving with distance, will never mature into a blooming love, once unshackled by proximity.

Less than a month later, a teeny four-week-new tuxedo kitten suckles eagerly from the bottle I hold in my hand, a wet soul patch of formula soaking his scruffy chin. I've named him Kafka, a somber moniker for this little furball with claws. This new addition has love-bombed me, stolen my heart with his shell-pink nose and cotton candy toe beans—a fluffy, final declaration that this chapter in my life is over. Adopting Kafka, without Edmond, adds a period to the final sentence we've already written.

In the years after, I can't help wondering, *What if I had been braver? What if I had made the move to Seattle, pushing all reticence aside?* I shouldn't examine love through the lens of risk versus reward, but I can't help imagining what saying, "Yes, Yes, Yes" would have cost me. We possess a unique connection, certainly, but it takes more than a bond of recognition between two slightly fucked-up souls to persevere through the worst bits of cohabitation.

I envision my alternative life in Seattle, marred by never feeling up to the mark of his expectations. To live in a city with too much rain and cold—so different from my California-girl life—would require me to relinquish an integral part of myself. Slogging through the rain on perpetually grey days would result in a diluted and grey Julie. A move would mean selling my condo—likely never to own a home in California again, the one possession that promises "security" in my mind. Making Seattle my home base would require relinquishing lifelong friends, starting another job search, and transferring what credits I can to a fourth college. If and when our inevitable end arrived, I would have lost more than Edmond, slinking back to Southern California to live where exactly, to do what exactly? There is no net beneath me, except of my own making, and, to ensure I retain that safety, I can't relinquish my sense of security for a relationship already beginning to malfunction.

Edmond, in contrast, would contentedly continue his life in Seattle, working at his current job, walking the same streets, socializing with familiar friends, with the added bonus of a girlfriend nightly in his bed. What would he be risking if I move? Nothing, from where I stand, and that doesn't feel like a partnership to me.

I claim he broke my heart—he retorts I broke his. After a few months, the grapevine, aka one of my fellow admins, Denise, admits she's heard he's been dating the woman from the befriended now-ex couple. My Spidey-sense rarely makes mistakes. Edmond continues to call me occasionally, even arrives on my doorstep unannounced one evening, but finally, Denise shares the news—he has married this new woman. I smile at the revelation, pretending to be unaffected, but a stone lands heavy in my stomach.

My older sister has a saying about the men in our lives: "They always come back." Really, I wonder, even when they've taken that final, decisive action to say, "I do"? I lift Kafka to my lips and kiss the tip of his pink gumdrop nose. "You'll never leave me, right?"

four

PALATE CLEANSER

∘∘∘

LOVE:
IN COMPONENT PARTS

A DEFINITION

"Define love," my friend Todd asks while doing his best philosophy profes-sor impression. "Explain how your definition has changed from your earlier notions."

I answer quickly, regurgitating statements I've made previously, "Contentment with my partner, contentment with who I am around this person, contentment with our similarities as well as with our differences, contentment with each other's values and perceptions of the world." Contentment, contentment, contentment.

I've used that G-rated C-word before, as an attempt to describe the slippery and difficultly defined emotion of love, often to the annoyance of boyfriends for utilizing that particular word. I've learned this friction stems from divergent inter-pretations of contentment's meaning. On the surface, contentment can describe the apathetic mindset, "I've accepted my lot in life. I'm good with this mediocrity. I'm unmoved to strive for better." So, it's entirely understandable lovers would balk when I respond to "How do I make you feel?" with an answer sounding like, "I've accepted the mediocrity of our relationship."

If you peel back contentment's onion further, however, the word's deeper meaning is unveiled: a pervasive sense of tranquility and harmony that springs from feeling at ease with myself, my surroundings, and my relationships, without a yearning for more or a different life.

Contentment involves gratitude for what I have, as well as recognizing that true happiness and fulfillment cannot be found by endlessly searching. Content-ment does not mean complacency or stagnation, but rather a balance between the ambition to search for more or different and the ability to appreciate the present situation. If, when wrapped within a lover's arms, I am imbued with such a feeling, doesn't that embody at least one form of love?

Love's various versions merely complicate my quandary further when describ-ing this intangible and mutable emotion. Familial love, often mixed with exas-peration—even potentially anger or derision—is quite different from passionate, amorous love. I'm sure you've heard that, in the Arctic regions, the Inuit/Yupik languages possess a rich vocabulary for the various aspects of "ice" and "snow." The myriad weather conditions they encounter require a lexicon to accurately paint various Arctic environments. Likewise, we should, in fact, have a similarly diverse vocabulary for love in all its permutations. How can we capture love's faceted multitudes within one four-letter unidimensional term?

In ancient times, the Greeks employed several distinct words to differentiate various types of love. For instance, *eros* referred to intimate, passionate love, *philia* denoted deep friendship and affection, *agape* represented unconditional, selfless love, *storge* referred to familial love, and *philostorgia* denotes the love of a pet or animal. They even used the now-immoral man/boy *paederastia*.

Before venturing beyond my well-worn definition of contentment, I realize that what Professor Todd seeks isn't a philosophical exploration of love in all its forms—he's after my take on romantic love, stepping beyond contentment into something deeper. Something more profound.

LSAT – Love Scholastic Aptitude Test

Essay Section: Students are expected to provide a thoughtful and coherent response by developing a clear thesis statement, providing supporting evidence and examples, and demonstrating effective organization and language use. Begin with a clear and concise introductory sentence that captures the reader's attention. Provide at least three supporting sentences that include evidence, examples, or further explanation to support and develop the main idea presented in the introductory sentence. Finish with a conclusion that wraps up the paragraph by summarizing the main points or restating the main idea in a concise manner.

Q: Without using the word "contentment," define romantic love. Explain how your definition has changed from your earlier notions.

My concept of love remains far from well-defined. How can I expound upon an emotion, from my perspective, often elusive and ephemeral? Does one define love based on the effects of the relationship on the individual: I feel X because I receive Y? I once attended a wedding where the couple wrote their own vows. Sounds romantic, right? Well, the groom spoke of how his soon-to-be wife made him feel, what she did for him, how she supported him, how she allowed him to be himself, with nary a word about his feelings for her. Wouldn't that be labeled "selfish love"? They're heading toward divorce now, if that provides any indication of this being the correct definition.

Perhaps love should be solely based on how the other person feels? On closer inspection, though, would we label that "unconditional love"? While not inherently bad, this specific version of love can lead to unhealthy boundaries, a lack of self-love, and unbalanced dynamics. I've learned the lesson one should never love to the point of losing self (see "Brett" chapter coming up), even in the frequently referenced parent/ child dynamic. If you love and care for yourself first, you are available to love others fully. If not these two versions—taking all for yourself or giving all of yourself—then, conceivably love could be a verb, like Stephen Covey proclaimed in The 7 Habits of Highly Effective People, *the self-help book that adorned every executive's bookshelf in the 1990s. In Covey's definition, love is not an emotion you feel. Love is a verb. You love when you "do" for another person, regardless of whether you feel love for them or not, a "fake it till you make it" variety of love. I believe Mr. Covey is mistaken. When love is involved, there are kindnesses and actions organically exchanged, but these same actions, without the emotion behind them, become merely the veneer of love, not the deeper emotion. Alternately, my younger self erroneously believed love must be enveloped in red-hot passion. This conflagration of love is a double-edged sword. The fire of passionate romance quickly flares into wildfires of anger and quite possibly hate. I've been charbroiled by this pelean embodiment of love, suffering the effects of more infernos than one woman should be forced to endure. The older, wiser version of myself would arrest passion's heat, tempering ardor with the word "desire" in place of "passion."*

So, what, really, defines love for me? Is the question best left to the poets and songwriters to illustrate? Throughout this writing exercise, I've been pestered by the earworm of Haddaway's 1993 pop hit, "What Is Love" followed by "What's Love Got to Do with It" by Tina Turner.

I'm not lacking the ability to declare affection, ardently expressing my love for another, but once our bond has been stretched and broken and I find myself healed from the heartache, I reflect, concluding my ardor was not the L-word after all. I'm frightened that I'm intrinsically incapable of love—at least to the level of poems, songs, and what we see in films. Is that dramatized version an unattainable, unsustainable love?

If you had asked me for love's recipe, rather than its definition, I would gratefully employ knife and cutting board in lieu of pen and paper. I'd concoct a hearty stew of desire and harmony (since the C-word is verboten per the instructions above), with a few cups of shared values, a sprinkling of mutual attachment, and a good glug of respect—or the pot would remain empty, love as a figment, a chimera—the nihilistic version of love that rears her head in my musings, usually between partners.

On second thought, don't ask me for I haven't an answer. I don't know shit about love.

A DISEASE

Love is a malady, a sickness, ravaging our soul and divorcing us from our wits and self-possession. It disorients us, causing delirious bewilderment. We are entranced, alienated from ourselves and our dignity. This infection leaves our identity a hollow shell. We become strangers to ourselves and, when this illness has run its course, we are left without even our inner self to comfort us. Who are we once this fever passes? We are defeated, undone.

A METAPHOR

This heart of mine is strictly feline. Treat me as you would a house cat. If you want to win my affection, don't approach me straight away or attempt to tightly wrap your arms around me, for I am certain to recoil and wiggle free. Don't croon my name and pat your lap expectantly. I am no one's property. If you coax, I will snub, finding far more interesting things to occupy my time. I will nap or clean myself, even stare blankly at the wall, rather than acquiesce to your beckoning.

If you are seeking my affection, you would do well to ignore me. Your disregard is catnip to my heart. Become absorbed with another pursuit. Only then will I adamantly and persistently demand your unmitigated attention, sprawling myself across whatever else, or whoever else, has caught your notice. Leave that spot beside you on the couch available, but do not wait on tenterhooks for my arrival. When you're distracted, I will find my way beside you, in due course, on my own terms. Once I have decided to stay, then you may adore me, and I will purr with contentment (there's that word again). Do not fuss too much. Hold me too tight or keep me too close and I will flee to my haven of solitude. Lock me out of a part of your life, like a closed door, and that's where I'll want to be. Understand my terms, display patience, do not frighten me, and I will show you how I love: loyally, enduringly, and deeply, but always like a cat.

AN OBSERVATION

"My Velcro heart unwittingly snags those men, frayed and tattered, who happen to brush past."

I wrote that a handful of years ago, believing it was happenstance, this bad luck of mine that snares the ragged and unraveled hearts of the world, my misfortune of drawing unhealthy partners to me. I've come to understand it's a talent, a finely honed skill. Chance is not involved. I possess a preternatural ability to home in on the damaged, the unavailable. Like a parlor trick, I'll enter a room with one thousand men, and I'm drawn to the solitary marred soul like a magnet. Shit, I don't even require a room…let me peruse an array of online dating photos and, like an eyewitness scanning mug shots, I'm pulled toward the one incapable of connection. "Officer, that's your man right there." It would be a neat trick, if it weren't my defenseless, beating vulnerability on the line.

AN ADMISSION

I can't help staring at him, transfixed. His perfect Dutch face—high cheekbones, full lips, mutable blue-grey eyes, alabaster skin—dissected diagonally, from his left eyebrow, across his nose to the right of his chin, by a jagged, pink, angry scar.

He. Is. Beautiful.

I blush when those eyes catch me looking.

ooo

Three decades have passed since meeting my Dutch Boy and scars still fascinate me. Rather than flaws, I see them as character, turning unremarkable symmetry into something unique, exquisite. In addition to their visual interest, each scar carries a story—nature's version of a tattoo, without any say from its owner in the final artwork. My Dutch Boy's particular fissure, his story, was the result of smashing through a windshield.

I find the invisible scars just as beautiful, the ones carried inside. We hide them from the world, afraid we'll appear disfigured, imperfect, damaged. However, they're what make us truly remarkable. A smooth cabochon is lovely, but a faceted stone, with its one thousand cuts, is more precious, flickering with unfathomable fire. There's no need to hide your damage from me—it's what draws me. Scars, both the visible and unseen, tell the world we have lived…and survived.

I won't love you despite them; I'll love you because of them.

A WARNING

Beware of Prince Charming. He's quite possibly a sociopath.

Confession time: I watch my fair share of true crime TV and documentaries, from Netflix's *American Murder: The Family Next Door* to *Dirty John* to *Dateline* to old reruns of *Cold Case Files*. In fact, if I can't sleep, true crimes are my go-to bedtime stories. This became a habit during my most recent career as an event manager. Hotel television in other countries is often a handful of terrible shows, usually in the country's native language. However, regardless of where I've traveled, I can usually find a channel playing back-to-back episodes of *Forensic Files*. At a half hour each, they are just long enough to provide the necessary background noise to send me off to dreamland. And although I'm unsure if it's intentional, true crime hosts tend to possess a soothing voice—Keith Morrison, Lester Holt, Bill Kurtis, Peter Thomas—that jettisons me off to snooze-land within no time. Yes, this does mean I sometimes crawl under the covers clutching a kitchen knife or pepper spray in lieu of a teddy bear.

I've noticed these stories—predominantly wives or girlfriends who have been conned of their life savings, often murdered, or had some other atrocity committed upon them by their partner—initially describe the perpetrator as "charming." Hello, Ted Bundy. Interviewers of the unsuspecting neighbor or family member will hear, "I don't understand what happened. He was so charming."

Having dealt with my own "charming" partner who eventually exposed himself to be an accused liar, philanderer, and psychological abuser, I often relate closely to these women, from feeling cherished in the first month to changing the locks on all the doors during the final days.

I'm not alone in recognizing "charming," a word little girls grow up believing describes the perfect man, should actually be a big ol' red flag. A simple Google search of "Charming Beware" or "Charming Red Flag" shows charming behavior is often a precursor to abuse, whether physical, mental, emotional, or a combination of these. In fact, there's a name for these men—Charm Syndrome Men.

"Dave was a charming, outgoing, hands-on dad."

Sandra Horley, author of *Power and Control: Why Charming Men Can Make Dangerous Lovers*, writes, "At first it seemed astonishing, but soon repeatedly, I was making the connection between these two apparent opposites, charm and abuse, which seemed to run like two threads intertwined into women's lives. It might be the charm of Dr. Jekyll or the abuse of Mr. Hyde, and just as in Stevenson's novel, the activities of Mr. Hyde are protected by the character of Dr. Jekyll.

Women invariably remember the charming side of their partners, the side they fell in love with. They describe them as loving, tender, funny, and considerate. More often than not, they explain that between bouts of abuse, their partners revert to being charmers. They can beg forgiveness, smother them in affection, and promise they will never behave badly again. And because the women still care, they agree to give them one more try...The word "charm" has cropped up again and again."

Interviewer: *"Was Tom charming?"*

Victim's Best Friend: *"Very charming. Larger than life."*

Charm is an affect employed to convince the outer world this person is a good egg. If this man is truly of good character, no affect or convincing is needed. True character will shine via their deeds and consistent right actions. When recalling my healthiest relationships, the words I use to describe my partners would be "kind," "loyal," "dependable," and "thoughtful." Prince Dependable, however, doesn't have the same ring.

A MALFUNCTION

"Welcome to Dating Diagnostics. My name is Beatrice. Do you have an appointment?"

"Um, no, sorry. I didn't make an appointment. I read the Walk-Ins Welcome sign and decided to give it a shot."

"And your name is?"

"Julie."

"OK, Julie, what brought you here today?"

"It's my man-picker. I think it's broken or needs recalibration or something. Honestly, I'm convinced it's never worked correctly. I should have brought it in while still under warranty, but, back then, I assumed it was functioning correctly. Now, after all this time, I've realized its calculations are completely askew from everyone else's—my friends, my siblings, my coworkers. Could it be faulty wiring or a misalignment?"

"First day of your last menstrual cycle?"

"Why do you need that? It's my man-picker I'm here about."

"For our records. First day of your last menstrual cycle?"

"I dunno. My period ended two Sundays ago, so, count back five or seven days…like Monday or Tuesday of that week?"

"March fifth?"

"Yeah sure, March fifth sounds as good as any other date."

"Wait in room two, Julie. The technician will be in to see you shortly."

Forty-one minutes later…

"Hi, um, Julie. I'm Technician Bob. It says here in your chart you believe your man-picker is broken? That would be extremely unlikely, indeed. It's an almost unheard-of diagnosis, very uncommon. Were you looking up your symptoms on WebMD?"

"Well, Bob, you see, I've begun to notice…"

"First day of last period?"

"I don't know why that matters. I think it's in my chart alr…"

"First day of last period?"

"March fifth."

"OK. Can you tell me, in your own words, Julie, about your symptoms?"

"Up until now, I've been blissfully oblivious to my man-picker's shortcomings, never considering there might be a glitch, a malfunction, even when the device convinces me, time and time again, to push aside kind, generous, obviously smitten, emotionally strong, financially secure, and lovingly supportive options for ineligible, financially unstable, closed-off, emotionally distant males with latent misogynistic tendencies."

"Hmm. I see. Go on."

"My friends call me the embodiment of a perfect wingwoman, never vying for the attractive, stable, well-dressed businessman at the bar, instead leaning toward the tattooed, underachieving yet overly confident bartender on the other side of the counter. Eros face-palms each time my picker makes a choice, shouting in my mistuned ears, 'No, not him. You've screwed up yet again,' as my picker leads me, stumbling, once more toward impending disaster. I'm at my wits' end. Can it be fixed?"

"Did you try powering down and then powering it back up again?"

"Yeah, my friend told me to try that. It didn't seem to help."

"CTL+ALT+DEL?"

"I did that, too. No change."

"I'm going to show you three inkblots. I'd like you to describe what you see. OK? Here's the first one."

"Umm. I see a self-absorbed, petulant underachiever who self-medicates standing in a field of eggshells—Yum, he's a dish."

"Hmm. Interesting. Now, here's the next one."

"Oh, that's definitely someone who is cheating on their spouse—but I'm sure he has a reason."

"OK. Thank you for your answer, Julie. Anything else?"

"Nope. One-hundred percent justified adulterer."

"And the last one. What do you see here?"

"Oh, that's Andrew from the mail room. We've been dating for a few weeks. I have such a huge crush on him. He's forty-two, still lives in his mom's basement, and drives her car because his was repossessed—it was either pay for the new tattoo or the car…so, well, he went with the ink. I see tons of potential in him. He's just trying to figure things out and doesn't want to be rushed. He keeps insisting, "Don't push me." He has two master's degrees and writes beautiful sonnets. The mail room job gives him the freedom needed to write and think big thoughts…

and whatever else he's doing at night when I can't get in touch with him for hours. He swears he falls asleep on the couch and can't hear his phone in the other room. Isn't he adorable? He's continuously correcting me when I say or do something he loathes, but he promises me it's for my own improvement. Any arguments his criticism stirs up are my fault. Andrew says I'm too touchy—like most women he's dated. Yesterday, I caught him emailing a dick pic to Brandi in Sales. I started to get upset, but he admonished me for overreacting to harmless flirting. He assures me I'm the only one for him."

"Alrighty. Thank you for your participation, Julie. It's my diagnosis you need a full man-picker transplant, immediately. I'm writing up a referral to a specialist. In the meantime, be sure to avoid any situations where you're in contact with the opposite sex. See Beatrice on the way out for payment."

TARTS

in component parts

ooo

*I call this section "Component Parts" because I've provided the
tart building blocks: four of my go-to shell recipes with five of my most
requested fillings. Mix and match shells and fillings to make your own
tart creations. Each filling comes with my recommendation for a garnish
or accompaniment, but feel free to interchange options here as well.*

EASY SHORTBREAD SHELL

Yield: One 9-inch tart shell

This is the easiest of all tart shells, using packaged shortbread cookies. If I had a little self-control, I'd keep a package of cookies on hand so I could whip up a tart without having to visit a store, but, alas, I'd end up eating all the cookies.

Ingredients
- 10-ounce package shortbread cookies, such as Lorna Doone
- ¼ teaspoon kosher salt
- ½ cup (1 stick) unsalted butter, melted and cooled

Directions
1. Preheat oven to 350°F. In the bowl of a food processor, pulse shortbread cookies and salt into crumbs. Add melted butter and pulse until mixture resembles wet sand.
2. Pat mixture evenly along bottom and up sides of a 9-inch tart pan. Place on a baking sheet to catch any butter leakage and bake about 15 minutes or until golden. Remove from oven and transfer to a cooling rack.

EASY NUT SHELL

Yield: One 9-inch tart shell

This is the same as the Easy Shortbread Shell, substituting some of the cookies with ground nuts.

Ingredients
- One-half 10-ounce package (5 ounces) shortbread cookies, such as Lorna Doone
- ¾ cup toasted nuts of your choice
- ¼ teaspoon kosher salt
- ½ cup (1 stick) unsalted butter, melted and cooled

Directions
1. Preheat oven to 350°F. In the bowl of a food processor, pulse shortbread cookies, nuts, and salt into crumbs. Add melted butter and pulse until mixture resembles wet sand.
2. Pat mixture evenly along bottom and up sides of a 9-inch tart pan. Place on a baking sheet to catch any butter leakage and bake about 15 minutes or until golden. Remove from oven and transfer to a cooling rack.

GRAHAM CRACKER COCONUT SHELL

Yield: One 9-inch tart shell

The addition of coconut to a graham cracker shell adds a unique coconutty twist to a familiar standard.

Ingredients
- 11 full sheets of graham crackers (1½ cups crumbs)
- ½ cup sweetened shredded coconut
- ½ teaspoon kosher salt
- ½ cup (1 stick) unsalted butter, melted

Directions
1. Preheat oven to 350°F. In the bowl of a food processor, pulse graham crackers, sweetened shredded coconut, and salt into crumbs. Add melted butter and pulse until mixture clumps together.
2. Pat mixture evenly along bottom and up sides of a 9-inch tart pan. Place on a baking sheet to catch any butter leakage and bake about 15 minutes or until golden. Remove from oven and transfer to a cooling rack.

PAT-IN SHELL

Yield: One 9-inch tart shell

This is another easy shell. The beauty of this recipe is that you get a classic pastry shell without the need for a rolling pin. You can pat this shell directly into your tart pan.

Ingredients

- 1⅓ cups all-purpose flour
- ¼ cup granulated sugar
- ½ teaspoon kosher salt
- ½ teaspoon lemon zest
- 9 tablespoons (1 stick plus 1 tablespoon) unsalted butter, melted

Directions

1. Preheat oven to 350°F. In a medium bowl, combine all-purpose flour, granulated sugar, salt, and lemon zest. Add melted butter and stir just until you can see no dry flour.
2. Crumble dough evenly over the bottom of a 9-inch tart pan. Pat dough along bottom and up sides of pan. Place on a baking sheet to catch any butter leakage.
3. Bake for about 35 minutes for tarts with refrigerator fillings that do not need additional baking time. Bake shell about 25 minutes (10 minutes less) if you need to bake the filled tart a second time, like the Pink Grapefruit Tart. Remove from oven and transfer to a cooling rack.

KEY LIME TART WITH RASPBERRY COULIS *Yield: 10-12 servings*

Ingredients

<u>Key Lime Filling</u>

- Easy shortbread or pat-in tart shell
- 2 14-ounce cans sweetened condensed milk
- ½ cup full-fat Greek yogurt
- ¾ cup fresh Key lime juice (not bottled)
- 1½ tablespoons Key lime zest
- Sweetened freshly whipped cream
- White chocolate shavings and Key lime zest for decoration (optional)

<u>Raspberry Coulis</u>

- ½ cup granulated sugar
- 3 tablespoons water
- 12-ounce bag frozen raspberries, thawed
- 1 tablespoon raspberry or orange liqueur (optional)

Directions

1. Preheat oven to 350°F. In a medium bowl, whisk together sweetened condensed milk, Greek yogurt, Key lime juice, and Key lime zest. Pour into baked and cooled shell.

2. Bake for 10-12 minutes, until tiny pinhole bubbles burst on the surface of the tart. Do not brown. Remove from oven and cool on a cooling rack for 30 minutes. Transfer to the refrigerator and chill tart thoroughly before serving.

3. Make coulis: Combine sugar and water in a heatproof liquid measuring cup. Microwave on high for two minutes, stirring to ensure all sugar crystals are dissolved. Combine sugar mixture with thawed raspberries in a blender. Blend until smooth. With a rubber spatula, stir and push puree through a fine-mesh strainer to catch the seeds. Add liqueur, if using. Store in the refrigerator up to a week.

4. To make whipped cream: Beat together 1 cup heavy whipping cream and 2 tablespoons confectioners' sugar until soft peaks form.

5. Decorate tart with freshly whipped cream, white chocolate shavings and Key lime zest, if using. Drizzle raspberry coulis on individual plates. Place tart slices atop coulis.

TRIPLE COCONUT TART WITH BERRIES

Yield: 10-12 servings

Coconut in the shell, along with coconut milk and shredded coconut in the pastry cream, ensures coconut lovers won't be disappointed.

Ingredients
- Graham Cracker Coconut Shell
- ½ cup granulated sugar
- 3 tablespoons cornstarch
- 2 tablespoons all-purpose flour
- ¼ teaspoon kosher salt
- 2 large eggs, beaten
- 1 cup whole milk
- 1 cup canned coconut milk (unsweetened)
- 2 cups sweetened shredded coconut
- ¼ cup (½ stick) unsalted butter, cut into 1-inch pieces
- 2 teaspoons vanilla extract
- 1½ - 2 cups assorted fresh berries
- ¼ cup apricot jam
- Sweetened freshly whipped cream
- ½ cup toasted coconut

Directions

1. In a medium saucepan, whisk together sugar, cornstarch, all-purpose flour, and salt. Whisk in eggs, milk, coconut milk, and shredded coconut. Place over medium heat and bring to a simmer, stirring constantly, about 8 minutes or until custard is very thick. Remove from heat and whisk in butter and vanilla extract. Transfer custard into a bowl, press cling film against the custard's surface, and chill in refrigerator until cool.

2. Spoon coconut filling into baked and cooled shell and smooth top. Mound with fresh berries.

3. In a small bowl, heat apricot jam for 1 minute in the microwave. Strain any large chunks from jam and then brush berries with smooth jam. Decorate with sweetened whipped cream and toasted coconut. To make whipped cream: Beat together 1 cup heavy whipping cream and 2 tablespoons confectioners' sugar until soft peaks form. Refrigerate tart until ready to serve.

CHERRY ALMOND TART

Yield: 10-12 servings

Toasting the almond flour brings out the flavor, and it's easy—toast the flour in a dry skillet over medium heat, stirring constantly until the flour turns golden and you can smell the almonds. Remove from heat and cool.

Ingredients
- Pat-in Shell

Cherry Filling
- ¾ cup water
- 1 cup dried tart cherries, chopped
- ¼ cup granulated sugar

Almond Cream
- ½ cup (1 stick) unsalted butter, softened
- 1¼ cups almond flour (lightly toasted and cooled)
- ¾ cup confectioners' (powdered) sugar, plus more for dusting
- 2 large eggs, beaten
- ½ teaspoon kosher salt
- ½ teaspoon vanilla extract
- ¼ teaspoon almond extract

Almond Topping
- ½ cup sliced almonds
- ¼ cup turbinado sugar, such as Sugar in the Raw

Directions

1. Make cherry filling: Preheat oven to 350°F. In a small saucepan, combine water, dried cherries, and sugar. Bring to boil and cook over medium-high heat, stirring occasionally, for about 8 minutes or until water is partially absorbed. Set aside.
2. Make almond cream: Whisk butter until light and fluffy. Whisk in remaining ingredients, one at a time until combined. Cover and set aside. (Refrigerate if the cream will not be used within an hour.)
3. Assemble tart: Drain and then layer cherry filling on the bottom of cooled shell. Spread with almond cream, then scatter with sliced almonds and turbinado sugar. Place on a baking sheet to catch any butter leakage and bake until puffed and brown, about 40 minutes. Remove from oven and place on a cooling rack. Once cooled, dust with confectioners' sugar.

Variation: Replace cherries with other tart dried fruit such as Blenheim apricots.

MINI FRUIT TARTLETS

Yield: 18 tartlets

These add a wow factor to any buffet table, although to be honest, I like popping them in my mouth one by one when no one else is looking. You can make the component parts over a few days, then assemble the tartlets the day of your party. White chocolate between shell and pastry cream helps keep the shell crisp and adds another layer of flavor.

Ingredients

Vanilla Pastry Cream

- ⅔ cup whole milk
- 3 tablespoons granulated sugar, divided
- Pinch kosher salt
- 2 teaspoons cornstarch
- 2 teaspoons all-purpose flour
- 2 egg yolks
- 1 tablespoon (scant) unsalted butter, cut into small pieces
- 1½ teaspoons vanilla extract

Tart Shells

- Pat-in Shell dough, unbaked
- ¼ cup white chocolate morsels
- 2 cups assorted sliced fruit and berries (kiwi, mango, nectarines, blueberries, raspberries, etc.)
- ¼ cup apricot jam

Directions

1. Make pastry cream: Heat whole milk, 2 tablespoons sugar, and salt in a medium saucepan over medium-high heat until hot, but not boiling. Blend cornstarch, flour, and remaining 1 tablespoon sugar in a bowl. Beat egg yolks into sugar mixture. Pour hot milk over egg mixture slowly, whisking constantly, to avoid scrambling the eggs. Pour entire mixture back into saucepan. Bring to a simmer while continuously whisking. Cook over low to medium-low heat until thickened. Remove from heat. Add butter and vanilla extract. Transfer pastry cream into a shallow pan, cover with cling film touching the surface, and chill for 1 hour.

2. Make shells: Follow the recipe for Pat-in Shell dough. Form dough into a disk, wrap in cling film, and let rest on the counter for 20 minutes. Preheat oven to 350°F. Using a rolling pin and working from the center out, roll dough between two pieces of parchment or waxed paper to a thickness of $\frac{1}{6}$ inch, sprinkling with flour as needed to avoid sticking. Cut with 2½-inch round cutter and gently press into the bottom and up the sides of mini-muffin cups (the dough will be soft). Chill shells in the muffin tin in the refrigerator for 20 minutes. Bake for 18-22 minutes or until golden brown. Remove from oven and cool for 10 minutes. Remove tartlet shells from tin and cool completely.

3. Make tartlets: Melt white chocolate morsels by heating them in a small bowl in the microwave for 30 seconds to 1 minute, stirring every 30 seconds. Spread a very thin layer on the bottom of each tartlet shell. Scoop pastry cream into a pastry bag and pipe over white chocolate or carefully spoon over white chocolate. Decorate with fruit.

4. In a small bowl, heat apricot jam for 1 minute in the microwave. Strain any large chunks from jam and then brush fruit with smooth jam to create a glaze. Chill tartlets until ready to serve.

PINK GRAPEFRUIT TART

Even people who say they don't like grapefruit love this tart. If you want the tart to look a little pinker, use a drop or two of red food coloring.

Ingredients

- Easy shortbread or pat-in tart shell
- 3 large eggs, beaten
- ⅔ cup heavy whipping cream
- ⅔ cup granulated sugar
- ¼ teaspoon kosher salt
- 1½ teaspoons pink grapefruit zest
- ⅔ cup pink grapefruit juice
- Sweetened freshly whipped cream

Directions

1. Preheat oven to 350°F. Beat together eggs, heavy whipping cream, sugar, salt, and grapefruit zest. Stir in grapefruit juice, and pour filling into baked and cooled tart shell.

2. Bake tart about 30 minutes or until filling jiggles only slightly in center. Remove from oven and transfer to a cooling rack for 30 minutes. Transfer tart to the refrigerator and cool completely. Decorate with sweetened whipped cream before serving. To make whipped cream: Beat together 1 cup heavy whipping cream and 2 tablespoons confectioners' sugar until soft peaks form.

Tip: It can be unnerving to transfer a shell filled with sloppy liquid from counter to oven. Instead, place your shell on the oven rack, pour in your filling, and push the rack inside the oven.

five

FOOLISH RECONNECTIONS: EDMOND, PART II

Age 42–49 (9 years post-breakup)

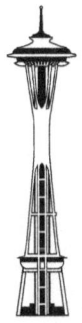

ACTIONABLE

In last night's 6:30 vinyasa yoga class, sitting cross-legged, with strong, straight back and shoulders, I set my sankalpa—my yogic vow or intention. Last evening, my yogic manifestation was an uncharacteristically nebulous "Love," forgoing my customary litany of qualifiers: committed love, reciprocal love, healthy love.

Damn, that is heady stuff, like snorting a line of uncut self-actualization straight up my nose. This morning, Edmond's email is waiting, bold and black at the top of my inbox. Long-lost love. Impossible love. Foolish love.

My brevity was careless. Next class, my sankalpa will be crafted with finer precision: Actionable Love.

CHOICE

Julie,

Somehow, I knew that when I accepted Denise's friend request on Facebook that this moment would come, that I would see your face smiling at me under the heading, "People you may know," and I'd be compelled to reach out. I cannot tell you how many times I have thought of writing you only to stop mid-sentence and erase everything I'd written. Why, you ask? I cannot say.

I sincerely hope that all is well. I hope that life has brought you much happiness, both personally and professionally. For my part, I am well and living the life which I have chosen.

Take care. Best.
Edmond

I am dumbfounded to find his email waiting in my inbox this morning after almost a decade of silence. As my brain processes his first and last name in black, bold Helvetica on the screen, my hands freeze, two ice-sculpture swans poised above my keyboard. My warming lifeblood beelining from my left hand straight to my heart to deploy the deflector shields and, from my right, to my guts to fire up engines on high alert, as if Captain Kirk on the bridge commanded, "All hands to battle stations."

As my digits slowly return to a cozy 98.6°F, I pull out a worn and creased handwritten list from my wallet. After reading the heading at the top, "Top Five

Ex-Boyfriends I'd Wish Were Prisoners on a Romulan Warship," I scan the short list to number three. Edmond's name stares back at me, this time in Arial, confirming I hadn't misremembered my experience of our time together.

Our relationship back then was fraught with difficulties almost from the beginning. When he decided he "needed time to think," I felt rejected, as if I'd failed as his partner. Yet, these issues weren't enough to make the list of lamentable liaisons. I soon forgave him for falling out of love. But instead of moving on, he continued to pluck my heartstrings for the next twelve months while sorting out his own romantic life: calling me in the dead of night, pulling me from my dreams to whisper sweet nothings in my ear.

One evening, the doorbell rang and I opened the door to find Edmond on my porch, unannounced, having, as he commented, a *"High Fidelity* moment." In my kitchen, while I baked gingersnaps, he remarked on my distance, my folded arms across my wary heart, as he invaded my personal space, standing too close for comfort in my culinary Shangri-la. Month after month, he continued to pull me like taffy, toward him with his sugarcoated words and then away with weeks of silence. And still, I didn't add him to the list.

I only added his name after that last afternoon I called him, desperate for his comforting voice, while my father lay behind the hospital curtain, gravely ill and a slip of the man of my youth. I choked out one message before my ICU visit and another after, my words diluted by my flood of tears. Edmond never returned either call. Ever. He just…disappeared.

My father survived that hospital visit, my fondness for Edmond did not. His lack of compassion or concern during one of the most difficult moments in my life left me not only pained and confused, but fuming. That time, I couldn't forgive.

Yet here I sit at my desk, nine years later, with his message staring back at me, and my spleen toward him surprisingly vaporized. His words upon my computer screen again after all this time. My father is dead, my mother lost in a haze of Alzheimer's. I've moved out of the beige condo to a home in a vibrant city, I have a new career in corporate events, I've started blogging, college is long finished… and I've managed to forgive Edmond.

He tells me he is *"living the life which I have chosen."* He is a writer. That odd choice of phrasing isn't happenstance, but I have no interest to pull the curtain back in search of the subtext. I know he is married now. That is his life, and this is mine.

He says he hopes life has brought me happiness. I can't imagine he'd hope to find me otherwise—I've done nothing to warrant his schadenfreude. My life is good, fulfilling, easy, and I am grateful.

I catch, for just a moment, a quick flash of a silent and dimly lit apartment living room, splashing Seattle rain streaking the slider window, and Edmond, with door shut, sulking in the other room over something I said or did or failed to do to his liking. That image quickly fades from view.

Yes, I am happy with my choices—and I'm surprised to discover I hope Edmond is, too.

FALLING ON HIS SWORD

What is the value of gallantry after the blood-soaked battle is waged, the fair maiden rescues herself from the stone tower, the formidable dragon lies slain? Edmond kneels on the floor before me in supplication, nine years too late, conceding only now that he was scared, immature, and intimidated by the "passionate, erudite woman" who stood before him those many years ago. In the communications that follow his first after years of silence, he accepts blame and sings ballads of my praises.

But this is not the truth. Sentimentality is wagging his tongue today.

He imagined me, at first glance, to be the fairy princess of storybooks, conjured into existence to stand beside him, yet one step behind, the foot to fit the glass slipper carried in his satchel. A second look and he realized I was merely human, not so magical after all, and, by his third and final glance, my every utterance and action elicited his contempt. Prior to our magic island getaway, he had discovered these cracks in my veneer, certain all faults rested with me, unwilling to admit this was no portrait he gazed upon, but a mirror. Confidences are rarely held. Tongues wag and I've heard accounts of the offences Edmond had heaped upon me, at the time accepting no fault himself. His heart had already turned toward the princess from another land who, soon enough, he would deem to call his wife.

Like others before Edmond, he envisioned me as a knob of clay, unblemished by thought or deed, a golem ready to be molded by his hands into an ideal mate—or a girlfriend to Pinocchio, made flesh and waiting to be imbued with his preferences and dispositions. Then, once he discovered I was fully formed with my own ideas and self-determination, no maiden in need of rescue or molding, he stumbled back, stammering, "Witch, I've been tricked. She is not what I imagined."

I don't condemn Edmond for falling out of love with me. This greatest of human emotion cannot be commanded like a king to his army. He was entranced by a chimera of his own making and found himself, one short year later, with a creature fully formed, intricate and complex, standing on her own, a woman full of faults and foibles, a maiden-not-so-in-distress. He no longer adored me and, although that realization placed another nick into my much-trampled heart, all is well as he circles round me with his words once more. Edmond tied himself to another who won his heart. I'm waiting to find my own king: a man who sees me for the treasure I am.

There is no need for Edmond to fall upon his sword today. I no longer mourn his loss.

THE GAME OF FORGIVENESS

The board rests on the wooden table between us, multicolored paths wind across the surface, reminding me of an overhead view of a coral snake (in the grass? I wonder). I'm positioned on the "Start" square in my plum-colored convertible, my lone pink peg piece in the driver's seat. Edmond selects a shiny black SUV, of course, blue peg similarly placed. He spins the dial...*bizuzuzuz*...and moves six spaces to the right, he doesn't even glance my way. I spin next and move a single space to the left, landing on the "Indignation and Perceived Abandonment" square. I lose a turn. Within a few moves, he picks up a pink peg, places it in the passenger's seat, and disappears from my sight.

I avoid the "Get Married" square and the squares dedicated to babies: add a boy, add a girl, twins. I focus inward, dabbling around the Buddhism squares for a few years, meditation, journaling, yoga. I land on squares about midlife career changes, buying a home, and caring for aging parents: hospitals, housing, final breaths, and trusts. Culinary school is just a square or two ahead.

After almost a decade, we've managed to arrive, simultaneously, at the same square. I glance into his car expecting to feel my previous rancor, yet, after the initial shock, I'm pleased he's reached out. This is not alchemy at work. I've spun the wheel and chugged down these paths, taking detours: twists, turns, and lessons learned. Youth faded and time mellowed my sharper edges.

Just as Edmond believed I was deficient in some essential girlfriend gene, that

I was somehow failing him, I recognize now that I expected him to become other than he was as well. Edmond possessed nothing more to give to the relationship than what he had. We held each other at gunpoint, demanding "gimme all you got," disappointed with our haul of some loose change, a linty roll of Life Savers, and a ChapStick missing its lid. We were judging the other by the path each of us had decided to take.

Once I stand up and take a step back from the board, I can appreciate him based upon his locus and the squares he traveled to get here, not by my path. It's more than just my new perspective of the road. This ability now to forgive is rooted in my nine-year journey. As I move further along, my capacity to forgive expands. Almost a decade ago, given the chance, I would have spat out some hurtful retort to Edmond, thick with anger and recrimination, but not today, not today.

THE PERSISTENCE OF MEMORY

Edmond's image in the photo peers at me, and I cannot help staring back, arrested by this unfamiliar topography. I recognize the vista before me, yet this is not the terrain I once wandered. It is altered, changed, youth's softness worn away.

The east wind whispers above my ear, "You can never go home."

I search for familiar landmarks. The plains upon his cheek remain unchanged. Yes, I know this geography and the rugged scrubland across his jaw. I inhale deeply, recalling his scent—freshly washed laundry drying in the breeze. The ravines zigzagging toward the chocolate oases of his eyes surely must be tricks of light. Not faint, but strong, deep furrows. These Nazca Lines traverse his temples, both right and left.

These glyphs caution, "You can never go home."

Were I to steal an hour, perhaps while he is sleeping, my fingers would roam unhindered across this unfamiliar undulating landscape, intimately examining time's signposts for myself. With my forefinger, I'd trace the outline of his nose, landing in the trough above his lips. My pinky would skim along his cheek, like a zephyr wandering a plateau. I'd plumb the vertical relief of his nascent arroyos, the side of my fingernail a surveyor's tripod. I'd dare to traipse through the silver birch forest growing thick just past these furrows to convince myself this misty patch of wood is not some conjuring of the Brothers Grimm.

A lone crow squawks from a high branch, "You can never go home."

My memory's persistence has melted all the clocks, like in the famous painting by that fellow from Spain. Yes, years have meandered across our vistas and we have aged, but before this moment, it remained abstraction, and idea unrefined. Edmond is still beautiful, but he is no longer the boy I once knew.

We can never go home.

THE DEEP END

"I won't let you go," my father assures me, his voice firm.

"I'm not going to dunk you," he adds, attempting to convince.

I'm clinging to the lip of the Holiday Inn's pool in Flagstaff, AZ, my fingertips pumiced pink by the rough concrete coping. I kick below the water line while gripping the edge for dear life, mock dogpaddling around the pool's perimeter. My father is attempting to cajole eight-year-old me to allow him to shepherd me to the pool's middle and deep end. I grip my cement refuge, resolute and petrified, imagining him letting me slip from his grasp or dunking us both underwater—some no-nonsense literal version of "sink or swim." His bald head shines in the late afternoon light, his bare chest a tangle of salt-and-pepper hair. This is the first and only time I've seen him in a swimming pool. Our negotiations continue as I attempt to weigh his promises' sincerity.

An older neighbor kid pushed me into a pool when I was quite young—five years old—and I retained a phobia, not of water, but of other people, what they could or would do to me around a body of water. On that particular slightly overcast Sunday, I found myself floating through the turquoise world below, coolly musing, *So, this is how I die.* Quite the drama queen and not even in kindergarten yet. The kid's brother pulled me out after what seemed like minutes, but was probably less than thirty seconds. I ran, shivering, crying, with a feeling of betrayal, to the safety of Mom and home, right next door.

Granted, this afternoon I'm swimming with my father, but his track record with me isn't much better than the neighbor, a shaky foundation of trust, at best. I eventually relent, allowing him to ferry me around the deep end in his strong, tanned arms. He keeps his word, not releasing me or taking me below the water's surface, but I still feel relief when my pruney fingers grip the pool's secure coping once again.

I don't learn to swim until the summer I turn twelve.

For me, trust is allowing another person to carry me into the deep end of life. I gingerly step down the concrete stairs into another's arms, cautiously assured my escort means me no harm and is adept at navigating these waters.

How, I wonder, should I approach the trust of someone, like Edmond, who has disappointed me more than once: blindly, warily, or resolutely refusing to release the wall?

"I won't let you go," he coos from the safety of his emails. I hope this time is different, and yet, I cannot shake the image of myself alone on the muffled quiet of the pool's floor, my lungs burning with the effort not to breathe, Edmond, once again, nowhere to be found. So, as I begin to release my grip from the edge, I ponder which fate is worse: allow myself to drown or lose trust completely.

WORDS

I check my inbox, like I do every morning now, anticipating my daily word from Edmond, reminiscent of when we were a couple long ago, but today is not like our past. Edmond is Happily Married Now. Those three words keep me in check. I refuse to be "that woman."

I'm sated by Edmond's written words—our preferred playground. It's my version of a male revue show: fully dressed, reading written passages. Chippen-Tales, porn for the literary lady.

How easily we've fallen back into old patterns after brief vows of contrition. Nose to nose, we argued; word to word, we painted our own secret world. And we've rediscovered our world once again.

From the safety of our computer screens, we feed each other morsels from our daily lives and serve up long-held dreams. We weave each other stories as if...as if our history doesn't sit on each of our shoulders. We meant those words, "I love you," and our passion singed both our hearts. We circumvent this truth today, playing the roles of reunited friends who lost touch, but I remember his caress, his scent, his desire. And I know he remembers, too.

"I don't get it," my good friend Todd says one afternoon. "So, you guys just have email sex all day?"

"No, it isn't like that. It's *cerebral*." I emphasize the word. "I hunger for his finely wrought wordcraft," I joke. "And he does not disappoint."

"Ah, so you wanna fuck his brain, then. Is that it?" A wry smile plays on Todd's lips.

I attempt to explain. "You know how when you're in the first blush of a new relationship, you can text or talk on the phone for hours without running out of things to say? Everything the other person says is funny and fascinating and the conversation just flows?"

"Yeah, it's been a while for me, but I get what you're saying," Todd replies.

"It's like that, but rather than having that kind of conversation for a few weeks or months, we've been talking like that for years now."

"So, no sexy talk?"

"No sexy talk. He's married."

But once Todd has gone home, I can't help but wonder, Is she aware? Has Edmond confessed to our almost-daily emails? If "Our Conversation," as we've grown to call it, is as benign as we pretend, what could be the harm in telling her? I've convinced myself my actions are guileless. Surely, this isn't cheating or infidelity, I lie to myself.

Culinary school is finally within my grasp, and Edmond's counsel is the one I seek. All other opinions, including Todd's, are moot. It's an aspiration that's jangled around my head for decades ever since I watched those Tante Marie Cooking School students through the windows, but I'm already in my forties with a successful career outside of the culinary realm. What would be the point? Yet, it all aligns. There's one opening. A student has dropped out a week before class is to begin. At work, I'm directed to cut employee hours. Why not my own? "Yes," Edmond advises. "Yes?" I ask my employer. "Yes," I tell the school. Never in my wildest dreams did I imagine Edmond would help me make such a crucial decision more than a decade after our breakup.

The school shrewdly requires students to pay the twenty-thousand dollar tuition in advance—otherwise I probably would drop out during the first few weeks. Twice as old as most of the other students, I feel every one of the six hours on my feet. And learning a skill from a right-handed instructor as a left-handed student is always challenging, knife skills, it seems, even more so. The truncated class curriculum purportedly condenses the Culinary Institute of America's eighteen-month course into six months by assigning all book work as homework and delegating dishwashing to a dedicated staff member. I arrive at school by 8:15 a.m., grab a quick coffee, attend class until 2:30 p.m., then change from chef's whites to professional attire and head to the office, reeking of garlic and onions, where I work from 3:00 until 7:00 p.m. The executives at the office remain supportive, even attending my "final exam," a restaurant we create the last two nights of class. Weekends are reserved for homework and translating class notes. This school/work balance is grueling at the beginning, but I find my footing around week five, and the remaining months fly by.

After graduation, I settle back into my old familiar pattern of my suburban, corporate life, but that is upended by the loss of two loved ones in quick succession. I am lost, isolated, apathetic to life. During the months that follow, Edmond's words provide me with an escape. We don't talk much about what has transpired, but we talk about books and food, as well as the ephemeral. Never suffering any loss himself, he's not good at offering me comfort, but our conversation provides the respite I desperately need from reality and the necessary balm to allow me to find my groove again.

The years tumble on, one after the other.

For a year and a half, I manage to keep a boyfriend, but, besides that, my attempts at dating are unsuccessful. Edmond gives me ninety-five percent of what I need from a man, and the other five percent, the physical, I get from some sort of battery-operated appliance in the nightstand drawer.

I'm certain I'll be hurt again. I don't blame him. It's my heart—always enamored by the fantasy, always disappointed by the truth. Ironic, that reeks of the similar crime I accused Edmond of committing—reality versus the imagined. We are living in a fantasy of our own making, a diversion from the grind of daily life. Were he here, beside me, barriers of distance and marriage removed, I'm certain our fire would have burned out years ago. It's the safety, the distance, the fantasy that keeps our connection alive.

TELL ME GOODBYE—A MESSAGE TO EDMOND

If you choose to disappear from my world again, please leave me with one thing.

No, not an explanation. I'm quite aware, to avoid candor's jagged edge, you will hand me your story couched in downy half-truths and white lies: fictions to assuage hurt feelings, untruths to save face. Don't lean on your special darlings, your beloved "lies of omission." Deceit, even wrapped in good intentions, offers me no succor. Dishonesties abrade my skin and assault my ears.

Practice with me, right now: "Goodbye." Two syllables. Pronounced, guhd-bahy.

If you decide to leave, just tell me goodbye.

I will sit with your decision upon my lap, like a sleeping cat, unquestioned and unchallenged. Tell me goodbye so I comprehend you are gone, so I don't wonder if something dreadful has befallen you or that my words have in any way offended. Tell me goodbye so I can move forward—or jump back, to my life before you appeared, again. Tell me goodbye so I abandon my endless waiting for a line from you, checking email for your daily notes that ask, *"How was your day?"*

Please, do this one thing as a favor to me.

If you must leave, tell me goodbye. This time, I deserve to hear at least that.

A SLIPPERY SLOPE

I'm scheduled to fly to Seattle for a conference. I'm not sure who suggests it, but Edmond and I decide to meet for coffee. We've been emailing for seven years now, seven times longer than our romance. I consider Edmond my best friend, and he knows more about my life now than anyone. What harm could there be in meeting for coffee?

I'm nervous to see him again, but that feeling soon dissipates. I'm reminded of Jesse and Céline in the movie *Before Sunset*. They appear stiff and unsure how to be around each other after all this time, but soon their conversation becomes easy, strolling the streets and alleyways of Paris.

For us, coffee becomes a walk through Seattle, around the Olympic Sculpture Park, ending up at Pike Place Market. As we slurp freshly shucked oysters at a seafood vendor's stand, I glance over at Edmond and swallow a briny jolt of realization—my feelings for him are more than mere friendship. I've been lying to myself. I've been lying to Edmond. I make up some excuse about needing to get back, frightened by my epiphany.

Edmond walks me back to my hotel, and we hug goodbye. He leans in to kiss my lips, and I pull away, allowing him to chastely kiss my cheek instead. We are not Jesse and Céline, and this is not a movie.

Alone in my hotel room, competing thoughts run through my brain:
What have I done? I did not mean for this to happen.

Oh, come on, you must have known you were falling for him on some level.

Maybe, I just avoided thinking about it.

You cannot be responsible for ruining a perfectly happy marriage—especially not with your track record. Edmond would be alone within the year.

We speak on the phone later that night, agreeing something like today cannot happen again, but I wonder, How can I pull my heart back from the precipice to the safety of just being friends again?

CHOCOLATE

I like chocolate. That's an understatement. Truth be told, I'm surprisingly enamored by chocolate these days, fallen for it head over heels again, it seems.

Okay, I admit it: I *love* chocolate.

I indulged in its melting bittersweetness over a decade ago, but I must keep a healthy distance now. Still, you'll find me in the chocolate shop Monday through Friday, and many times throughout those days at that. The chocolate beckons me, "Julie, come inside and see what we have for you." As I open the door, I catch a heady whiff of the cocoa liquor–scented air and swoon. I slowly meander around the display counter, admiring the truffles and bonbons nestled in their pastel paper beds behind the glass, tiny gems filled with magnificent crèmes and caramels and decorated with pyramids of fleur de sel, an iridescent sugar pearl, or a blizzard of shredded coconut. Within the dessert case on the back wall, there's an array of chocolate tarts and cakes: *Chocolate Almond Tiramisu Cake*, *Hazelnut Mocha Tart*, a *Chocolate Raspberry Tart with Pistachio Crust* pavéd with fresh raspberries.

I sigh, recalling the sensation of velvety cocoa butter melting across my tongue. I salivate while daydreaming of gorging myself, unrestrained, on the delights ensconced behind the glass, playing out the role of the Comte de Reynaud in the film *Chocolat*. I treasure my minutes within the shop, but it is also maddening. Very soon, I'm convinced, the shop's proprietress will notice me loitering and banish me forever.

I'm content with just looking, merely smelling the liquor, I assure myself, unshakable in my resolve. My willpower will never falter, succumbing to my desires for one tiny little bite. But is this wise, I wonder, to surround myself with this temptation? Wouldn't it be better to fall smitten for the doughnuts in the shop down the street? I have no restrictions on doughnuts, but crullers don't interest me presently.

HEARTBREAK

Heartbreak.

His, this time. An aortic valve. Tests. A rush to operate. Decisions to make. Pig valves or metal and ceramic?

I am not there.

To comfort him. That's her job. And his family's unaware I exist for him once more. Worried faces around the hospital bed, holding his hand, kissing his knotted brow.

I am not there.

How will I know if your heart fails you? I ask. How will I know to grieve? Will I sense it in the dusty Santa Anas blowing past? I will not.

I am not there.

He left me once without a word. He will leave this world the same way.

Because I am not there.

But not today.

Weeks, months of recuperation. A cerise scar from sternum to abdomen. Tending hands to offer succor. I stand outside the hospital curtain, miles away, behind the glass murky with my fingerprints, craning my neck for a glimpse.

No one knows I'm here.

This half-romance cannot continue. My timing could not be worse. Or maybe it's perfect. *Worry about healing and cherishing those around you. I'll be fine.*

But I cannot be there.

ADDICTION

I type *goodbye* on the keyboard. The word, its meaning resolute, appears ambiguous on my screen.

I've typed that word to Edmond before, not once, not twice, but by my tally, there's been six previous goodbyes over the past seven years, when the guilt would overwhelm me, when I grew tired of being second best, when he would retreat. I'm weary of it. I release him to his wife—and his life.

Like a smoker saying "I quit" yet again, I wonder if this time it will truly stick.

Lucky number seven.

EDMOND

the chocolate recipes

MODERN BLACK FOREST CAKE

Yield: 12-14 servings

This cake, which had been banging around in my head for a while, is a modern reimagining of that 1970s classic. If you'd rather not make a mirror glaze, just use ganache to frost the cake.

Ingredients

Brandied Cherries (make the night before)

- 1½ cups morello sour cherries in syrup, drained and cut in half (available online)
- ⅓ cup granulated sugar
- ⅓ cup cherry-flavored brandy, such as Kirsch

Chocolate Ganache Frosting

- 10 ounces (scant 1¾ cups) semisweet chocolate pieces
- 1 tablespoon light corn syrup
- 1 cup heavy whipping cream
- 1 tablespoon cherry-flavored brandy

Cake

- 2¼ cups all-purpose flour
- 2 cups granulated sugar
- 1 cup unsweetened cocoa powder
- 2 teaspoons baking soda
- 1 teaspoon instant coffee granules (optional)
- ½ teaspoon kosher salt
- 2 cups cold water
- ⅔ cup canola oil
- 1 tablespoon vanilla extract
- 2 teaspoons white vinegar

Filling

- 8-ounce container mascarpone cheese
- ⅓ cup heavy whipping cream
- 3 tablespoons confectioners' (powdered) sugar
- 2 teaspoons cherry-flavored brandy

Mirror Glaze (optional)
- ½ cup plus 1 tablespoon cold water, divided
- 1 envelope (2¼ teaspoons) unflavored gelatin
- 1 cup plus 2 tablespoons granulated sugar
- ½ cup heavy whipping cream
- 4 tablespoons unsweetened cocoa powder

Directions

1. Make brandied cherries: Combine cherries, sugar, and cherry-flavored brandy in a small saucepan. Heat and stir until sugar dissolves, cover, and let steep overnight.
2. Make chocolate ganache frosting: Place chocolate in a microwave-safe bowl with corn syrup and heavy whipping cream. Heat in microwave about 90 seconds, stirring every 30 seconds, until fully melted. Add cherry-flavored brandy. Cover and cool to room temperature. Before using, beat for 2-3 minutes to lighten and whip to spreading consistency.
3. Make cake: Preheat oven to 350°F. Line three 8-inch cake pans with parchment paper and lightly grease paper.
4. In a large bowl, sift together flour, sugar, cocoa powder, baking soda, coffee granules (if using), and salt. In a liquid measuring cup, combine water, oil, vanilla extract, and vinegar. Slowly whisk wet ingredients into dry. The batter will appear very wet.
5. Pour the batter evenly into the prepared pans and bake for about 20 minutes or until a tester inserted in the center of the cake comes out clean. Cool in the pans for 15 minutes, then invert onto cooling racks, carefully remove parchment paper, and cool completely.
6. Make filling: Place the mascarpone cheese in a large bowl and beat until smooth. Gradually beat in the heavy whipping cream and confectioners' sugar to make a creamy, spreadable frosting. Beat in the cherry-flavored brandy.

7. To assemble, place the first cake layer on a cake plate. Spread with half the mascarpone filling and cover with half of the brandied cherries. Cover with second cake layer, remaining mascarpone filling and cherries. Finish with top cake layer. Frost the sides and top of the cake with the chocolate ganache and smooth well. Refrigerate.

8. Make mirror glaze (if using): Place 1 tablespoon cold water in a small bowl. Sprinkle gelatin over water and let soften 5 minutes. In a saucepan, combine ½ cup water, sugar, heavy whipping cream, and cocoa powder. Simmer, but do not boil, for about 20 minutes until mixture slightly thickens. Remove chocolate mixture from the heat and whisk in gelatin until thoroughly combined. Set over an ice bath and whisk until the glaze thickens and reaches 80°F. Pour mirror glaze over cake and quickly smooth with an offset spatula. Decorate as desired with additional cherries, chocolate, whipped cream, or other decoration. Refrigerate until ready to serve.

CHOCOLATE RASPBERRY TART
WITH PISTACHIO SHELL

Yield: 10-12 servings

I highly encourage making the raspberry coulis. Its tartness helps to cut the richness of this decadently sinful dessert. A bit of espresso powder intensifies the chocolate's flavor.

Ingredients

- Pistachio shell, baked and cooled (see Easy Nut Shell for recipe, using toasted pistachios)
- 1 pound (16 ounces) dark chocolate
- 1¾ cups heavy whipping cream
- 7 large egg yolks, beaten
- ½ teaspoon instant espresso granules (optional)
- ½ cup seedless raspberry jam
- 12-ounce container fresh raspberries
- Raspberry coulis (See Key Lime Tart for recipe)

Directions

1. Preheat oven to 350°F. Chop chocolate and place in a microwave-safe bowl. Microwave in 30-second bursts, stirring in between, until chocolate is fully melted, about 2 minutes. Set aside to cool slightly.
2. Whisk together heavy whipping cream, beaten egg yolks, and instant espresso granules (if using). Slowly add melted chocolate, whisking constantly, until fully combined.
3. Fill baked and cooled shell with chocolate mixture and bake 25-30 minutes until top is firm to the touch, but center still jiggles slightly. Remove from the oven and cool on a cooling rack for 30 minutes before refrigerating until completely cold.
4. When tart is cool, heat seedless raspberry jam in a small bowl in the microwave until it is liquid, about 30 seconds. Brush top of tart with warm jam, arrange fresh raspberries on top of jam, and brush raspberries with more jam to glaze. Refrigerate until ready to serve. Serve tart with raspberry coulis.

CHOCOLATE ALMOND TIRAMISU CAKE *Yield: 12-14 servings*

Layers of dark chocolate cake soaked with almond liqueur and fluffy mascarpone frosting result in a richly satisfying cake.

Ingredients
Cake
- 2¼ cups all-purpose flour
- 2 cups granulated sugar
- 1 cup unsweetened cocoa powder
- 2 teaspoons baking soda
- ½ teaspoon kosher salt
- 2 cups cold water
- ⅔ cup canola oil
- 1 tablespoon vanilla extract
- 2 teaspoons white vinegar

Drizzle
- ¼ cup almond liqueur such as Disaronno
- ¼ teaspoon almond extract

Frosting
- 3 8-ounce containers (24 ounces total) mascarpone cheese
- 1⅓ cups heavy whipping cream
- ⅔ cup confectioners' (powdered) sugar
- ½ teaspoon almond extract

Amaretti Cookies (optional)—or purchased Amaretti cookies such as Lazzaroni
- 1½ cups almond flour
- ⅓ cup granulated sugar
- 3 tablespoons confectioners' (powdered) sugar, plus ½ cup for coating
- pinch kosher salt
- 1 large egg white, beaten
- ¼ teaspoon almond extract

Directions

1. Preheat oven to 350°F. Line two 8-inch cake pans with parchment paper and lightly grease paper. In a large bowl, sift together flour, sugar, cocoa powder, baking soda, and salt. In a liquid measuring cup, combine water, oil, vanilla extract, and vinegar. Slowly whisk wet ingredients into dry ingredients. The batter will appear very wet.

2. Pour the batter into the prepared pans and bake for about 30 minutes or until a tester inserted in the center of the cake comes out clean. Cool in the pans for 15 minutes, then invert onto cooling racks, carefully remove parchment paper, and cool completely. Slice each cake in half horizontally to make 4 even layers.

3. Make drizzle: Combine the liqueur and almond extract in a shallow dish. Set aside.

4. Make frosting: Place the mascarpone cheese in a large bowl and beat until smooth. Gradually beat in the heavy whipping cream and confectioners' sugar to make a creamy, spreadable frosting. Beat in the almond extract.

5. Lightly brush the cut side of the bottom cake layer with the almond liqueur mixture, spread with about ½ cup frosting, and top with another layer. Keep layering the cake and frosting. Frost the top and sides of cake with remaining frosting. Decorate with Amaretti cookies (optional). Chill until ready to serve.

6. Make Amaretti cookies (optional): Combine the almond flour, sugars, and salt. Add the egg white and almond extract and stir until the dough holds together. Shape into a thin disk and refrigerate for 30 minutes. Preheat oven to 325°F and line a baking sheet with parchment paper or a silicone sheet.

7. Roll small teaspoons of the dough into balls (about 10 grams each). Roll the balls in confectioners' sugar and place on the baking sheet. Gently press down each ball to flatten slightly. Bake for about 20 minutes until they've cracked slightly, are golden under the sugar coating, but are still slightly soft when pressed in the middle. Decorate cake with cookies.

HAZELNUT MOCHA TART

Yield: 10-12 servings

This recipe was the result of a last-minute decision to cohost a progressive dinner. I started with the concept of a pecan pie-type filling, substituting hazelnuts, then added a bit of instant coffee and some leftover bittersweet chocolate. Loaded with toasted nuts, rich coffee, and dark chocolate, this tart was a hit.

Ingredients

- Easy Shortbread Shell or Pat-in Shell
- 1½ cups roasted unsalted hazelnuts, roughly chopped
- ¼ cup bittersweet chocolate, chopped, or semisweet chocolate morsels
- 1 large egg plus 1 large egg yolk
- ¼ cup light brown sugar, lightly packed
- ¼ cup light corn syrup
- 1 tablespoon instant espresso granules
- ¼ teaspoon kosher salt
- ¼ cup (½ stick) unsalted butter, melted
- 2 teaspoons all-purpose flour
- ½ teaspoon vanilla extract
- ¼ teaspoon flaky sea salt, such as Maldon
- Lightly sweetened freshly whipped cream or vanilla ice cream (optional)

Directions

1. Preheat oven to 350°F. Cover baked and cooled shell with hazelnuts and chocolate. In a medium bowl, beat together egg, yolk, brown sugar, corn syrup, instant espresso, and salt until brown sugar dissolves and filling is the color of hummus. Beat in the melted butter, flour, and vanilla extract.
2. Pour filling mixture into shell over nuts and chocolate and sprinkle with flaky sea salt.
3. Bake about 30 minutes until the filling is browned along the edges. Remove from oven and place on a cooling rack. Cool tart completely before slicing. Serve with lightly sweetened whipped cream or vanilla ice cream (optional).

Variation: Replace hazelnuts with any type of nut you prefer, such as pecans or walnuts.

six

A SLICE OF SINGLEHOOD: MR. X

Age 43

SOME MEN ARE LIKE SHARPIES. Good or bad, they leave an indelible black scrawl upon my heart—like Jason. Others are like whiteboard dry-erase markers. Although vivid at the time, their fleeting imprint on my memory is soon smudged and blurred, finally to be wiped away and forgotten completely. The following chapter is based on one of these dry-erase men. I recall neither his name nor his face. He captures my heart, but not for more than a moment. Let's call him Mr. X.

TUESDAY

I'm smitten. He is adorable…by my peculiar measuring stick, anyway. Physically speaking, I'm drawn to tall, rail-thin men, accessorized with a pair of geek-chic glasses. If he happens to sport a visible angry pink scar, so much the better. The French term is *beau-laid*, or "handsome-ugly." This certain guy ticks all those boxes: tall, thin, glasses. He's also clever, witty, and an artist, in other words, *parfait pour moi*.

Mr. X has been dancing across my thoughts, disrupting me from checking nary a project off my to-do list today. Each time he limbos under my skull and Fred Astaires across my brain, I replay his flirty, playful words, unable to stifle the grin that blooms across my face. He emailed me his photo yesterday. Could this be a deliberate ploy to keep me enthralled? This afternoon, I printed and strategically taped his likeness to the edge of my computer monitor, smack-dab in my sight line, with the aim of discouraging a repeat of this morning's clicking of my inbox every fifty-seven minutes, just to sneak another dreamy, doe-eyed glance at his mug. At least now, if my boss saunters by, she's assuaged by my intense stare at the spreadsheet displayed on my screen, unaware I'm gazing, besotted, at Mr. X's pic smiling back at me.

I'm determined to decipher the strength of his feelings; are his sentiments reciprocal, or is he solely playing games with my easily won affections? We met for caffeine and a cozy conversation a few weeks back and have continued to text-tango since then, yet we haven't reconnected face to face. A day or two after our coffee date, he caught a plane to the East Coast for a family visit. He's only been gone two weeks plus a handful of days, yet I wait for his return like a sweetheart waiting for her man to come home unharmed from the war. He's coming back in three days. Finally.

Shy and unable to throw the invitation out myself, I search each of his messages for a second date request once he's returned, impatient to decode him and clarify his interest level.

Yet, conversely, his ambiguity breeds my desire, stereotypically wanting those I cannot have. I know only a handful of his qualities, erroneously coloring in his character's terra incognita with assumptions mirroring my own predilections. I love that quote I heard on TV about humans, on the whole, being better in the abstract. Reality often disappoints. Yet, I yearn to untangle him, unable to endure this knot of uncertainty much longer.

THURSDAY

Why did he send me that damn photo? I haven't been able to shake thoughts of him from my head since. Now his texts and emails have gone silent. For the last three days, I've checked my phone for a line, glimpsed the blank screen, and my mood turns melancholy. Admittedly, he's still traveling. He mentioned he's flying home tomorrow, but it's not as if he doesn't own a mobile phone. How taxing can it be to take a moment in his day to type a line or two? We're chatting daily, we're connecting, he emails me the cutest selfie, and then…crickets. What is he playing at? Is he truly traveling? Does he email that photo to every woman he's stringing along? I've read certain types of men will do precisely that—send the same message to multiple women. Less work, more potential for reward.

It's time for tough love brought to me by my gut: *"What did that book teach you— you know the one—if he's not calling, if he's not dying to see you, well…*He's Just Not That Into You. *It's time to erase him from your brain."*

I understand it's a waste to linger, yet I must confess I've fallen for him a bit. Why does this constantly happen—the ones who capture my attention never share my feelings? I glance over to my bulletin board at the typewritten list posted there, "Washing That Man Right Outa My Hair." I read down the list, making mental check marks as I go along: #1 Stay busy. *Check.* #2 Pamper yourself. *Check.* #3 Make plans with friends. *Check.* #4 If your mind wanders to thoughts of him, gently direct it toward other things. *Hesitant check.* #5 Remove his contact info from your phone to avoid temptation. *I'll do that tomorrow.*

We were never a couple. This isn't a breakup. I'm not pining for him so much as the possibility of what might have been.

FRIDAY

There's something to be said for the etiquette of Jane Austen's Georgian era, when women were proper, ankle-hiding ladies practicing the pianoforte in the drawing room and gentlemen would gallantly pay a visit in hopes to woo them with tempered ardor and a bouquet of freshly gathered flowers.

Wait, huh? I can hear the needle drag across the record. Yes, I'm aware the scene I just painted is a distortedly rosy view of that time—decidedly not what a self-reliant feminist like me would pine for, but indulge me for a minute, please.

My resolve failed me today and I texted Mr. X. How long was I supposed to linger, waiting for a word? Weeks? Months? Years? Well, I lasted scarcely thirty-six hours. I'm aware the plan was to forget him and soldier on, but in a minute of weakness, I shot him a brief text and promptly, if not surprisingly, received one in response. Among other tidbits, this is what he wrote: *"I am trying to make next Sunday 'free' for fun. Just throwing it out there."*

Hold on, what? Did he just ask me out? I believe he wants to hang out, but I'm not certain. Could he be any vaguer? Free for fun with *me*...or just free for fun, in a very general way? *"Just throwing it out there,"* as in "Just throwing it out there to see what sticks?" Am I unworthy of a proper request: *"Do you want to hang out this Sunday?"*

And, damn, I'm *not* available on that day, regardless. My new post-culinary school steakhouse job beckons from noon until midnight. I respond, proposing the alternative of Saturday, and am awaiting his reply.

And waiting...

And still waiting...

The authors who wrote that book, *The Rules*, would disown me. I'm sounding desperate—and neurotic—even to myself. Why can't we return to those golden days when Mr. Darcy, with a slight bow, would politely ask over tea, "Miss Bennet, would you be so kind as to accompany me on a ride in my barouche this upcoming Sunday? The weather should be fine and my sister, of course, will accompany us to avoid any blemish to your unimpeachable reputation. We will call at half past ten, should you be so inclined, as I am quite certain the most beautiful, accomplished, and witty member of the fairer sex who I have ever had the pleasure to encounter stands before me now. I would be honored by your presence, if only for this one afternoon."

Why don't they say that anymore?

MONDAY

Monday morning. No word from him all weekend. I'm hiding in my tiny office, the melancholy rainfall drumming insistently against the cold windows behind me. His photo lies crumpled in the trash can. I stare unblinkingly at the computer monitor. Its harsh glare, combined with another restless night, burns my bloodshot and palsied eyeballs.

Last night's fitful slumber has left me emotional and fragile.

After completing culinary school and reading Bill Buford's restaurant-slave memoir, *Heat*, I envisioned myself earning my culinary chops honing my inchoate talents on the weekends in a friend's steakhouse. But Sunday nights in the bustling kitchen leave me buzzing like I've snorted lines of cocaine off the cutting board. Sleep eludes me until well after 1:00 a.m., not conducive for 9:00 a.m. Monday morning "all-hands" meetings. Why didn't I take a personal day this dreary morning? I could be nestled at home right now, clad in my PJs, napping on the couch with a blanky and roaring fireplace.

My door is shut. I prefer this silent cocoon to the boisterous laughter and banter of my coworkers on the other side of my barred office door. No word from Mr. X. I'm disheartened. In my fantasy, I envision us as a good match, finally breaking this dry spell of mine. However, it takes two.

TUESDAY

And waiting…

THURSDAY

I texted Mr. X once more yesterday afternoon to dangle this Saturday as an option to connect (I know, I should be excommunicated from the feminine wiles, hard-to-get club. So much for considering myself a model member). This was his response:

"I'm going to plan [his emphasis] *to actually compose some prose and send your way after I get home from the office late tonight. My weekends are usually free. So, I say we aim for Sunday the 23rd."*

Based on the above, any woman would rightfully expect to find a message waiting in her inbox this morning, yes? My inbox was full of crap, but nothing from him (obviously my inbox wasn't the only thing full of crap). Sundays are not an option for me, as I've already mentioned more than once. And based on his unenthusiastic initiative to see me, I have no impetus to find a replacement to cover my shift.

So, watch me let him go…

For good this time…

I promise…

Truly…

As I incessantly check my inbox for a message from him.

FRIDAY

Mr. X may be no more than a fleeting chapter in my story, but it's humiliating and painful to be toyed with, regardless; yet that won't stop me from trying again. I dust off my dating profile, change a few phrases, upload a new photo, and off I go.

Eeny, meeny, miny, moe.

Catch a dry-erase man by the toe.

If he doesn't text you, let him go.

Eeny, meeny, miny, moe.

My mother said to pick the very best one, and you are not it. So, O-U-T spells out you go.

…Ready or not, boys, here I come.

MR. DARCY'S LEMON VERBENA
EARL GREY THINS

Yield: 4 dozen cookies

These crisp cookies are a unique and sophisticated combination of citrusy-floral lemon verbena and Earl Grey tea with a hint of warming, earthy nutmeg, reminding me of a proper British tea. Lard gives these cookies a crisp, flaky texture.

Ingredients

- 1¼ cups granulated sugar
- 3 tablespoons fresh lemon verbena leaves, roughly chopped (or 1½ teaspoons lemon zest)
- 3 cups all-purpose flour
- 1½ teaspoons baking powder
- ½ teaspoon table salt (not kosher)
- ¼ teaspoon nutmeg
- 2 Earl Grey tea bags, opened and tea leaves removed
- 1 cup lard (you can substitute vegetable shortening in a pinch)
- ¼ cup (½ stick) unsalted butter, softened
- 1 large egg, beaten
- 1 tablespoon limoncello or brandy

Directions

1. In the bowl of a food processor, process sugar and fresh lemon verbena leaves (or lemon zest) until leaves are finely ground and the size of the sugar crystals.

2. In a medium bowl, sift together flour, baking powder, and salt. Stir in the nutmeg and Earl Grey tea leaves.

3. In the bowl of an electric mixer, using the paddle attachment, beat together lard, ¾ cup lemon verbena sugar (reserve remaining ½ cup lemon verbena sugar), and butter until light and fluffy, about 4 minutes. Add the egg and limoncello or brandy and beat until combined. Gradually beat in the flour mixture on low, in three additions, just until combined. Don't overmix or the dough will become tough. Form dough into two bricks, wrap in cling film, and refrigerate for at least 30 minutes.

4. Preheat oven to 350°F. Line two baking sheets with parchment paper or silicone sheets. In between 2 sheets of parchment or waxed paper, roll out one brick of dough to a ¼-inch thickness. Keep the remaining brick in the refrigerator. Cut out cookies (I use a 2-inch square cutter). Place cookies on baking sheets and chill for 10 minutes.

5. Bake cookies until just barely golden and set, 10-12 minutes. Remove baking sheets from oven, let cookies cool for 1 minute, and then carefully toss them into the remaining lemon verbena sugar. Place on cooling rack until completely cooled. Repeat the process with the second brick of dough. Store in an airtight container.

seven

THE REBOUND: BRETT

Age 44-46

LUPINES

I first visited Mount St. Helens in 2000, two decades after the devastating blast in May 1980. The landscape didn't appear changed from the stark images I saw in *Life* magazine after the eruption. Except for the blue sky, it was as if I had driven into a black-and-white photo, shades of ash and smoke surrounding me. Waves of fallen monochromatic grey tree trunks remained scattered across the somber mountainside, reminding me of images I'd seen of the Civil War dead. The area appeared decimated, lifeless. But once I parked at the visitor's center and started to stroll along the paths, signs of life became apparent: dun-colored grasses, knee-high alder saplings, amethyst lupine, all punctuated by a few scurrying grey squirrels. Slowly, life was reemerging from the destruction.

A decade later, in August 2010, my mother died, her adult children surrounding her. It was closely followed by another devastating blow to my heart, another loss, unexpected, unlike my mother's, just two days later. Two people torn from my life in the span of forty-eight hours.

In the weeks and months following these losses, I numbly went about my routine, elbowing waves of grief into the periphery, feeling as obliterated as St. Helens's landscape.

Then, two and a half months later, in mid-November, Brett and I met online. Opening myself up to a new relationship was like the first violet lupines popping their heads above my ash-covered earth. I was tentatively taking the first steps toward reawakening, acknowledging I'd likely be hurt in the end, but possessing an optimistic soupçon of impetus to try.

ooo

When I arrive at the wine bar for our first date, the afternoon sun is shining directly through the front windows, blinding me and obscuring Brett in shadow. As I turn around to finally see him, my back toward the window, I feel like the bachelorette on *The Dating Game* when Bachelor #3 rounds the corner and she can't wipe the tinge of disappointment from her face. He reminds me of Pedro Pascal—if Pedro has been on a five-year drug-and-alcohol bender.

Brett is shorter than he professed in his dating profile—about five-feet-nine—and his teeth are in a terrible state, with a prominent chip in the front. "An unfortunate run-in with a fork," he confesses. His eyes are a pale sky blue, his complexion ruddy. I note and approve of his style—Vans sneakers, Levi's, and a rockabilly plaid shirt. I glimpse a tattoo on his wrist. I'm a sucker for a tattoo.

We chat over wine. Him: lost his job, then his wife. Father of two kids, a son still at home and a daughter on her own. Me: a recent culinary school graduate, no kids, never married, mother of an ornery cat, Kafka. After two glasses each, we venture across the street to what Brett insists is "the Best Gelato in Orange County." And I have to admit, he isn't wrong. The proprietor, Brett mentions, studied gelato-making for a month in Italy. The gelato is indulgent, but not heavy, the flavors unique, the owner blissfully happy. I confess to Brett my newly minted fantasy of my own month-long gelato adventure under the Tuscan sun. As we walk to my car, my ambivalence toward him lingers in the air. I had a nice time. Nice. We hug goodbye and Brett doesn't lean in for a kiss. I don't dislike him but remain firmly planted on the fence about continuing. If he never texts me again, my self-esteem will take a blow, but I won't be crushed.

I am uncertain our evening will lead anywhere, but this attempt to open my heart once more feels like a beginning, like the alder saplings and grasses unfurling from their safe cocoon beneath the St. Helens's ash. Time heals, we survive, and eventually poke our heads above life's greyness, renewed.

SECOND BASE

I almost don't agree to our second rendezvous, even canceling once. I pull up to the Oaxacan restaurant, find him waiting for me outside, and am startled to feel my heart cha-cha-cha in my chest, *Yeah, he's kinda cute.*

After sharing a dinner of *tlayudas* and *pollo con mole negro*, he leads me to his favorite dive bar in Fullerton—packed with barflies, blue collars, and tattooed chicks in tank tops. Two stools, lit by the glare of blue Bud Light neon, are open at the bar. He orders us Cuba Libres.

As we sit, our jeaned thighs lightly graze against each other and then rest, knees touching. Lust stirs between my legs at the sensation of our bodies testing this chemistry. He brushes his arm against the back of my hand, gently places his hand for a brief moment on my thigh as he speaks, as if not deliberately. Alcohol has made me bold. I stroke the soft inside of his tattooed arm and rest my hand in his, fingers entwined. Enough of this game.

He kisses me. He doesn't ask permission. He doesn't hesitate. He leans toward me, his lips on mine, his tongue inside my mouth. Mmm…Yes. I like the way he tastes.

He isn't afraid to kiss me in this public place. His burning hand caresses my lower back, my waist. He kisses me with passion, his day's worth of stubble leaving my chin raw.

A wrinkled regular at the end of the bar shouts, "Give her back her tongue!" We laugh, but I am unsettled by Brett's intensity, this lack of modesty among these strangers.

We kiss and drink and share secrets, finishing another round. It is late and we decide to leave the bar's seediness, weaving our way across the parking lot toward my blue convertible. I lean back against the rough cinder-block wall, pulling him with me, kissing him, being kissed. We move to the side of my car. I feel him, hard and hot, pressed against my own desire. His chest is firm beneath my hands. I am drunk off rum and yearning. Too fast, this is going too fast. My logic and this ache for him doing battle, I plead, "Let's make this last. Let me know your brain before I learn your body." He doesn't want to comply.

He asks to see me the next day. I make him wait until next weekend. A daytime date—an attempt to slow us down. He wants my body. I want something more.

Oh, but I do like the way he tastes.

ROUNDING THIRD

A midday date, following a week-long hiatus, my endeavor to slow the pace, a pause between the Wham, the Bam, and the Thank you, ma'am, a chance to build anticipation and an opportunity to buy a new outfit, something I imagine he'd like. Only two dates in and I've run out of cute datewear. I buy a 1940s retro-inspired red polka-dot top with a Peter Pan collar and pair it with jeans and crimson wedges: retro casual to match his rock 'n' roll style.

At Brett's recommendation, we meet in the strip-mall parking lot of an Argentinian sandwich shop in Anaheim. Caught in an almost magnetic reaction, I bounce toward him, a grin spreading across my face. I am uncertain about how to greet him: a hug, a kiss, a friendly punch in his arm? Last weekend's hot and heavy make-out session still lingers in my mind. I go in for a hug, he garnishes it with a brief kiss on my lips, confirming there are no regrets from him about last weekend. "Look how cute you are!" Brett exclaims. My new outfit's a winner.

An Argentinian sandwich virgin myself, we are here so Brett can show me the ropes. We enter the crowded shop and Brett orders us a *chori-bondi* sandwich to share, with extra chimichurri sauce on the side. This masterpiece of meatiness is a combination of smoky grilled chorizo sausage and slices of flavorful slow-cooked pork. We take our sandwich and the red wine I'd hidden in my water bottle to a small café table outside the store. I load my sandwich half with a hearty drizzle of garlicky green chimichurri and hand the remainder of the sauce to Brett. The vehicle for the meat is a combination of thin, crackling crust and tender, pillowy-soft bread within. If the perfect sandwich roll exists, this is surely it. As I take my first bite, flakes of the crisp crust fall like snowflakes into my lap. After this first experience with this magic called Argentinian sandwiches, I make a solemn vow to visit my local Argentinian market for pan de campo rolls whenever I plan to make hot sandwiches at home. Why hasn't America caught on?

ooo

Standard Sandwich Bread Failings:

Pre-Sliced Bread: It's the Clark Kent of sandwich breads: no texture, no flavor, just blandness disguised as convenience. Might as well put your filling between two kitchen sponges. Exceptions: A must for nostalgic egg-salad sandwiches with crusts removed, PB&Js, and fried bologna with mayo.

Baguette: A Frenchman would slap me for saying this, but while this Gallic staple has many uses, the chewy exterior requires too much jaw work for a sandwich. And while their length is unparalleled, their girth leaves much to be desired...and girth is important to a woman. Exception: The ultimate pairing for any sandwich filled with melty brie cheese like roasted turkey, brie, fig jam, caramelized onions, and arugula. Mmm.

Focaccia: Overly thick, skewing the bread-to-filling ratio. How many focaccia bottoms have been needlessly thrown away with the wrapper because there's just too much bread? Exception: When squashed mercilessly in a panini press like a boob in a mammogram machine, focaccia magically transforms into the perfect canvas for flavor-packed fillings.

Bagels: No, just no. Leave the bagels for breakfast and schmear.

Pita Bread: With a "pocket" thinner on one side than the other, trying to use the bread as intended, stuffing the pocket with falafel or shawarma and all the condiments, ensures you'll end up dealing with an inevitable baba ghanoush blowout. Exceptions: Roll it, taco-style, around the fillings, instead.

Brioche: Like trying to build a sturdy house with cotton candy: flimsy, sweet, and not meant for the rigors of sandwich construction. Exceptions: Burgers and breakfast sandwiches.

ooo

After our lunch, we head off on the second part of our adventure, to what Brett affectionately calls the "Monkey Zoo." The officially named Santa Ana Zoo is a small, eclectic collection of animals in Prentice Park a few blocks from my house. The grounds consist of a petting zoo, a tired elephant kids can ride, a few injured animals found alongside rural area roads, and an aardvark enclosure—the mascot for the nearby college, UCI. And monkeys, monkeys, and more monkeys. Because of the haphazard and somewhat sad collection of creatures, I call it "The Land of Misfit Animals." The zoo is slowly raising money to improve conditions for the inhabitants—and they do their best—but I am confident the animals dream of a one-way ticket to the much-lauded San Diego Zoo and Safari Park down the freeway. It is odd to find a zoo tucked within Orange County's urban sprawl. Brett calls it the monkey zoo because the original founder, Joseph Prentice, has included a stipulation in the land deed donation. The "Prentice mandate" requires that the zoo have at least fifty monkeys at all times and, although there are fewer than fifty, the majority of the animals are indeed simians.

For our purposes, we choose this particular zoo because it's a nearby, public, family-oriented daytime date, a safe venue to deter us from tearing our clothes off at first sight, or so we believe.

While craning our necks in an attempt to get a glimpse of the ring-tailed lemurs hiding in the shadowy back corners of their enclosure, Brett catches me unaware and kisses me. Not the chaste peck of pre-Argentinian sandwiches, but a real kiss with the intensity my body recalls from the previous weekend. My fingertips tingle in response and I willingly acquiesce. His scent and the warmth of his body against mine eclipse any lingering tipsiness from the earlier wine drinking. There is a cloud of pheromones wafting about our entwined bodies and, when we finally wrench ourselves apart, five pairs of glowing golden lemur eyes are pressed against the enclosure, watching this mating dance of their distant cousins. For those behind the enclosures, Brett and I are the exhibition at the zoo this day.

Holding hands, I notice we pick up our pace through the remainder of the zoo. "If you've seen one monkey, you've seen them all," we seem to say. Two hours later, the sun beginning to set outside the window, I find myself in my own bed, sated and lying naked in Brett's arms, tracing the tattoos on his chest with the tip of my finger. So much for trying to slow us down.

VANILLA

Vanilla sex isn't anything like the similarly labeled ice cream flavor. With the ice cream variety, one knows what to expect. Sure, there may be some subtle differences between French vanilla, vanilla bean, Bourbon vanilla, Madagascar vanilla, or the good ol' classic, but, by and large, if you order a double-scoop vanilla cone, the flavor on your tongue will be exactly that.

Vanilla sex, on the other hand, is undeniably in the eye of the beholder. So, when Brett admits he likes his sex "vanilla," I stop mid-fellatio in disbelief.

As a former writer within the Larry Flynt empire, his repertoire, I presume, includes an array of positions and toys I have only seen, uh, in passing on Pornhub. I anticipate facing a steep sexual learning curve along with daily sets of runners' lunges if I am to ever persevere in whatever sexual escapades he had in his arsenal.

Relieved, and I must admit, to a certain degree, disappointed, I discover after our first few nights beneath the sheets, his idea of "vanilla" matches my own—straightforward and somewhat lacking in experimentation, even after those years writing for *Hustler*.

I was similarly surprised when I slept with a yoga instructor a handful of years prior. I envisioned Sting's seven hours of tantric ecstasy, yet participated in some of the most banal sex of my life. Sleeping with Brett isn't like that; it isn't unsatisfying, we have fun, it just isn't exceedingly experimental.

He divulges that, from time to time, he screwed his ex-wife, entirely with her permission, while she was passed out on Ambien, her habitual nighttime state. It's safe to say any form of mutually participatory sex with me, however lacking in "flavor," will be an upgrade from a passed-out and unconscious partner. Brett has no fetishes, or ones he willingly admits to, anyway. Sexy lingerie or none, hairy bush or shorn, whatever enticements I may or may not employ are of no consequence. He gallantly ensures I am satisfied first and then finishes with eyes closed, as if imagining there is someone else beneath him—his estranged wife, perhaps? This habit ignites my insecurities, but I pretend not to notice.

SCARLET LETTERS
Brett is branded with a scarlet letter...

There's an imaginary *S* for "Separated" tattooed on his hirsute chest. His marital status didn't concern me when I clicked the "like" button on his dating profile. Of course, the length of the marriage, twenty-two years, in comparison to the shortness of the separation, eight months, caused me pause once he told me, but I'm trusting he's been candid about the breakup, assuring me that door is closed, he's never going back to his wife.

I'm astonished, however, when a friend accuses me of committing *adultery* by involving myself with a separated man. I consider myself an ethical and honest individual—sometimes it takes me a minute, like with Edmond, but I eventually get there. My moral compass would never lead me to sleep with a married man, happily wedded or not, but I suffer no ethical quandary about sex and the separated. His wife gathered up her clothes, stuffed them in the trunk of their car, and drove away without a backward glance at Brett or their teenage son still at home. She wanted out. She left him. Her actions could be equated to discarding a used couch in an alley—if I see its vintage appeal, I'm entitled to shove it in the bed of my pickup, give it a spritz of Febreze, and arrange it in my own living room.

Even so, I acknowledge dating The Separated is sticky business. I have labeled the two biggest snags as the Rs. Numero Uno *R* is "Rebound." Brett made a home, raised two kids, and built a life with this woman for more than two decades. I'm doubtful he wants to immediately burrow into another partnering that consists of anything more than frivolity and fun. Like it or not, I am his Rebound Chick. The remaining *R* is "Reconciliation." Separated isn't the same as divorced and, after having a dozen months of single-girl fun, his estranged wife may choose to come home to the comfortable refuge of familiarity and Ambien sex. On our first date, Brett shared that she hit the eject button—he remained committed to the marriage and making it work. He's the injured party, and I'm convinced he'd take her hot ass back (my friend Todd said he knows her and she's "really sexy"), if that's what she decides.

In addition to the two Rs, Brett's dealing with a pile of messiness: finding his footing with his newly minted singlehood, trying to remain cordial with Ms. Sexy Former Spouse, parenting a bewildered teenage son, and processing his grief over a failed marriage. He emphatically declares his enthusiasm at starting this next chapter, yet I suspect he's in denial of how entrenched he remains. Twenty-two years is a long-ass time. I can't recall committing to anything for more than two decades. Brett is lost and fucked up, whether he acknowledges his situation or not.

Another emotionally fucked-up man? No wonder I'm drawn to him, like the proverbial moth to the flame.

Consequently, where does that leave me in this picture? Branded with a scarlet *V* across my breast—Vulnerable. Spelled out above in black and white, my first inclination is to run like hell. Our odds are slim, 22-to-1 slim. If I was handicapping at Del Mar Racetrack, I'd cross that gelding out on the racing form, especially with a zero-win jockey like me, but that's my fear murmuring in my ear, isn't it? I'm doubtful my battle-scarred heart can withstand another direct hit. I'm continually wincing from the fear of added pain—like when the air is charged with static electricity and you hesitate to grasp another door handle, certain of the outcome. Yet, how can I step over the threshold from past disasters to promising future intimacy without taking the gamble? I have an equal chance of getting zapped by a single man who's never been married. Mr. Never Married is as liable to dump me as Brett, even more so, since he's never committed to a woman long term. At least with Brett, I know he's capable, even if he's not currently willing.

KNOTS AND TANGLES

My stomach just landed a double Axel, triple toe loop.

I met Brett through the online dating site OKCupid, *the* site for creative, artsy singles in the aughts and teens of the new millennium. Online dating is the modern version of dumpster diving for Love—picking through messages and "likes" from the unwashed and incompatible, yet hopeful to unearth a treasure, like a response from the Long Beach Buddhist painter with cheekbones that could cut glass (so what if he's vegan and I wax poetic about *Bacon, Cheddar, and Green Onion Scones?*).

Call me a serial dater. Once I've found a compatible partner, I stop looking, thankful to climb out of the refuse bin. Thus, once Brett and I begin sleeping together, I only revisit OKCupid to read new messages in my inbox, and only then, out of curiosity. I haven't dug for a better find, leaving those messages unanswered (ignored messages—see, Mr. Vegan Buddhist Painter, we *do* have something in common after all). I'm poised to hit the delete button on my profile, removing myself from this dating (cess)pool. My search is over, at least for the near future. With my rose-colored spectacles firmly planted atop my nose, I behold Brett, an intelligent, funny, forthright man who causes my long-neglected body to reawaken underneath his touch.

I'm reminded of a book I read about "maximizers" and "satisficers." That's the word—*satisficers*—not a typo. Maximizers are individuals who strive to make the best possible decision by thoroughly researching all available options and making sure every possible alternative is considered before deciding on a final choice. They are often perfectionists and can be exceptionally hard on themselves if they feel they made the wrong decision. Satisficers, on the other hand, are individuals who are content with making a decision that is "good enough." They are less concerned with finding the absolute best option and are more interested in finding a solution with as little fuss as possible. They tend to be more decisive and are happier with their choices.

Vote now: press "1" if you are a Maximizer or, if you are a Satisficer, press "2."
I press 2. I am a satisficer. I'm happily content with my choice.

So, why are my guts doing somersaults?

There was another message waiting for me this morning, so I log on to OKStupid out of curiosity. I see it immediately—before I even click on the email. On the front page, under the heading, "Your Matches," Brett's profile and the green dot in the right corner with the words "Online Now" splashed across the bottom of his picture. I feel a wave of prickling along both arms and a slight constriction arise in my belly, but I pacify my body's reaction into submission by acknowledging the undeniable fact I am logged on at this very moment too. Brett has every right to be online: goose, gander, and all that.

Lest he notice the green dot next to my name, I quickly log out. Ten minutes later, I enter my name and passcode again, merely to sneak a quick look. Yep, Brett is online. My guts tuck and roll. I promptly hit the "Log Out" button a second time. I attempt to work on my expense report while green "Online Now" dots dance across the spreadsheet. After twenty minutes, I close that screen and once again click on OKCupid,ThanksForRuiningMyDay.com. He is still online. I sign out for a third time. I amble to the break room, pour myself a fresh cup of java, heavy on the cream, chat with my coworkers in Creative Services about a project, my computer screen, and that damn website, beckoning me from a few steps away. Back at my desk, my hand involuntarily reaches for the "Log In" button. You can guess who is still online.

Vote now on my behavior: press "1" for "warranted," press "2" for "compulsive," or "3" for "stalking."

Like passing a car wreck on the freeway, I want to look away, focus on something—anything—else, yet I am compelled to look again, grasping to comprehend what my eyes are seeing, my intestines plaiting themselves tighter each time I am confronted with the words "Online Now."

My insides are now knotted and tangled like the computer cables beneath my desk. Thank goodness I've saved myself the embarrassment of telling my friends and coworkers about him. Well…a handful of distant friends and coworkers on the keycard-accessed second floor haven't heard about him, anyway.

I've never understood that axiom, "When you ASSUME, you make an ass out of you and me." Yes, I get the ASS + U + ME part, but how often does the other party actually feel like an ass? There's only one of us who's chagrined in this current situation—and it isn't Brett looking like a donkey's booty. We spent the entire weekend together. I slept at his place both nights. We went out for breakfast Sunday morning at his favorite café. We've already solidified plans for this Thursday. We agreed on exclusivity—at *his* suggestion. I assumed, *hee-haw, hee-haw,* things were progressing. Meanwhile, my knotted guts indicate that he is working from a different assumption.

My mind, the most rational part of my anatomy, counsels me to stop this nonsense: stop logging in, avoid overreacting, play it cool, ignore my guts, get back to work. It's only been a few weeks. It's shiny and new and unfamiliar and a little frightening, for both of us.

On nights we spend together, I still slip out of bed at dawn while he's sleeping to brush my teeth, dab on a little lip gloss, fix my hair, and wipe the crusties from my eyes before heading back to bed, pretending an hour or so later that I always

GLUTEN FOR PUNISHMENT

wake up looking this fabulous, like some housewife from the 1950s. In other words, we are not yet entirely comfortable together.

My brain gently reminds me Brett's also untangling himself from a long-ass marriage. Naturally, he wants to look around to see what else is on the menu. Unfortunately, my inner voice, the one I can't seem to silence and that doesn't connect to my brain, insinuates I'm not enough for Brett, that I'm an amuse-bouche rather than an entrée, that he's merely biding his time with me. Why else would he still be looking?

ooo

Head, heart, guts, and that niggling inner voice are always jockeying for my attention. It's crowded in here. After my meltdown above, my rational brain snatches the reins from my intuitive guts before the horse can bolt. I don't confront Brett, although in hindsight, that certainly should have been my next move, calling him to ask, "Hey, knucklehead, I noticed you were on OKCupid today and I was as well, to read an email. Just trying to figure out where we stand. Are we exclusive or not?" Nor do I deem our future futile and run for the hills. I play the stoic and don't act at all. Scratch that, that's not entirely accurate—I remove my profile from OKWhyBother. I don't press delete from a misguided expectation of reciprocity, hoping he'll respond in kind. I quietly wipe myself from the site and don't mention a word of my decision to Brett. He gives no indication he's noticed, either, yet when I anonymously check his profile the next day (yes, my head is resolute, but my heart is weak), his profile is no longer there. Crisis averted. The horse is safely back in the barn.

SHERPA—A MESSAGE TO BRETT

Here we lie, side by side, a brief sojourn from our trek, sprawled in the tall grass. My profile is down; your profile is gone, too, silently agreeing, yet not speaking the words, "I want to be with you—only you."

"For now, at least," I hear the qualifying whisper on the wind. The downy hairs on the back of my neck prickle. I am naked and laid bare.

We've chosen a precarious path, strewn with minefields and deep ruts. It's never a straight shot when our hearts tag along with us like headstrong children. I suspect I'm in greater peril than you as we gingerly tread forward. I know this terrain. I've been here before, and I've chosen to walk closest to the precipice, my heart in tow. I've let you in.

Separation is never easy. Raw from your split, you're limping along, unable to acknowledge the ache—a limb has been severed, gone to live in another house in another city. Hurt and confusion fester beneath your skin, in your joints and muscles, yet you convince yourself all is fine. We're not ready to set out on this trek, not really. Still, you're resolved to move forward, determined to regain your footing, assessing the ground's solidity with each step, assuring me you are fit for this journey while I eye your unsteadiness. You're convinced you are ready to venture out—and I am your first. I am "The Rebound," and that frightens me. I've stumbled down similar roads with others, always leading to dead ends, disappointments, disillusionments. I haven't the fortitude to retrace my steps and start yet again, battered and bloodied heart cradled within my arms.

Why have I chosen you, of all my options, and why now? I've managed this journey as a solitary traveler for countless years. I desire you. Our palpable chemistry is undeniable, but it's beyond that. Trust. I trust you—my Achilles heel. Have you earned it? No, not yet, but I long to believe I can trust you, and so I do. Even with my faith in you, should we be traveling this path together? Do our destinations align? I'm uncertain. We've little in common. We both like music, but different genres—and, besides, everybody enjoys music of some kind. We're both "foodies," but how far can our palates carry us? We adore reading books, but we've already had those conversations. I've no interest in surfing the blue waters of the Pacific like you. You've never loosened soil to ready a plot for perennials.

You casually introduce me to your friends, and I recede, awkward, out of place, aware they view me as an outsider, an interloper. Especially the women. "Can I *help* you?" the first asks when she notices me hovering quietly in your orbit. Another friend remarks how "brave" I am to don a shirt of horizontal stripes. Yet another digs her fingernails deep into my inner wrist, looking me in the eyes, eager to make me flinch, as she "demonstrates" the pain of a tattoo needle. I am unwelcome here, and I follow you throughout the night, hugging your side, silent, my hand shoved deep in your back pocket. These females are the stalking mountain lions, watching and waiting for me to stumble. Protect me, Brett.

Our destination remains hazy. Outwardly, we venture forth in lockstep—you require a lover to mend your heart, your ego, and I'm eternally captivated by broken things, and you are, at this moment, shattered. Then again, you don't ask me those customary new-lover questions, those queries that build a durable foundation, touching on past loves and future hopes, my likes and dislikes. Is my role solely to fill your wife's shoes until you are ready to forge on, complete, renewed, abandoning me on the roadside? Or, even more troubling, do you simply deem me the antithesis of her, something new and different? Dig below my smiling and acquiescent veneer. You'll discover a complex, nuanced creature. Appreciate me for who I am, not just how I differ from her.

Are we hiking this road together, or am I merely your sherpa?

One sunny day, trekking hand in hand, I admit out loud that I like hanging out with you. You confess you like hanging out with me, too. You reveal I make you happy. I attempt to play it cool and not react. I know one day I'll say or do something (or for no concrete reason at all) that will leave you flinching. You'll want to run, screaming, "She is not what I want!" So, I keep one foot pointed backward toward base camp, taking this journey one week, one step, at a time, prepared to bolt, like a startled doe, when the need arises. I'm trying not to cling to you, not to panic. Men can smell panic. I'm endeavoring to let our journey unfold naturally, not pressuring you, but I am "The Rebound," and I'm frightened.

UNDENIABLY FAZED

I cannot endure this uncertainty. Why must relationships make hearts feel so unsettled? Brett and I spent an ideal weekend together. Saturday night, naked, spent, and wrapped around me in bed, he looks into my eyes and tells me he is happy. What more do I need to assuage my doubts?

He introduces me to more friends, a married couple. These two, contrary to the others, give me thumbs-up, at least. This week, however, I'm sensing Brett pulling back. He's mentioned vague plans for tonight or tomorrow, nothing we've solidified, and I haven't heard a peep from him today. I'm checking my phone obsessively for his call or text. Is it worth canceling Thursday's me-time yoga practice for a tentative, maybe-perhaps date?

Also, at my gut's insistent pestering, I perform a deeper online dive (stalking) and discover his dating profile isn't down at all. On the contrary, he's merely shrewdly hidden it from me, but not from the rest of the available women, ages thirty to fifty, with a penchant for tattooed musicians sporting a chipped-tooth smile. The seismograph in my stomach is sketching the Himalayas across my innards.

How have I allowed myself to be this vulnerable? This persistent uncertainty haunts me. I've permitted Brett to fill my heart and brain, leaving room for little else, my only distraction my continuing online conversation with Edmond. I loathe myself for allowing my own emotional fortitude to slip away so effortlessly. Todd, always the loyal friend, assures me I'm tough and unfazed by the intricacies of relationships. If he only knew the complicated truth. I am the antithesis of unfazed. I've tethered myself to Brett, in a manner that doesn't feel mutual, like I hooked my carabiner on his belt loop without permission. I can't reside in this ambiguity much longer—suspended, waiting, unsure. I must endeavor to give him his space. He evidently doesn't feel the same as I do. I need to refocus myself on my work, on my yoga, on my baking, on anything but him.

CONSUMED

Thoughts of Brett consume me. I'm unable to think, to write about anything else. I attempt to update my blog, but I've grown uneasy writing about my life with him. We're now "an item," and sharing our romance's intricacies online feels like betrayal. He doesn't know about my blog, the only other secret, besides Edmond, I've kept hidden from him.

It seems dishonest to disclose my reflections on Brett unbeknownst to him. I could easily remedy my quandary by mentioning the blog, yet I'm simultaneously horrified, lest he read my posts and my deranged behavior regarding him. I envision Brett recoiling as he reads my slightly unhinged musings. He'd likely grab his jacket and head straight for the door.

Without mentioning Brett, however, my mind and the page remain blank, because my life, as I've known it, is gone. Strip away our exchanges, our dates, my musings on him, and I become a ghostly creature. That's terrifying to admit: Julie has ceased to be, except when in his orbit. How did I manage to shed my identity so effortlessly, so completely—after barely two months, and to a man I was initially dubious about dating?

This plot twist, frankly speaking, cannot be laid at Brett's feet. Prior to dating him, I merely subsisted in my world for quite some time, tired of the same conversations with familiar faces, indifferent to my usual diversions, searching for a painless, no-fuss remedy for my ennui. It's #1 on my to-do list.

<u>TO-DO</u>
1. Revamp life
2. Clean litter box
3. Pick up jacket from the dry cleaner
4. Drop off Amazon return at UPS
5. Schedule facial

Peeling off my tired, uninteresting old existence and redressing myself as Brett's girlfriend is a simple solution for the daunting task of remolding my daily life into something fulfilling, my version of sweeping the dust bunnies under the rug rather than lugging out the vacuum. I've always been easily distracted from overwhelming projects that interest me little.

"Time to dust the bookshelf. Oh, look at this new catalog."

"Time to rejigger my life. Oh, I think I'll waste more time with Brett."

Brett called me a "pleaser" last week. I bristle at that moniker. To me, a "pleaser" subjugates their wants and needs for another. At this juncture, I seem to possess neither wants nor needs of any significance. Apart from where we dine, my input concerning Brett-and-Julie time is nonexistent. We go to Brett's shows on weekend nights, watch the movies Brett fancies, camp with his friends, but not mine, spend Sunday afternoons and vacations fly-fishing, Brett's hobby—although I confess I enjoy, and often encourage, our fly-fishing adventures. Brett even jokes that we've yet to step foot inside a museum, an activity he knows I adore. The blame lies not with him. I willingly accepted this new existence, gladly exiting a life formerly known as "Julie." Yet, do my newfound circumstances with Brett satisfy me more? I'm tired of ruminating and dissecting, so I find myself, if not content, then complacent with my new situation.

Last Saturday night found me alone and, without Brett, feeling *lonely*. What new horror is this? Ah, a glimpse onto the flip side of relinquishing my identity to another. I've whiled away dozens of Saturdays alone with nary a second thought, yet now the silence is deafening. This is not me. Besides, how can Brett continue to like me if the woman he fell for no longer exists?

I shouldn't bank on Brett to fix my apathy, but to not think, to not endeavor, to avoid striving for a different kind of existence has been a nice break. I've employed Brett as my crutch to hobble along in this half-life.

It's time to rediscover myself.

I'd do well to reacquaint myself with the writer lurking within. I devoted yesterday to the garden, my back turned away from the page, and from Brett, cleaning up the mess winter left behind: raking leaves, pulling weeds, cutting back dead plants. Four and a half hours of moving meditation. Today, I've locked myself inside my writer's retreat, commanding the torrent of words and thoughts to leave my head and rain down on the page, proclaiming a decree of almost biblical intensity, "I Command Thee to Write," like Moses parting the Red Sea. My first attempt looks bleak:

> *"Brett, Brett, Brett, Brett, Brett, Brett, Brett, Brett, Brett, Brett, Brett, Brett, Brett, Brett, Brett."*

SCHRÖDINGER'S MIND

I have proven the Many-Worlds Theory of quantum mechanics, with a slight tweak Feynman and Hawking must have missed: the other worlds exist solely in my head.

Amateurs.

Based on the Schrödinger's cat hypothesis, the Many-Worlds Theory posits every potential outcome of a quantum event occurs in separate and parallel universes. According to this idea, our current reality remains one of an infinite number of coexisting universes, each with its own set of possibilities and branching timelines…in my head.

Brett and I are still walking hand in hand in the majority of these worlds, yet our narrative branches off in distinct yet parallel stories. In one awfully overpopulated world, we've agreed two households are senseless, and Brett boxes up his possessions and relocates into my cozy two-bed, one-bath house. "Brett" meaning not only him, but his smelly and ravenous teenage son, the two dogs requiring home-cooked special meals, one cantankerous cat, plus an African grey parrot with mental health struggles and remaining lifespan of sixty years. All descend on me and poor Kafka, my antisocial tuxedo kitty—all dressed up with no desire for company. In another scenario, Brett and his estranged wife tearily comfort each other, thrown together by a car accident resulting in the tragic death of that same teenage son. Reunited in grief, the estranged couple reconciles while I'm selfishly signaling from my empty house, "Hey, what about me?" In the next image, Brett walks out on me with a shrug, claiming he's incapable of conjuring more than superficial feelings for me, never glancing back, yet, in another scenario, he's shockingly proposing we marry, regardless of my own sentiments on such an unnecessary union.

Each world orbiting past my mind's eye churns up a swirling cyclone of emotions. A bit of a cynic when it concerns love, I find the harsh, bleak worlds of Jupiterian proportions eclipse the hospitable, pleasanter realms at an approximate three-to-one ratio. Living these multiple scenarios, if only within my brain, wrenches me from one extreme to another, as if I'm traveling through emotional wormholes. I'm struggling to confine the reactions stirred up from these other worlds to their respective biosphere, distinguishing them from reality, yet they seep in far too often.

I wish I wasn't prone to ruminations such as these. I wish I could exist in this reality and quit imagining what may or may not transpire, jettisoning these other possibilities from my head and far into space, focusing on the present for a change.

FANNING EMBERS

We don't have a blowout or anything. I won't even go so far as to label it a "bad weekend." The word that springs to my mind would be "perfunctory."

Brett's band doesn't have a show this weekend, so our calendars are blank white squares waiting for us to graffiti across them with our plans and adventures. Friday night's field of white remains empty, as does Saturday day. Brett makes an appearance Saturday night, after I invite him to my place for a casual dinner.

I choose one of my "looks fancy, but is incredibly easy" recipes, Hawaiian pork with steamed rice and sautéed cabbage. As I review the recipe, my mouth waters, recalling the sticky glaze, redolent of garlic, ginger, and Chinese five spice, coating bits of meltingly tender braised pork, reminiscent of a Hawaiian plate lunch.

Any recipe with the word "braise" in the title is usually a safe bet when you're avoiding being chained to the stove throughout a date. I don't make dessert, a surprising choice considering that's my comfort zone, but since graduating culinary school, I've been focusing on my savory dish repertoire instead. I could have whipped up my *Coffee Caramel Macadamia Pie* without much fuss, complementing the pork and showing Brett I made an effort, but I choose the lazier route.

During dinner, our conversation is stilted, both of us pouncing upon whatever trivial topic comes to mind. The CD on the stereo, I can't remember the band's name, fills in the heavy gaps of silence that crowd us. Anyone peering in the front window would label us an old married pair rather than a couple yet to celebrate their first dating anniversary. Give Brett a newspaper to hide behind and we'd be set.

Dinner progresses to a movie, *The Fighter*. No canoodling like in the early days, just a comfortable entwinement on the couch while focused on the screen. I steal glances over at Brett on occasion, but his eyes stay fixed on the film, rarely turning in my direction. After the credits roll and dutiful goodnight kisses, Brett ties up his Vans and heads home. I stand at the squeaking screen door, flummoxed, as I raise an apprehensive hand to say goodbye. No sex, no discussion of sex, no real hint of why he's leaving, only a hollow excuse about feeling tired and the dogs being home alone.

This is not what I signed up for. I'm not saying sex is preoccupying me, but we haven't missed a weekend horizontal romp yet.

I don't see him again for the remainder of the weekend. This is the first time our fairly routine schedule varies, reawakening that doubting inner voice inside of me.

What changed? Have I made myself too available? I'm reminded of the story about Hershey's employees and free fun-size chocolate bars on their lunch tables. New employees ravenously gobble them down like kids on Halloween, but long-time workers, surrounded by the taste and scent of chocolate for years, turn away, no longer able to stomach another bite. I've heard, by the way, this is an urban legend, but it's an apt illustration of my point. The first month Brett and I dated, he would ask me out for the following weekend during our date. Gobble, gobble, gobble, he couldn't get enough of me. The next month, in November, he slowly began asking me out no sooner than midweek. Today, I'm surprised if the topic is discussed prior to Friday afternoon, as if he assumes I'm available and, alas, I always seem to be. Is this what being a couple looks like?

I recognize I've been relying on Brett—to ask first, to come up with the date particulars, something he readily acknowledges isn't his forte. His wife, it seems, organized all their plans, which causes me to ponder which part of the man's brain is extracted when hetero men undergo that elective surgery called "marriage." These men give the impression they've lost the capacity or the desire to devise and implement a plan to navigate simple aspects of daily life. I'm guilty of generalizing here, I'll admit, but I've dated a handful of separated/divorced men, and witnessed the inner workings of dozens of marriages. When it comes to the planning, I often hear, "Oh, my wife was in charge of that." I Googled it. The term is "forgetting by retrieval failure."

But I digress.

Disregard Brett's former uninvolved role in his now-defunct marriage. In our current situation, he feels pressured with the full responsibility of planning, and he's requested I step up. I pinky-promised him I'd make more of an effort, take more of an interest going forward. As an event manager by profession, arranging social calendars often feels like a busman's holiday for me, and, as I've already mentioned, I've been apathetic about activity specifics in general. Whatever Brett wants to do during our couple's time is fine with me, but I'll step up with the planning. It's ironic to denounce married men's indifference when I'm committing the same blunder.

These past months, I've shoved my former doubts out of reach, but this lackluster weekend has enabled an uneasiness to creep near me once more. Our disconnect would be understandable if we argued, but we never fight, not once, not even a little snippy exchange. In the beginning, this constant harmony reassured me of our compatibility, yet now I'm convinced it's more likely a warning sign of mutual apathy—a disastrous foundation for building an enduring bond.

LOOK NOW

"Relationships sparkle, fizz, bubble, flash, subside, ignite, combust, sputter, fizzle, burst. It just depends on when you are looking."—Todd

I want to scribble out my recounting of last weekend with a thick, red Sharpie. I wish I could convince you my hours with Brett are near perfect. I want to sanitize and social-media the fuck out of that entire lackluster turd of a weekend: Here's a pic of me working my magic at the stove, *click*. And aren't you jealous we're eating this mouthwatering, time-consumingly prepared meal, smiles, *click*. Rather than going out, we prefer each other's company, watching our movie, snuggling, smiling, a kiss, *click*, include a clever caption crafted to suggest we never finished the movie (wink, wink). But these tableaus of my various relationships, like Brett, that I rip, bloody, from my memories and smear across these pages aren't the whitewashed fictions you usually see on social media.

I'm ashamed for highlighting the banal reality of our dinner and movie, as if I envision each minute to be Instagram-perfect and blame Brett when we fall short. I'm further mortified, wondering, if he stumbled upon these words, how would my depiction make Brett feel? Is this an accurate microcosm of our greater relationship? I've opted to chalk that evening's ennui up to an off night, or even an off weekend, rather than the death rattle of a sputtering romance. My sage of a friend, Todd, is right. This connection we're building is a kaleidoscope of moments, and what you see depends on when you're looking. So, today, I turn the object chamber again, create a different image, and encourage you to look through the eyepiece now:

There's a certain moment, often in the smallest morning hours, which finds us lying face-to-face, our moonlit features inches from one another. And as I gaze upon his countenance, day-old stubble, scars, and lines I recognize well begin to soften and change. His eyes shine clear, blue, and guileless, time's furrows soften along his temples and forehead, his smattering of childlike freckles multiply like stars along his cheek, and I am, at that moment, consumed with love for this man.

This paragraph, these words above, are the ones I would want Brett to read.

ENTWINED IN DOUBT

Last weekend, in our chilly cabin snuggled in the Big Sur woods, Brett clung to me as he slumbered. We haven't been so entwined since our first few weeks together. And, back then, it was me, and not he, so wrapped (or rapt?). His arm cradling my head, his leg thrown over my bare thighs, a hand entwined with mine, his warm breath on my neck, I felt safe and wanted, like I belonged there.

I wake to a nightmare early this morning. A vision of Brett that's left me rattled, the details escaping like vapor into the morning mist. As the dove-grey dawn seeps through the thin gold drapes, I yearn for those arms, that leg, his kiss of breath to soothe my troubled mind, but my fingers grasp cold sheets on his side of the bed. I settle on a walk through the neighborhood to remove this swirling dread.

Could my foreboding and portentous imaginings solely be the result of insomnia and my choice of pacifier? From 2:00 to 4:30 this morning, I lazed on the couch, awaiting sleep and my bed to beckon me, absorbed in reruns of *Sex and the City*. I gazed at the glowing screen, relating, as Carrie never receives the unreserved affection she needs from Mr. Big. Realization blossomed as I emphatically nodded, commiserating with her exasperation.

If I don't scrutinize what we've built too closely, squinting a bit, our bond is flourishing, but exchange kaleidoscope for microscope, and this is what I observe:

- We've been monogamous for seven months, and Brett has managed to utter the term "girlfriend" exactly twice. He's capable of pronouncing two-syllable words, so it's not that "girlfriend" is beyond his physical abilities.
- The last time he shared his feelings with me was New Year's and he said, "I like you, a lot." Neither his sentiments nor his vocabulary has expanded since then. Almost five months later and we're stalled at "a lot."
- His daughter (his favorite kid) and father (his favorite parent) are in town, but there's been no talk of introducing me (his supposed favorite girlfriend).
- Brett and his no-longer significant other haven't begun divorce proceedings, and he hasn't broached the topic in months. I can't help but speculate he's holding out hope they will reconcile.
- He talks about his former wife often, not necessarily fondly, but her name escapes from his lips frequently. Does she still consume his thoughts?
- Lately, I practically envision myself as a friend with benefits rather than his lover. Our time together has an air of detachment and remoteness I try to ignore.

The brisk morning air during my walk does not revive me. This terrible sensation of calamitous prescience hovers near throughout my day, yet I'm scared to say, "I need you tonight," loath to be seen as needy. So, I vow to wait patiently for tomorrow, our usual Wednesday night together, and plan to wrap myself around him tighter still.

COMFORTABLE COMPLACENCY

If you were watching a film, the director, at this point, would cut to an idyllic nature scene resembling somewhere in the Northeast. You'd see trees shimmying their emerald leaves like flappers dancing in the mild summer breeze, songbirds twittering away as they hop from branch to branch. Bright sunlight would glint on the babbling brook running through the tableau. Slowly this picture would morph into sunset-hued leaves gently suiciding from their branches onto the brittle, camel-colored grasses below. The dazzling sun would grow long and golden and then dim, as the trickling brook freezes over, and the trees become bare skeletons keeping watch over the silent, windswept, snow-dusted landscape. All of this representing time moving, seasons passing. But this is not a movie, and I'm in Southern California, where the changing of seasons is imperceptible to all but the very few of us who label ourselves native Californians.

Whether he recognizes it or not, Brett seeks an existence as closely aligned to his previous married life as possible, so we fall into a groove, becoming comfortable with each other before our first year has passed. We'd been on an even keel, devising a weekly pattern that doesn't often deviate. Wednesdays, we take turns cooking dinner and spending the night at each other's places. His band usually has a show on Saturday, and I sit dutifully in the "wives and girlfriends" section, supporting him into the wee hours, even though the other wives and girlfriends act like they'd rather I was elsewhere. We spend Saturday night together, eat breakfast or dim sum at one of Brett's favorite spots on Sunday, usually with his son in tow. Afterward, the two of us fly-fish in the afternoon and say goodbye in the early evening. This predictability lures me into a sense of comfort.

Brett eventually introduces me to his entire family, including the elusive daughter and father, and he braves my family gatherings as well. We travel on vacations together. The relationship is effortless. Brett's words or actions never bring me to tears. We don't even become irritated with one another. Our companionship fills a hollowness in each of us, yet we are mistaken to rely on each other to fulfill that need. We should have focused on self-care, first, only starting a romance once we were each whole, rather than two broken halves. Brett looks to me to stand in for the role of "wife," without laying out any emotional investment himself. I am no less culpable. I've become bored with my life; bored with my hobbies, my friends, my job, and rather than focusing on revamping my own life, I've become a fixture in his. I am called to neither kitchen nor writer's retreat. I have abandoned myself, utterly.

UNWELCOME SURPRISE

I awaken to the soft cooing of a mourning dove. I can't recall the last time I heard that plaintive cry, befitting a day like today. It's 8:00 a.m. on a Saturday, three hours before I'm usually stirring, but this Saturday is different.

Brett left me yesterday.

We spent last weekend together, ate dinner out, had sex, enjoyed dim sum Sunday to celebrate Chinese New Year, and spent the remainder of the day lounging on the couch.

We chatted over email and text on Monday, on Tuesday, and part of Wednesday, but then he never responded to my last text, a completely innocuous question, "Did you ever try the Have'a chips I bought you?" How can Have'a chips trigger a breakup? They're made with "Joy, Love, and Light," if their packaging is to be believed.

Brett and I didn't have our usual dinner on Wednesday. I didn't hear a word from him on Thursday either. Friday came and I called, my guts crooning, *something is wrong-ong*. We talk, text, or email every day. My initial call went to voicemail. Unusual. I called again a few hours later, voicemail yet again. Uh-oh. I emailed; no response, my trepidation building with each passing hour. I eventually received a call back in the afternoon. Brett was standing outside Panera Bread, ready to order a salad. I closed my office door.

"What's going on with you?" I asked.

"I don't have feelings for you," he replied simply, "and I feel really guilty about that."

That was it. That was all he had to say to wriggle out of "us." No face-to-face, "we need to talk" conversation, no blowup, just a phone call, as if he was canceling his streaming service. "Thanks, but I've decided to go with Netflix instead, and I feel really guilty about it."

I wanted to ask why, I wanted to scream at him, but the words remained locked within. I managed to croak out a mousy "Alright" before I hung up the phone.

I'm not sure why they say love resides in the heart. It's lower, in the solar plexus. There's a dense hollowness as if Brett took his boot and kicked me squarely in that spot. I cannot eat, the heaviness blunting all desires for food. I cannot stay home today. I'm caged, wanting to socialize, get my hair cut, buy new clothes. Yet, I do no more than crawl into a ball and cry. I didn't know I possessed so many tears. These salty drops of my anguish continue to arrive, unbidden, raining down my cheeks in drizzles and downpours while this leaden ache rests stubbornly inside me. I can't speak the words, "Brett has left me," to another soul. I'm too fragile. I suffer alone.

THE HOUSEGUEST

Melancholia unexpectedly arrives upon my doorstep this weekend, barging in, making herself at home, sleeping beside me, leaving her stuff all about the house, dispensing an unmatched bleakness more potent than my initial days without him. Back then, my doses of despondency were diluted with disbelief and a dash of hope Brett would change his mind. Today, my sadness has been distilled to an unction by insomnia, persistent rain (I knew contentment once, hearing raindrops on the roof, wrapped safely in his arms), plus the thirty-day anniversary since he said those words, "I don't have feelings for you."

Happy anniversary, Brett.

Melancholia (I soon begin calling her Mel) stands resolute in my living room, goading me into her ill-conceived plan for a night out at the gastropub off the Orange Circle—Haven. It seems a sound proposal, at the time. Unaware of her true intent, I convince myself her companionship would temper my newfound unease at going out alone. We flat-iron our hair, apply makeup, don jeans and cute blouses, and make our way to Haven.

Predictably, people swarm about the place, so Mel assures me luck has shone on us when we nab two seats at the bar. I order a glass of red and short rib tacos, my first meal of the day. To bastardize a certain refrigerator magnet axiom—I'm only one breakup away from my goal weight. Mel consumes not a bite, merely sipping her water, while she hovers watchfully as I nibble on mine. Chatting twenty- and thirty-somethings press in on all sides, yet no one speaks or even acknowledges we exist. The tattooed bartenders, annoyed by my food order, pay us the minimal notice required to perform their job. Mel's perfume of misery wafts about us both, holding everyone at bay. Finding a haven at Haven remains outside my grasp. Mel doesn't speak a word to me, so I stare awkwardly at the bottles lined up behind the bar and check my phone every few minutes for texts that never materialize. That single glass of wine goes straight to my head, the result, I'm certain, of eschewing food throughout the day.

As we depart Haven, Mel finally opens her mouth, cruelly prodding me to call Brett, a tad drunk on a Saturday night. She assures me he would welcome a drunk dial, an ideal occasion for admitting I still miss him terribly and tearily demanding to know how it's possible he cannot miss me. I ignore her counsel, the vestiges of common sense I still possess winning that tussle, thank god.

This morning, Sunday, Mel pours salty despair down my cheeks as she follows me on my walk and again while she tightly embraces me throughout the day. Her relentless attention forces me to cancel dinner plans with friends, knowing she would tag along, mortified for them to meet her.

Instead, we mope about the house. Mel shows me Brett's photos on Facebook, playing with the band on Friday night. She notes how handsome he looks in his new haircut, and also mentions he looks fit, like he's started working out. "Most likely," she says, derisively, "in hopes of attracting someone younger, prettier, smarter, more interesting. Maybe he met someone that night? Doesn't he look as cute as he did on your second date, waiting for you outside the Oaxacan restaurant? Remind me, didn't you fall for him that night?"

Yes, I've been stalking him online—at Mel's insistence. I know it's not healthy for me to look, but this weekend, Mel has hidden my resolve and determination somewhere in the house. We even take the freeway to his town this afternoon. In hopes of what, I'm not sure. Mel coerces me but doesn't divulge her intentions. The familiar freeways and off-ramps mock me. "This isn't your route anymore. Stay out, intruder." It's the first time I've ventured in his direction since he said goodbye.

I'm a mess tonight, feeling utterly lost. I happily basked in the life I built with Brett, but he doesn't want me. I never expected to encounter that simple and bleak truth. What is the point in sharing my predicament with any other friend besides Mel? They cannot save me. They will not save me. I am tasked with rescuing myself. Mel departs in the morning, but she threatens to call and text throughout the week, lest I attempt to forget him.

SPRING CLEANING

The mornings remain too quiet. I don't remember feeling this miserable when my parents died and, as Brett would say, "I feel really guilty about that." I brew fresh coffee. That was Brett's job weekend mornings—making coffee. He'd carry our steaming mugs, mine with exactly the precise amount of milk, to our nest of tousled sheets, and we'd lie there, naked and talking until noon…or until his teenage son would inconveniently knock on the bedroom door and stand at the foot of Brett's bed, chatting with us, while I hid my lack of PJs under blankets pulled up to my chin.

The first fingers of anger are slowly choking the remaining life from my sadness. I've been nothing but kind to Brett, by his own admission. And yet, I'm treated like I'm disposable, like I meant absolutely nothing, worthless like a dirty McDonald's wrapper crumpled and discarded in the gutter. I deserve more regard, more elucidation, more contrition than a pre-lunch phone call from Panera's parking lot. I can barely swallow a bite of food for weeks, while he, conversely, dumps me then orders a Citrus Asian Crunch with chicken to go.

It's not lost on me that he strategically timed his exit to happen after the holidays, but before February 14. I'm sure he justified the careful timing as an act of kindness, yet I view it as stomach-turning evidence of a well-devised plan. Precisely when, I ponder, did he conclude he wanted out? Was it during the New Year's party, or maybe before we spent Christmas with my siblings? Possibly it was as early as Thanksgiving with his family.

I'm keen to discard the clutter and detritus of sadness that persists in enveloping me. Everything reminds me of him—everything. I throw away music CDs and the gifts he bought me for Christmas, my fly-fishing gear, the books he gave me. I erase Brett's number from my phone, purge his email address from my computer, block him on Facebook. *Eternal Sunshine of the Spotless Mind*: I would sign up in a second. Erase it all, the good and the bad together, because, truly, the good bits are the most painful…or the memory of them. A spotless mind, that's what I need.

These feeble attempts at erasing him are insufficient. His ghost still haunts these rooms. I'm determined to reclaim this bedroom, at least, as my own. My pink and plum Parisian boudoir is no more. I've stripped the bed of every pillow where he may have lain his head. I've thrown away the plum velvet duvet and sheets stained with his desires. More than merely washing away his morning scent, they now reside in the garbage, where Brett belongs. The pile of throw pillows we joked were too numerous have been rehoused in the trash bin as well.

I've exchanged it all for slate grey-green bedding flecked with gold, brown, and terra cotta—stark, deep, and calming, more masculine than my last set. I've removed the thin, golden drapes that seeped in sunlight, the drapes Brett pulled aside in the morning to spy on the backyard critters. I've swapped them for thick, chocolate-brown blackout drapes that fool me into thinking it's midnight when twilight still winks outside. Their weight makes them difficult to pull back, like fortified wooden doors. I've found replacements for the chair, the mirror, the lamp,

GLUTEN FOR PUNISHMENT

even the vase near his side of the bed. I consider taking a baseball bat to them, but donate these items to charity instead.

I've even replaced his side of the bed, starfishing from one corner to the other, claiming every inch as "mine." It's my haven, my cocoon, again—and I haven't slept more soundly.

FORENSICS OF A BREAKUP

On the driveway outside my front door lies a shoe print, the waffle pattern of a Vans sneaker. Over the months, I've sauntered by this imprint 6,726 times, give or take, whether to slide inside my car to drive to work or step over it to wheel the trash cans to the curb. This stamp upon the concrete used to make me smile, this insignificant mark, knowing what it meant—until the day Brett left. It's the pattern of *his* shoe, of course.

Suddenly, its significance has transformed. Those interlocked hexagons mock and needle me, "Don't forget him, Julie, don't forget." I wait patiently for the first rain of spring to rid me of this pesky reminder. And, in time, heavy clouds drop a week's worth of buckets on my city, bathing the dusty trees lining the streets and Waterpiking grime from roof tiles, clogging neglected gutters with swirling leaves, muck, and a flotilla of discarded cigarette butts in the process. This storm is what I need. The warming sun eventually pokes his head through the cloud-filled skies and licks the raindrops from my neighborhood.

To my chagrin, the imprint remains.

A half-dozen storms visit after Brett leaves, and as each departs, I step onto my porch and gaze upon the concrete, confident the latest downpour possessed sufficient force to erase the greasy remnant, and another of my memories of Brett, away. My hopes are dashed. Each time, it remains.

Todd asks, "Is it pointing toward the house or away?" A strange question and, frankly, I never took note. I inspect the imprint today—the answer is away. Brett was walking away, prophetic.

I grow weary of waiting for Mother Nature's help in moving on with my life. There's a scrub brush swirl where his shoe once walked. Simple Green is my wingman today, since Mother Nature balked at my request. Someday I'll need to eradicate the swirl as well.

For now, this is enough.

CASKET

I bring home a large, sturdy cardboard box from work. In its previous life, it contained the new fuser drum for the Creative Services Department's copier. I place the container on the bare wooden floor of my living room and fold back the thick flaps so I can peer into the emptiness inside. On the bottom, I place Sunday's newspaper, carefully folding each sheet to fit snugly into the corners. On top of the newspaper, I place my ex-boyfriend, Brett, bending his arms and legs as needed to fit.

Around my former partner, I tuck in our memories. I stuff in the water bottle that held the red wine we surreptitiously drank on our third and fourth dates. I add his England sweatshirt, the one I wore whenever I was cold, and my favorite photo of us that sat proudly inside my office for over a year.

I squeeze in the shumai we enjoyed on alternating Sunday mornings, and the night I soaped him up and scrubbed him down in the shower after his sweaty show with the band. I fold in his personal ad that caught my eye and pour in his morning scent, along with our first kiss in the bar, the day he taught me to fly-fish, and the torrent of tears I've cried these past two months. I pack every last trinket and memory inside until the contents bulge against the cardboard sides.

I fold the flaps closed and push them together with my knees tightly as I tape the seams. One long strip across the length and three perpendicular to the first, ensuring it is sealed. I smooth the tape firmly with my hands and mark the box using a thick Sharpie with the word "PAST." I write the word in large block letters on the top and all four sides. I lift this cardboard casket of our relationship, heavier than I expected, and carry it into the garage.

By stepping on an old, wobbly chair, I hoist my memories and my dreams for our future into the rafters, but I can still read the word "PAST" from my perch on the chair. I grab the broom leaning along the wall and use the blue, wooden handle to push the box farther and farther back, as far as the broom will reach with me outstretched and on my very tippy toes. I push these remnants of my affection into the darkest corner of the rafters, home to thick layers of dust, the black widow webs, and the big brown cockroach nest, until I can barely see the tip of its corrugated corner. I step down from the chair, place the broom back against the wall, switch off the garage light, lock the door, and wash my hands in the kitchen sink. The box, and all it contains, will soon be forgotten there.

BRETT

the recipes

COFFEE CARAMEL MACADAMIA PIE   *Yield: 8–10 servings*

This pie is inspired by Kona coffee-glazed macadamia nuts: a little salty, a bit sweet, with a dash of bitter coffee to compliment the buttery richness of the nuts.

Ingredients

Crust

- ¼ cup (½ stick) unsalted butter, cold
- ½ cup shortening
- 1 large egg white
- 1 tablespoon cold water
- 1½ teaspoons white vinegar
- 1½ cups all-purpose flour
- ½ teaspoon kosher salt

Filling

- ¼ cup (½ stick) unsalted butter, melted
- ½ cup light brown sugar, lightly packed
- ½ cup light corn syrup
- 2 large eggs
- ¾ teaspoon vanilla extract
- 1 tablespoon (generous) instant espresso
- ½ teaspoon kosher salt
- 1¾ cups roasted, unsalted macadamia nuts, well chopped
- Confectioners' (powdered) sugar for dusting (optional)

Directions

1. Make crust: Chill butter and shortening until very cold by placing both in the freezer for 15 minutes. Beat together egg white, water, and vinegar in a small bowl and set aside. Place flour and salt in the bowl of a food processor. Add chilled butter and shortening to flour and pulse until mixture resembles coarse meal (you can also combine the flour and fats using a pastry blender if you don't want to drag out your processor—more effort, less cleanup). Add egg mixture and pulse just until dough begins to clump. Don't overwork dough.

2. Pat dough into a disk, wrap in cling film, and freeze for about 20 minutes. (If you will not be using the dough within 45 minutes, chill in the refrigerator instead.)

3. Preheat oven to 350°F. Sprinkle dough with flour and then, between two sheets of parchment or waxed paper, roll out the dough, starting at the center and working your way out into a 11- to 12-inch circle. Once the dough is the correct size, peel off the top layer of paper and, using the bottom sheet, transfer the dough to a 9-inch pie dish. Flip the dough over, peel off the bottom sheet, and gently press the dough into the dish. Trim dough so the overhang beyond the pie plate lip is only about ½ inch. Fold edge under and crimp decoratively. If the dough is too soft, pop it back in the freezer for 15 minutes before baking.

4. To blind bake crust, cover dough with parchment paper and fill with pie weights, uncooked rice, or sugar. Bake on the bottom rack for about 20 minutes or until the crust just begins to color and looks dry. Carefully remove parchment and weights and return crust to oven for about 5 more minutes until edges begin to look golden. Transfer to a cooling rack and cool completely.

5. Make filling: Beat together the melted butter, brown sugar, corn syrup, eggs, vanilla extract, instant espresso, and salt about 2 minutes or until frothy and the color of peanut butter. Sprinkle macadamia nuts over cooled crust and pour filling over nuts. Bake for about 30 minutes until the sides are set and the center is still slightly wobbly. Remove from oven and transfer to a cooling rack to cool completely. Dust with confectioners' sugar (optional) and serve.

BACON, CHEDDAR, AND GREEN ONION SCONES   *Yield: 16 scones*

With three sticks of butter in the dough, no additional butter is needed. These scones are best when eaten the day they are made.

Ingredients
- 8 strips bacon, cubed
- 1 bunch green onions, sliced, white and light green parts only
- 4 cups all-purpose flour
- 1 tablespoon granulated sugar
- 1 tablespoon baking powder
- ½ teaspoon baking soda
- ½ teaspoon kosher salt
- 1½ cups (3 sticks) unsalted butter, very cold and cut into cubes
- 1¼ cups buttermilk, divided
- 1 large egg
- 1¼ cups grated sharp cheddar cheese
- Flaky sea salt, such as Maldon

Directions

1. Cook bacon in a skillet until crisp. Remove bacon from pan. Add green onions to bacon grease in pan and cook until softened. Add onions to bacon and cool both. Line two baking sheets with parchment or silicone sheets.

2. In the bowl of a food processor, combine flour, sugar, baking powder, baking soda, and salt. Add the cold butter and pulse until the butter is pea sized. Pour into a large bowl.

3. In a liquid measuring cup, measure 1 cup buttermilk. Beat in egg until well blended. Pour buttermilk and egg mixture into dry ingredients and gently combine with your hands until dough barely comes together. Add bacon, green onion, and cheddar and gently combine. The secret to flaky scones is not overworking the dough.

4. Shape the dough into two disks about $5\frac{1}{2}$ inches wide by $1\frac{1}{2}$ inches high. Freeze for 20 minutes.

5. Preheat oven to 350°F. Cut each disk into 8 wedges and place wedges on the baking sheets about 2 inches apart. Brush scones with remaining $\frac{1}{4}$ cup buttermilk and lightly sprinkle with sea salt. Bake about 40 minutes until scones are golden brown. Cool on baking sheets for 5 minutes then transfer to cooling racks. These scones are best served slightly warm.

THE MORNING AFTER
VANILLA SEX DANISHES

Yield: 12 Danishes

By grating the butter and performing all "turns" at the same time, I've simplified the classic process of making danishes, although this version still requires chilling and proofing. If you don't want to wake up at the crack-o'-dawn to make these, you can follow the recipe up through step 5 the night prior and finish them in the morning to ensure they are at their peak of buttery, flaky crispness.

Ingredients

Dough

- 1 cup (2 sticks) unsalted butter, cold
- 2½ cups all-purpose flour
- ½ teaspoon kosher salt
- ¼ cup granulated sugar
- 1 packet (2¼ teaspoons) instant yeast
- 1 cup whole milk
- 1 teaspoon vanilla extract

Vanilla Pastry Cream

- 1 cup whole milk
- ¼ cup granulated sugar, divided
- Pinch kosher salt
- 1 tablespoon cornstarch
- 1 tablespoon all-purpose flour
- 3 large egg yolks, beaten
- 1 tablespoon unsalted butter, cut into small pieces
- Seeds from 1 vanilla bean or 2 teaspoons vanilla extract

Egg Wash

- 1 large egg white, beaten
- 1 tablespoon water

Glaze

- ¾ cup confectioners' (powdered) sugar
- 1 tablespoon milk or water

Directions

1. Grate the cold butter into a small bowl and place in the freezer for about 15 minutes.

2. In a large mixing bowl, combine the flour and salt. Add the grated butter to the flour and toss to coat.

3. Add the sugar and yeast and gently toss to combine. Stir the milk and vanilla extract together, make a well in the center of the dry ingredients, and add the wet. Lightly mix until a shaggy dough forms. Avoid overmixing to preserve the butter pieces. Shape the dough into a block, wrap in cling film, and refrigerate for 1 hour.

4. Meanwhile, make the pastry cream: Heat whole milk, 2 tablespoons sugar, and salt in a medium saucepan over medium-high heat until hot, but not boiling. Blend cornstarch, flour, and remaining sugar in a bowl. Beat egg yolks into sugar mixture. Pour hot milk over egg mixture slowly, whisking constantly, to avoid scrambling the eggs. Pour entire mixture back into saucepan. Bring to a simmer while continuously whisking. Cook over low to medium-low heat until thickened. Remove from heat. Stir in butter and vanilla seeds or extract. Transfer pastry cream into a shallow pan, cover with cling film touching the surface, and chill for 1 hour.

5. Place the chilled dough on a well-floured surface. Roll it into a rectangle approximately 12 inches x 8 inches. Fold the bottom third up over the center and the top third to the bottom, like a letter. This is the first fold. Rotate the dough 90 degrees and roll it out again into a rectangle. Fold it into thirds. This is the second fold. Repeat the rolling and folding process two more times for a total of four folds. Wrap in cling film and refrigerate for at least an hour or overnight.

6. Assemble pastries: Place the chilled dough on a well-floured surface, and, working from the center, roll into a rectangle a little larger than 16 inches x 12 inches. This dough is sometimes difficult to roll out. Just keep rolling the dough from the center until you have the appropriately sized rectangle.

7. Using a 4-inch cookie cutter or a knife, divide dough into twelve 4-inch squares. Place the squares on 2 baking sheets lined with parchment paper or a silicone sheet. Fold the corners of each pastry square halfway toward the center, then cover the unfilled danishes with a proofing bag or cling film, ensuring the plastic does not touch the dough. Let rise in a draft-free area for about 90 minutes.

8. Preheat oven to 400°F. With your fingers, press down the centers of the dough to make a very large well, leaving the edges puffed. Spoon a heaping tablespoon of vanilla pastry cream into the well of each round.

9. Make egg wash: In a small bowl, whisk together the egg white and water. Brush the exposed edges of the pastries with the egg wash.

10. Bake pastries: Bake for about 18 minutes or until golden brown. Remove from oven and transfer to a cooling rack.

11. Make glaze: In a small bowl, whisk the confectioners' sugar and milk together and drizzle over cooled pastries. These are best eaten the day they are made.

Variation: You can make fruit danishes by substituting the vanilla pastry cream with your favorite jam. I particularly like using raspberry or homemade apple butter.

eight

NEXT:
GAVIN

Age 47

TWO TIMES THE FUN?

Swipe left. Swipe left. Swipe left.

After two months of this fishing excursion called online dating, I'm ready to fling my phone deep into the ocean, convinced there's little hope of reeling in any sort of prized catch. The fish in the sea may be plentiful, but with my hook baited to lure a coelacanth, I continue to come up empty.

My eyes and heart have never turned toward the societal standard of a good catch. Your everyday nine-to-fiver, football- and Bon Jovi-loving tilapia doesn't interest me. Disheartened and disillusioned, I'm convinced what I'm searching for has gone extinct—and if he does exist, on some remote island near Africa like our friend the coelacanth, he'll be of Brett's ilk, a dead-eyed shark hiding beneath fish's scales, callously breaking my heart in the end anyway.

After weeks of ignoring the messages piling up on OKCupid and automatically hitting the delete button on any IMs with *"Sup?"* or *"Hey"* in the subject line, I'm now questioning whether I'm deserving of a better catch than those who have nibbled my online-dating bait. Who am I to think I can attract the eye and mind of someone finer than this mélange of mediocre carp (carp, not crap)?

So, I throw my heart's ideal, along with my rationality, it seems, far into the depths of the Mariana Trench.

Convincing myself I have nothing to lose by saying yes, I'm willing to entertain anyone who looks my way, barring they don't possess Richard Ramirez's verminous smile or a teardrop tattoo beneath their eye. Swipe right. Swipe right. Swipe right. My hasty about-face has resulted in two confirmed dates this weekend, twice as many as my usual goose egg.

I agree to wine with Contestant #1 on Friday evening at a local wine bar, Bacchus, around the corner from my office. This plan requires no more than a quick touch-up of makeup before heading over. I enter the bar, see him poised at a table near the door, and feel the beckoning pull of my car parked just outside, the familiar sensation of instantaneous disillusionment washing over me. He is an old man.

Can I digress for a moment? Possibly attributed to some unresolved cognitive dissonance, I've convinced myself I'm in my early thirties. Birthdays may pass, and yet, in my head, I'm still well on the left side of forty. I'm not one of those women who misrepresents her age—I'm forty-seven. I also cannot quip, "You're only as old as you feel." I *feel* ancient—my knees are known to pop out of joint for no apparent reason, my lower back is a minefield of my generation's myriad aches and pains. People comment that I don't look my age, but I'm not deluded into thinking my wrinkles and sagging breasts don't exist. This cognitive incongruence is of another origin, something that causes my age to simply not register in my brain. I've recently read in *The Atlantic* that this abstract concept is common and has a name, "subjective age." My subjective age is thirty-two so I'm shocked when my ankles ache from wearing death-defying heels or when I do my best newborn giraffe impression as I attempt to stand after sitting on the floor. I'm loath to admit I'm no longer young and supple and lithe. When I look eye-to-eye with the woman in the mirror, noting the laugh-line furrows and purplish dark undereye blotches, I convince myself it's bad lighting…in my bathroom…in the restaurant bathroom…in Nordstrom's dressing room. The age printed on my driver's license and the age in my head just don't align.

Because of this, when I meet a man my age or older, like Contestant #1, I mistakenly believe he is old enough to be my granddad. I envision him eating dinner at 4:30 p.m. and watching Lawrence Welk while I'm out raving. In reality, I haven't raved for more than a decade.

Back to the wine bar, I'm staring across the table at grandpa. In actuality, he is fifty-seven, a mere ten years older than me. On paper, he ticks all the "good catch" boxes: successful job, enjoys good wine and traveling, kids are grown. He's polite and smart with a full head of distinguished grey hair—the characteristics I inexplicably eschew. Throughout my life, as I mentioned earlier, I've given a wide berth to the societal benchmarks of an ideal man. Strong and muscular? Nope. Wealthy and powerful? Not a chance. Masculine? Not even that. Consequently, I'm anesthetized by the man across the table. He is perfectly pleasant, but just another middle-aged, white-fleshed tilapia from Irvine. It's Friday night, after an interminable week. Rather than sitting across from this man, I long to be relaxing at home, my nose buried in this month's book club pick, a dinner of Trader Joe's Tarte D'Alsace baking in the oven, and a slice of *Mom's Strawberry Icebox Pie* to finish off the night. Instead, I'm trapped at this mini-mall pickup joint, staring at the embodiment of my rash, new dating mindset.

With Brett's label of "Pleaser" still rattling around my brain, I wonder if it's this urge to please, politeness, or guilt that induces me to accept the offer of a second glass. I acquiesce, hoping the alcohol will mask the disinterest pouring from my every comment. Why draw out this ruse of an evening? I'm not smitten and won't be smitten thirty minutes and five ounces of Pinot from now. I suppress a strong desire to exclaim, "You know, you would be perfect for my older sister." I believe I hear my friend Samantha whispering persuasions in my ear, "Aw, come on, give the guy a chance." A chance to do what, exactly? Grow on me? Sweep me off my feet? Morph into someone else? I've always considered it kinder to cut and run, and as soon as possible. After two glasses, I do just that.

After Friday night's disappointment, I'm dreading my date with Contestant #2 on Sunday. Feeling utterly defeated, I consider canceling. Why bother getting dressed and leaving my house when I'm convinced he won't be worth the effort? On my drive to yet another wine bar, this one in Long Beach, I blast Beck on my car stereo, trying to raise my energy to a sufficient level to face a second in a consecutive series of dating disappointments.

Not only don't I throw up in my mouth upon meeting Gavin, I surprisingly *like* him.

He isn't tall. I'm not sure exactly how short. Wearing killer three-inch All Saints heels (and by "killer," I mean they kill my feet as I hobble the half block to the wine bar), I tower over him. I'd guess he stands about five-feet-seven. His skin is the color of cream-laden coffee, confirming his Hispanic last name. He lounges in the booth across from me, his hands draped languidly across his knee, giving the appearance of being at ease in his skin and in command of his surroundings. A slight smirk plays across his lips as he speaks. A sensual assuredness exudes from his pores, but not in a cocky, arrogant vein.

In the throes of an acrimonious divorce, Gavin currently shares custody of a passel of high-spirited boys, ages eleven, nine, seven, and four. When he isn't meeting women for first dates, he spends his spare time in the chaste pursuits of Boy Scout master and figure skating novice. I can hear Samantha commenting on this one, "What the fuck? He doesn't sound like your type at *all*." Hold on, that wasn't just Samantha, but my own inner voice in chorus with hers. After Friday's fiasco, have I arrived at this date with an even lower bar—so low that anyone who doesn't make me physically sick will ignite a spark? Am I genuinely attracted to Gavin, or have I just given up on finding someone who suits me?

Admittedly, he's not what I had in mind. After Brett, I forswore dating another recently separated man. I've hung up my Rebound Girl cheerleading outfit. And kids? All boys? All still at home? Kids are foreign beings to me and not part of my current or future plans. Factor in the other squeaky-clean pursuits and Mr. Ice-Skating Boy Scout's wholesomeness score just shot off the chart. I've overcorrected from Brett's bad boy, tattooed, rock 'n' roll persona a tad too much, but I'm not deterred.

Ignoring the "He's not my type" argument for a moment, I truly enjoy my evening with him. The conversation (and Malbec) flow freely, and an attraction frizzles between us. I find myself salivating as I picture taking a bite from his smooth, sleek, café au lait arm muscles, mmm. Wanting to consume the man in front of me, like taking a big bite from an *Italian Cannoli*, is a powerful indication of the evening's success.

DECISION TIME

"We could go see a movie," Gavin suggests in his text.

Translation: Let's spend an innocuous night holding hands in a darkened theater with a post-movie make-out session.

"Or you could come over and watch a movie," he texts again, ten seconds later.

Translation: The movie will never get turned on. Instead, I'll turn you on, and we'll end up rolling around, sweaty and naked in my bed.

I've agreed to see him again on Wednesday. He offers up those two choices. It's been a long time since I've come over to "watch a movie"—eons, or only eighteen months, but it *feels* like eons. I really need to come over and "watch a movie," or even a series, Seasons one and two. Binge watch. I'm convinced that's why I haven't been sleeping—a pent-up lack of movie watching. Sure, I watch movies by myself, but it's not the same.

If I make the wrong decision, choosing option one over option two, I may not get an opportunity to come over and "watch a movie" again for another year and a half. Still, I hesitate. Am I ready to watch a movie with Gavin? We just met on Sunday.

After additional deliberation, including polling my coworkers in Creative Services on what I should do, I select going to see a movie, in a public theater with other people around—handholding rather than sweaty nakedness. My body is chanting, *His place, his place, his place,* but my mind is conflicted, asking, *Is it hormones, or is there an actual connection?*

WEDNESDAY

So much for my resolve. I end up going over to his place to watch a movie. We unsurprisingly don't make it to the movie part. We don't even make it into the bedroom.

He keeps exclaiming how "snug" a certain body part of mine feels. As the first woman he's been with after a wife who spit out four kids in quick succession, I imagine even a well-ridden porn star like Jenna Jameson would feel like a virgin in comparison.

THREE DAYS LATER—TOO FAST

He brings me flowers.

We never leave my house.

He asks me to be his girlfriend.

I say, "Too fast."

SOFTENED

My car blows its passenger tire on the 5 Freeway at 9:00 p.m. No, that's not another sex euphemism like "watch a movie."

I am trapped on the shoulder, inside my tiny two-seater, alone and in the dark, as speeding SUVs whizz by at a hair's breadth away. This distressed maiden is trapped in her stone tower, dragons breathing fire on the other side of the driver's door. With frazzled nerves, I jump at each roaring big rig, expecting the next one to slam into the back of my stranded vehicle, hazard lights flashing like a beacon calling, "Swerve this way. Take my life." Unable to conjure up a courageous knight to rescue me from this harrowing experience, I forge my own escape: beseeching AAA with the urgency of my predicament, negotiating a final drop-off destination with the apathetic tow-truck driver, answering questions as the highway patrol officer grills me dismissively and, finally, summoning and awaiting the cab driver in the unlit, deserted Allen Tires parking lot, the tow-truck driver long gone, unconcerned with my safety. I am deposited home sometime after 11:00 p.m.

As I crawl into bed and try to fall asleep, I recall the grubby, thick-fingered tow-truck driver, together with the highway patrol officer, with his bright flashlight and squeaking polished shoes, grilling me, accusatorially, about what I hit on the freeway causing the blowout. I sense reproach from both men for my predicament. When I respond that I don't recall driving over anything, they are incredulous, declaring with their vast, god-given, Y-chromosome wisdom that I must have hit an object to pop a tire. Okay, so why cross-examine me if you are already cocksure of the answer? I begin to doubt my own recollection. Maybe I ran over a pothole? I would have noticed hitting an object, wouldn't I? I was driving, my tire popped, I moved to the shoulder. My account of how events unfolded is a simple one.

The next morning, I awake spent and exhausted, dreading the gauntlet before me: finding transport to the tire store in Tustin, ordering a replacement that always needs to be summoned from another store, fidgeting in an uncomfortable plastic chair for hours, drinking sour coffee from a Styrofoam cup, surrounded by patronizing gearheads as I wait for them to perform tire surgery, and, eventually, sheepishly arriving at the office sometime in the late afternoon.

When Gavin hears my recount of the previous night's odyssey and my apprehension for the battle I still face, he extends his dutiful service to me. Contrary to my typical staunch self-reliance, I gratefully yield. He drives thirty miles from his office to my house, collects me, and escorts me to the tire store. He waits by my side and, when we discover it will be four or five hours before the car is ready—no surprise; no replacement in stock—he takes me to work on his trusty steed, twenty minutes in the opposite direction from his office. I am grateful and comforted by my rescuer's ministrations, a kindness almost unfamiliar to me.

Flashback to a year prior, Brett and I are lunching at a small Thai place in a Laguna Hills strip mall. After eating, to-go cups of Thai iced tea in hand, we depart the restaurant only to discover my car's deflated tire. The vehicle's trunk is too small to possess a spare, but it does contain the cold consolation of an air pump and patch kit. Brett fills the tire with air and then asks that I drop him back at his work. As I deposit him at his employer's doorstep as requested, my brief glance in the side mirror confirms air rapidly escaping from the puncture, the tire slowly morphing from donut to pancake before my eyes. Brett gives me a quick peck, wishes me luck, and saunters back into his office.

My heart sinks. I am drawn to Brett partially for his concern and kindheartedness, toward his kids, toward his menagerie of animals, toward his estranged wife. Where is his caring nature in concern of me? I am disheartened, but don't recognize his indifference for the red flag it proves to be. He leaves me to fend for myself.

Map apps aren't robust during these years. I can't conjure up Siri, like a genie, to find the nearest tire store. Idling in his office parking lot, I recall driving by a Just Tires on my way to the restaurant, so I drive my hobbled vehicle there first. No luck. They are out of the tire I need. The two guys behind the counter direct me to another option around the corner. That store doesn't have what I need either. Call me Goldilocks, trying tire store after tire store—this tire is too big, this tire is too small. By this time, I am wondering why purchasing a tire to fit my car is such a difficult endeavor.

The second store suggests I try Costco a few miles down the road: big selection, reasonably priced. Costco has the tire in stock—this tire is just right—but the solution to my predicament won't be instantaneous. The wait will be three hours and, in addition to the cost of tire replacement, I have to purchase a Costco membership. Left with no other viable option, I wait. How can I amuse myself for three hours at Costco? I've heard the chatter about their celebrated food court, although I'm convinced the raves are based solely on price and not quality. I'd ordinarily partake in one of their infamous giant slices of greasy pepperoni pizza at the low, low price of $1.99, but I am still digesting pad see ew. I can slowly and mindfully promenade up and down the aisles of big box nirvana for one hundred eighty minutes, but, as a single woman living in a modest-sized house, I don't have use or room for a thirty-six-pack of toilet paper. It won't fit in my trunk anyway. So, I sit in a plastic chair and wait while the hours tick by. I don't roll home on my bouncy new tire until after 6:00 p.m. and Brett never checks in to see how I am getting along. I'm deserted by Brett. And, only a few months later, he did, in fact, desert me.

In the handful of weeks since Gavin and I started dating, I've been questioning our longevity. He's outside my warped idea of a Knight in Shining Armor, and we seem to be pulled from two separate stories, from disparate worlds. He tells me about singing Paul Simon's lullaby, "St. Judy's Comet," to each of his sons, and I cannot relate to Paul Simon, to singing lullabies, to kids. I'm unmoved. I grew up listening to David Bowie. I can relate to singing "Cracked Actor" at age four, my older sister warning me not to sing lyrics about prostitution, blow-jobs, and heroin in public.

Today, however, this fair maiden's heart softens toward Sir Gavin and his acts of tire repair gallantry, if only a little and for this moment.

TWO MONTHS LATER

You would think, after a handful of decades as a serial dater, I would have mastered the art of the breakup. I envision a blend of firm resolve and tender compassion, recounting the essentials for a successful relationship, and enumerating our deficiencies in a calm and measured voice. I will actively listen to his entreaties, shouldering complete blame for this untimely collapse of our romance. With an affectionate hug, we part ways, unscathed—Gwyneth's "conscious uncoupling."

Yeah, right. I opt for the spineless abandonment approach instead, breaking up via text message. I'm appalled at my callousness. In retrospect, Gavin, at a minimum, merits a phone call. A two-and-a-half-month relationship doesn't require a face-to-face but warrants more effort than an indifferent three-sentence text. The words I type to Gavin, combined with the lingering remorse at my actions, reek of Brett's breakup with me. Am I as coldhearted and gutless?

Gavin's rescue from my car trouble hell and his continued acts of kindness couldn't keep my heart malleable for long. On paper, he has a lot to offer, but not when viewed through my clouded lens of male desirability. He is attractive and fit, kindhearted and attentive, virile and gainfully employed, yet I never manage to tumble head over heels in his direction. In fact, after the tire rescue, I scarcely venture his way emotionally at all. I should long to spend my final night in bed with him before my business trips. He should fill my brain when the wheels touch down upon my return. Instead, after being apart for two-and-a-half weeks during my last trip, I reschedule twice and nearly cancel on him a third time this Saturday. I should be imploring him to sleep over so I can wrap my body in his warmth, but in truth, I'm bathed in relief when he acknowledges he has to leave.

I recall the intensity of my adoration for Brett, misplaced though it proved itself to be. Yet, I am loath to conjure more than a halfhearted fondness for Gavin, who deserves more than my feeble attempt. It is unfair to persist in this sham—to him by feigning my affection while his devotion grows, and to me by denying myself choices, erroneously reminding my heart that mediocrity trumps solitude, when, in fact, solitude is exactly what I need.

GAVIN

the recipes

CHOCOLATE CHIP ALMOND CANNOLI

Yield: 12 cannoli

I'm not a big fan of traditional ricotta cannoli. I usually find the filling dry and slightly grainy and the chocolate chips to be too large and hard compared to the rest of the filling. This recipe replaces some of the ricotta with creamy mascarpone cheese and swaps finely chopped chocolate for the chocolate chips.

Ingredients

- 12 cannoli shells (available online or at Italian markets)
- 2¼ cups high-quality milk chocolate, finely chopped and divided
- ½ cup finely chopped candied almonds
- 1¼ cups whole-milk ricotta, drained in a sieve overnight
- 8-ounce container (1 cup) mascarpone cheese
- ⅓ cup superfine sugar
- ¼ teaspoon vanilla extract
- ⅛ teaspoon cinnamon
- ⅛ teaspoon table salt, not kosher
- Confectioners' (powdered) sugar

Directions

1. Prepare shells: Place 1 cup of the milk chocolate in a microwave-safe bowl and heat at 30-second intervals, stirring until melted (about 90 seconds total). Dip both ends of cannoli shells in chocolate then roll in the candied almonds until the ends are well covered with nuts. Place on a cooling rack in the refrigerator to set.

2. Make filling: Stir together ricotta, mascarpone, and sugar. Add the remaining chopped milk chocolate, vanilla extract, cinnamon, and salt and combine. Let rest for 30 minutes in the refrigerator to allow the sugar time to melt.

3. Fill the cannoli: Place filling in a piping bag fitted with a star nozzle. Pipe the filling into both ends of the cannoli, starting from the center and working out to ensure cannoli are filled completely. Refrigerate until ready to serve. Dust with confectioners' sugar just before serving.

Variation: Hazelnut Mocha Cannoli

Ingredients
- 12 cannoli shells
- 2¼ cups high-quality bittersweet chocolate, finely chopped and divided
- ½ cup finely chopped hazelnuts, toasted
- 1¼ cups whole-milk ricotta, drained in a mesh sieve overnight
- 8-ounce container (1 cup) mascarpone cheese
- 1 cup Nutella
- 4 teaspoons (1 tablespoon plus 1 teaspoon) instant espresso
- ⅛ teaspoon table salt, not kosher
- Confectioners' (powdered) sugar

Directions
1. Prepare shells: Place 1 cup of the bittersweet chocolate in a microwave-safe bowl and heat at 30-second intervals, stirring until melted (about 90 seconds total). Dip both ends of cannoli shells in chocolate then roll in the toasted hazelnuts until the ends are well covered with nuts. Place on a cooling rack in the refrigerator to set.
2. Make filling: Stir together ricotta, mascarpone, and Nutella. Add the remaining chopped bittersweet chocolate, instant espresso, and salt and combine. Let rest for 30 minutes in the refrigerator to allow the sugar time to melt.
3. Fill the cannoli: Place filling in a piping bag fitted with a star nozzle. Pipe the filling into both ends of the cannoli, starting from the center and working out to ensure cannoli are filled completely. Refrigerate until ready to serve. Dust with confectioners' sugar just before serving.

MOM'S STRAWBERRY ICEBOX PIE

Yield: 8-10 servings

As a kid, I always requested this pie for my birthday. Mom would spell out "Happy Birthday" in slivered strawberries across the top. Lucky for me, my birthday cake gets another candle at the beginning of strawberry season, ensuring peak strawberry flavor.

Ingredients
- 1½ cups graham cracker crumbs (about 11 graham crackers)
- 7 tablespoons unsalted butter, melted
- 4 cups marshmallows
- ¼ cup whole or 2% milk
- 2 cups heavy whipping cream
- 4 cups (about 1½ lbs.) cleaned, hulled, and thickly sliced strawberries, plus more for decorating (optional)

Directions
1. In a medium bowl, combine graham cracker crumbs and melted butter. Press crust along the bottom and sides of a 9-inch pie plate. Place in the freezer to chill.
2. In a large microwave-safe bowl, melt marshmallows and milk on high in a microwave for about 2 minutes, stirring every 30 seconds, until marshmallows are completely melted. Set aside to cool slightly.
3. In a large bowl, whip heavy cream until stiff peaks form.
4. Stir sliced strawberries into marshmallow mixture. Fold in whipped cream in four additions. Remove crust from freezer and spoon filling into crust until pie is generously filled. Decorate with additional sliced strawberries (optional). Chill in refrigerator for at least 4 hours before serving.

nine

PALATE CLEANSER

ooo

WITHERING

An Assortment of Last Dates,
Final Goodbyes,
and Wilted Romances

SCAPEGOAT

After four years without a word, I listen with cautious curiosity to Chad's voice on the phone, unexpectedly inviting me to meet him this evening. I am curious. What prompted this out-of-the-blue entreaty? At worst, I envision a slightly awkward, yet friendly, reunion over drinks—our past, at this point, water well under the proverbial bridge. I agree to meet.

I don't recognize his invitation as a ruse to lure me into a trap of condemnation. Three dirty martinis into the conversation, Chad accuses me of destroying his life.

Chad works as a second-rate Hollywood director of photography—known as a "DP" in the industry. He has a good eye behind the lens and has bootstrapped his way into the business. He has just returned to the States after working on a film for two weeks in the Czech Republic. While there, thirty-six-year-old Chad fell hard for a nineteen-year-old Slavic beauty who didn't speak a stitch of English. He doesn't know a word of Czech, yet, in Chad's mind, after fourteen days, through hand gestures and a well-worn Czech phrase book, they had bonded on a level beyond words.

His Czech belle broke it off this morning, over the phone, after his sheepishly mumbled confession that he was, in fact, a married man.

And it was entirely *my* fault.

I first met Chad at a '40s club in downtown LA, the Derby. We started up a conversation, and I found him well-spoken and clever, though not particularly magnetic. I offered transparency. We could date, but he wasn't the only man on my dance card. I wasn't promiscuous, but there was another man in another city and, rather than cheating, I offered Chad honesty. Our tepid chemistry didn't warrant exclusivity. I hoped my feelings of fondness for Chad would take root, growing into something stronger, yet they never did. I convinced myself he felt as I did.

No, that's a lie.

I *knew* he wanted more. Much more. He sought nothing less than to devour me, like a ravenous mockingbird eyeing a juicy, fat grubworm, another reason I kept a safe distance. He never proposed, "Let's be exclusive," and I chose not to recognize the paranoia and jealousy overshadowing his behaviors. As our romance progressed chronologically, yet never deepened emotionally, he concocted lurid fantasies in his head that I slept around—with his friend from the club, with a married member of the Derby's house band, and with every man I chatted up, apparently. We dated about a year, his imaginings of my infidelity working on his sanity, and, when it finally came to a head, it didn't end well.

It was entirely *my* fault.

Chad was seeing someone else, too, an British expat named Jane. He blamed my alleged cruelty toward him for awakening in him a nascent heartlessness toward her. She suffered as the innocent victim of *my* callous conduct. He may have been the conduit, but the cause sat squarely with me. A few months after we ended things, Jane had a run-in with US Immigration resulting in a scheduled deportation back to jolly ol' England. In an act of contrition for his unkindness, Chad agreed to marry her, solving her imminent immigration woes. For Chad, this union wasn't an act of love, but hair-shirt penitence. They were married at the courthouse on a grey, nondescript day and, after satisfying the two-year immigration requirements for a green card, he failed to ask Jane for a divorce, even though their union had ended long before she became a citizen.

So, four years later, I'm sitting across from Chad, drunk on martinis, and astonished by his accusations of my unalloyed cruelty which, in turn, triggered his indifference toward Jane, that morphed into guilt, resulting in a loveless marriage, that didn't proceed to divorce, prompting his teenage Czech to leave him.

Yep, it's entirely *my* fault.

CASUALTIES OF WAR

I cross enemy lines this weekend, into Major Misery's city. I camouflage myself and my convertible, infiltrating through a back road. I keep low to the ground and out of sight, glancing over my shoulders, on my mission to the downtown clothing boutique, determined to pick up supplies. In less than thirty minutes, I return to my homeland, escaping back over the border undetected, but not nearly unscathed. The maudlin minefields were everywhere, and they blew me to pieces as I rounded every corner and stopped at each streetlight, the memories of our time in this city still too fresh in my mind: breakfast there (boom!), dinner here (boom!) and the park where we first kissed across the street (boom. boom. boom!).

Six months have elapsed since the cease-fire, and my desire, truly, is to become a veteran of this damn war. I don't want to lament the breakup longer than we were together. I want to get on with my life, ending this shellshock. I convinced myself I was ready, that I could walk the streets we walked along together, feeling no residual pain. I was wrong, again.

The wounds may be scarring over, but I'm afraid there's shrapnel embedded beneath my skin forever so that, when I hear his name or visit our old haunts, a little twinge of pain will eternally make me wince. Soon, I will stop mentioning the ache, putting on my courageous face for friends and family, but the slight spasm of discomfort will always be there, silently reminding me of the wounds I've suffered—and diminishing me just a little more.

FROM THE MOUTHS OF BABES

"You seemed so happy."

"I *was* happy."

"So, why aren't you together anymore?"

"Well..."

I'm having this conversation with my ten-year-old niece. She's asking me about my ex. How do you explain to a child that just because one person is blissfully happy doesn't mean the other is feeling the same—or even if both people are happy, it still doesn't mean there's a happy ending to the story? How do you break it to them that life's not a fairy tale?

THREE-CARD MONTE

I stumble upon Mr. Ambivalence's dating profile again, that face I know so well. Not in a "type in his screen name and up pops his photo" manner, but in a legitimate "I'm scrolling through my options and, wham, there's Mr. A's mug" kind of way. Every time his image jumps up on the page, it's as if he has leapt out from a hiding spot behind the kitchen door. Startled, my heart constricts and trampolines into my throat. I cannot swallow, and a cold, clammy chill slaloms down my arms.

I've read that this visceral reaction to seeing an ex's photo is the fight-or-flight response kicking in, the same response I would experience if I turned the corner and came face to face with an angry bear. This instinctive reaction is my autonomic nervous system shouting, *Danger, bad situation ahead!* Even though it is merely a harmless photo on a computer screen, my gut is performing its job, reminding me, *Girl, you do not want to go there again.*

I'm unwilling to accept this fight-or-flight explanation in its entirety. Instead, couldn't this fireworks show of reactions be attributed to the validly crushing sensation of being jilted by a partner, passed over for anonymous women on a dating site? I'm flabbergasted Mr. Ambivalence is online again, that he prefers swiping left and right and insufferable first dates to me—to us—and the comfortable, warm, caring bond we were (I was) building together (alone).

It's easy enough to hide his profile from appearing in my searches, but I inexplicably hesitate taking that final action. Why this unnecessary self-flagellation, especially since my astute gut has convinced me he's hidden mine weeks ago, pushing himself as far away as possible? I scroll through the other men's profiles, thinking meh and then reread his and remind myself, *Yes, perfect, but not for you, missy.*

Am I so utterly defective that I don't deserve a healthy romantic partnership, someone I can show affection and support while receiving the same in return? Or, more likely, I'm not broken at all, but merely repeating a pattern of choosing wrongly, like a game of Three-Card Monte, Romance Edition.

Where is my partner to hold my hand at the movies or chat with me about our day as we make dinner, someone who enjoys my company? Where is the man I can curl into at night, sleeping soundly in his arms? Where is my King of Hearts?

The three slightly bent, well-worn playing cards are shuffled and placed upon the makeshift table, really just a cardboard box with a scrap of cloth draped over it. I hand the dealer another five-dollar bill. I point at the center card. "This one here." Wrong. I'm fooled yet again.

HANGOVER

I wake too early. My head hurts, my stomach churns, and my limbs are filled with lead. The poison lies just beneath my skin. I must rid myself of this sickness quickly, not allowing its fetid tang to fester in my mouth again. I tie sneakers on feet, position earbuds in ears, and step outside.

The morning sun sits low and bright, the air warm, the breeze light. I begin my exorcism. The sourness seeps from my pores and releases in noxious vapors exhaled from my lungs. This isn't alcohol polluting me; it's anger, bitterness, and my chagrin at being played, yet again.

I refuse to allow these toxins a refuge in my body once more. I will not give the poisoner permission to afflict me. There's a yogic belief that says unreleased emotions dwell in our hips. I swing mine rhythmically, breaking loose the rank bile lurking there. Malignant tumors trapped in my sacrum dislodge and travel up my spine, out the top of my skull, and float innocuously into the atmosphere. Within an hour, I am sweaty, calm, clear, and smiling. I have released his venom into the sunlight—and I am peaceful.

JASMINE

The buds of pink jasmine have emerged, proclaiming spring's arrival. This explosion of blushing trumpets amassed along twining jade filigree never fails to elicit my smile. *Spring has truly sprung,* they croon. I spy clusters of pastel blooms from my kitchen window, recalling their sweet perfume when I bury my nose within the ephemeral blossoms.

Barefoot, I step from the door and walk gingerly along the overgrown path, gathering clusters as a gift to cheer up the winter-weary house. Back inside those four walls, blooms in hand, the heady, cloying scent is too much—funereal.

A stifled sob escapes from somewhere low and dark inside me. My Love's goodbye has rendered me fragile, like these pale petals that now slip from my fingers. The sunlight through the kitchen window is too dazzling. The house is melancholy. We are all in mourning here.

MIDNIGHT IN THE KITCHEN

If only this barely beating, battered, bloodied nub of an organ could generously proclaim, "I hope you're happy now. I wish you luck with finding your consummate partner, your ideal mate. May you be well, and let's be friends."

But no, this indignant heart seethes with bubbling fury and schemes for your untimely demise.

I slowly stir a simmering cauldron of my salty tears, seasoned with a stolen yellowish pearl of your earwax, a tangle of your navel lint, a pinch of your nail clippings, and sprinkled with a soupçon of hairs, plucked from a werewolf's scrotum. As I stir this noxious brew, counterclockwise, I quietly murmur the incantation in a low, singsong cadence, my face red and sweaty from the glowing fire:

May your miserable life be wretched, my dear,
Without me beside you, to guide you and cheer.
An existence, sad, shrunken, and diminished now,
No buoy to lift you, no joy to allow.
You'll soon enough realize the error of your ways,
Once you're told of my victories, triumphs, and praise.
I hope your ears sting at the upbraiding cry,
'Dude, she was a catch; Why tell her goodbye?'
Search near and look far for an upgrade from me,
May the rest of your short life be soaked in MISERY.

A bead of sweat trickles between my bare breasts. I slurp a sample of my culinary prowess from the wooden spoon, and my mouth fills with piquant bile, balanced by the bitterness of my wrath. I catch a lingering hint of unquenchable ire, the slightest whiff of loathing. I squeeze in a few drops of snarling hyena spit for good measure. Just a few more minutes simmering and my brew will be done.

I eagerly await serving you, dearest, this dish of my glorious retribution, my vengeful vichyssoise, best served cold, they say. I glance over my shoulder at the tray of baked *Gingerbread Effigies*, a bit brown, some would even say burnt, waiting for me to add fitting, final decorations—a noose to the neck on one, a glass of fluorescent antifreeze to the lips on another, possibly a Lorena Bobbitt to the crotch of a third. A sly grin spreads across my face. Never fuck with a woman in an apron, my dear.

IF YOU RUN INTO YOUR EX, DON'T RUN

Instead...

LOOK FABULOUS. The odds are in your favor because this breakup has probably left you unable to eat and since he's moved on, you've suddenly found plenty of time for long solo walks, gym workouts, and yoga practice. You're possibly at your fittest. You've also, I hope, been drowning your breakup sorrows with retail therapy, which means a closet full of new clothes and sexy shoes, not to mention a sassy new haircut. In the initial days after the breakup, you are allowed seventy-two hours of all-day PJs, breakfasts of Pringles and Oreos, and nonstop Netflix. After that, it's walks, new jeans, and platinum blonde. When you are ready to step back into the world, strut back in looking and feeling amazing.

LOOK PLEASANTLY SURPRISED, not distressfully alarmed, or woefully longing when he catches your eye. Ideally, you'll make eye contact from across the room, and he's too cowardly to walk over in person. One time, I was at a restaurant when my recent ex caught my eye as he walked in the door. He saw me, turned around to hightail it out of the restaurant, and, from the sidewalk, called whoever he was meeting so they could eat somewhere else. That's the response you want: This is *your* town.

If your ex is ballsy enough to stay, give him a **FULL SMILE** (he always adored your smile, right?) and a **HALF HAND WAVE,** that wave celebrities give on the red carpet that says, "I don't know you, but thanks for being a fan of fabulous me."

If he erroneously reads that as an invitation to come over to chat, **TREAT HIM LIKE AN OLD BOSS YOU HATE** but must treat cordially because you need the reference. Your body language should say, *Our breakup didn't break me, and now I'm impervious to your effect.* If he goes in for the awkward hug, offer a halfhearted side-hug with a few back pats—you know, hug like your friend who "doesn't hug." Or, better yet, hug with your one hand pushing ever so gently on his chest so you avoid full contact. No matter how uncomfortable touching him again makes you, this will work in your favor because he can feel how firm and lithe you've become, plus he'll get a dose of your pheromones. Be sure you're the first to pull away.

When he asks how you're doing, tell him **"REALLY GOOD"** in the way Summer Finn tells Tom in *500 Days of Summer* that her weekend was "really good." It'll leave him guessing. A muted "okay" or "good" sounds like you're barely hanging on, at home every night waiting for him to come back. "Amazing," "great," or "fantastic" is too much, like you're faking it. "Really good" says, "I'm doing just fine without you," whether you are or not. Don't elaborate on what "really good" encompasses. As his partner, you shared every tiny tidbit of your life with him. Now is not the time to catch him up on what you've been doing since the breakup or details about your cousin's wedding last week. Sharing too much will lead him to suspect you haven't replaced him and you've been dying for a chance to pour out your life's minutiae for the last few months into his ear. Keep it light and short while keeping a tight rein on your real desire to either throw a drink in his face or jump his bones right there in public. Use your indoor voice; make him lean in.

Courtesy, if you want to be courteous, requires you return the question. Try **"HOW ARE THINGS?"** "How are you?" reads too much like "Are you able to cope without my love?" "How are things" will steer him down the path of talking about non-personal subjects: how his kids are doing, his current workload, or news about his pickup basketball team. You can listen to all of that with detachment, responding with an unenthusiastic **"THAT SOUNDS GREAT,"** which, to his ears, should translate into "I don't really care."

Now it's time to make your escape. Keep it simple, and repress the desire to keep chatting. If he broke up with you, this is your opportunity to **BE THE ONE WHO LEAVES** this time. Don't blow it. This is a better boost to your confidence than weeks of therapy. Something like "Well, it was good to see you but I'm going to a) refresh my drink, b) join my friends, or c) find the bathroom" should do the trick.

And, lastly, **DO NOT LOOK BACK.**

WITHERING

the recipes

CZECH KOLACHE FOR CHAD

Yield: 24 kolache

Samantha's Grandma Jo inspired this kolache recipe. Kolache (also spelled koláče or kolach) are a type of pastry that originated in Central Europe, particularly in Czech and Slovak regions. Traditionally filled with a variety of sweet fillings, such as fruit (apricot, raspberry, cherry), poppy seeds, or sweetened cheese, kolache are usually enjoyed at breakfast or for a sweet snack.

Ingredients

Dough

- 1 package (2¼ teaspoons) instant yeast
- 1¼ cups whole milk, room temperature
- ½ cup granulated sugar
- 2 large egg yolks
- 1 teaspoon lemon zest
- ⅛ teaspoon ground mace or ½ teaspoon vanilla extract (add preference as directed below)
- 3½ to 4 cups bread flour
- 1½ teaspoons kosher salt
- ½ cup (1 stick) unsalted butter, softened

Raspberry Jam (or ¾ cup purchased tart raspberry jam)

- 1½ cups frozen raspberries
- ¾ cup granulated sugar

Cheese Filling

- 8-ounce package cream cheese, softened
- ⅓ cup granulated sugar
- 1 large egg yolk
- 1 tablespoon bread flour or all-purpose flour

Posipka Topping

- 3 tablespoons granulated sugar
- 2 tablespoons bread flour or all-purpose flour
- 1 tablespoon unsalted butter, melted

Directions

1. Make dough: In the bowl of an electric mixer, using the paddle attachment, mix together yeast, milk, sugar, egg yolks, lemon zest, and vanilla extract (if using). Switch to a dough hook, add 3 ½ cups bread flour, ground mace (if using), and salt. Mix on medium speed. Add additional flour (up to ½ cup) until dough pulls away from the sides of the bowl. Add butter, a little bit at a time, and mix on medium speed. Continue mixing until dough is soft and elastic, about 10 minutes. Transfer to an oiled bowl, cover with cling film or a proofing bag and let proof in a warm, draft-free location until doubled in size, about 90 minutes. Make the fillings while dough proofs.

2. Make jam: Combine the frozen raspberries and sugar in a small deep-sided saucepan and bring to boil over medium heat. When the sugar is melted, increase the heat and boil for another 4 minutes. Remove from the heat. Leave to cool and set.

3. Make cheese filling: Stir together all ingredients until smooth. Refrigerate until ready to use.

4. Make posipka topping: Stir together all ingredients until topping resembles rough sand. Set aside.

5. Once the dough is proofed, roll into 24 balls (about 45 grams each), flatten to about 2½-inch disks and place on two silicone or parchment-lined baking sheets about 1½ inches apart. Cover with cling film or a proofing bag not touching the dough and let proof again for an hour. Preheat oven to 400°F. Make a very large well in each kolache with your fingers. Fill with about 1 tablespoon of cheese filling. Dollop cheese with about 1 teaspoon raspberry jam. Sprinkle kolaches with posipka.

6. Bake for about 16 minutes or until golden brown. Transfer to cooling rack to cool completely.

Variation: Substitute cheese filling with lemon curd.

GINGERBREAD EFFIGIES

Yield: 18-26 cookies, depending on size

This dough can become soft during the rolling and cutting process. If the dough becomes unworkable, pop it in the refrigerator for 10-15 minutes and the dough will become firm enough to work with again.

Ingredients

- 2¾ cups all-purpose flour
- ½ teaspoon baking soda
- ½ teaspoon kosher salt
- 1 tablespoon ground ginger
- 1½ teaspoons cinnamon
- ½ teaspoon nutmeg
- ¼ teaspoon ground cloves
- ¼ teaspoon freshly ground black pepper (optional)
- ¾ cup (1½ sticks) unsalted butter, softened
- ½ cup light brown sugar, lightly packed
- 1 large egg
- ½ cup molasses
- Zest from ½ orange
- Icing and candies for decoration

Directions

1. In a medium bowl, sift together flour, baking soda, salt, ginger, cinnamon, nutmeg, cloves, and black pepper (if using). Set aside.
2. In the bowl of an electric mixer, using the paddle attachment, cream the softened butter and brown sugar on medium-high until light and fluffy, about 4 minutes. Add the egg, molasses, and orange zest and beat on medium until well-combined.
3. Add the dry ingredients to the wet ingredients in three additions, mixing on low after each addition, until just combined. Do not overmix.
4. Divide the dough into two rectangles, wrap each in cling film, and chill in the refrigerator for at least 90 minutes, but overnight is preferable.
5. Preheat oven to 375°F and line two baking sheets with parchment paper (do not use silicone sheets). Working with one rectangle of dough at a time, roll out the chilled dough on a well-floured surface to about ¼-inch to ⅙-inch thickness. Using a cookie cutter, cut out gingerbread man shapes. Place the cookies on the baking sheets and chill for 10 minutes.
6. Bake for 9-14 minutes, depending on cookie size, until the edges are set. Remove from oven, cool on the baking sheets for 5 minutes and transfer to a cooling rack to cool.
7. Once the cookies are completely cool, decorate your effigies to your heart's content with icing and candy.

ten

DUPED:
DEXTER
Age 52–53

AMBIGUITY

"Read this." I turn my laptop toward my coworker. "Is he flirting with me? He's flirting with me, right?"

She leans in, her eyes scanning the screen, and raises an eyebrow. "Yes, Julie. That sounds like flirting to me. But what do I know? I've been married way too long."

I met Dexter a few weeks prior at a movie night with some casual acquaintances, my attempt at widening my social circle. He was welcoming, and we chatted a bit, as much as you can in a movie theater.

A few weeks later, Dexter's clever, well-crafted DMs begin arriving, hilarious, and suggestive, with a side of ambiguous flirtation.

I am out of the country, working, for the next fourteen days, leaving me no chance to use my decoder ring on Dexter in person, so I'm relying on my coworker to help me decipher his subtext. *Is* he flirting? Her analytical subjectivity guides me through his cleverly worded labyrinth of plausible deniability.

Two weeks later, I am back in sunny Southern California, nerves bubbling as I head to a dinner with this new group. Dexter will be there. He is hosting. actually, and I am determined to pull back the afghan of ambiguity he's managed to carefully wrap around himself. I enter the Mexican restaurant and immediately see him sitting in the middle of a long table—tall and lean, just as I remembered from our first meeting, with a head of silver hair. His face is a study in asymmetry, as if the tectonic plates of his cheekbones converged as a child, causing significant subduction. Todd calls him "Picasso Face," but I still think he's cute, maybe not traditionally attractive, but with an alchemical magnetic pull—my damn pheromones hard at work after a long, extended sleep.

Picasso Face grins and waves. I blanch and paste a fake smile on my face, finding him wrapped, not in an afghan as I have imagined, but in a young, vapid cupcake who looks surprisingly like Brigitte Bardot. She is busy snapping selfies of the two of them with her glittery bubblegum-pink mobile phone.

My question, it seems, has been answered. No, he was not flirting with me.

No man flirts with another woman when he's got Brigitte Bardot in his bed. Besides, if she's his kind of cream puff, then my brand of Louise Brooks–style, clever but cute, independent flair wouldn't even register for him. Plus, I am twenty years Brigitte's senior.

I retreat to the far end of the table, a haven where I won't lose my appetite with a front-row view of their canoodling. But my seating choice provides no relief. I've plunked down into an in-progress discussion on the very topic I'm attempting to avoid.

"At least he's past his woman-hating phase," my male seatmate remarks, echoing an earlier comment about Brigitte being young enough to be Dexter's daughter.

I brush those comments off as jealousy, an excuse not to dig deeper. There's no need—he's taken.

WHERE IN THE WORLD IS BRIGITTE BARDOT?

Brigitte hasn't been on the scene for weeks, and Dexter and I have returned to our DM banter. Perhaps it's the oxytocin surging up my spine in his presence or, more likely, my impatience after years without a meaningful physical coupling. Whatever the reason, I am getting fed up waiting for him to ask me out. I try luring him with flirty texts in response to his, before I learn I am a neophyte practicing my art on the master. I bake desserts with flavors I know he likes, like a *Chocolate Peanut Salted Caramel Tart* topped with clouds of whipped cream. I surreptitiously respond when he entangles his legs with mine on a crowded train ride home from the Del Mar horseraces, the train car too packed for our gang of friends to notice. Yet still, Dexter remains undecided, unmotivated, disinterested, one text to my three. I'm nothing more than a handy solution to his midweek monotony, like a half-eaten bag of stale popcorn for dinner during a Tuesday night Netflix binge.

After another night out with him and the gang, I receive the long-awaited text, *"Do you want to hang out some night this week?"*

The night is casual—ice cream at a dessert place barely a hundred feet from his back door and a leisurely stroll around the grounds of the local college campus. The international dating judges give him ten points for convenience (his, not mine), 5.4 on originality, and a somewhat generous 1.2 for his planning efforts. Outside my car, as he dismounts, he kisses me goodnight. *At last,* I breathe a quiet sigh of triumph. The kiss earns a solid 8.85 from me.

THE KEY

"What's the most important thing you look for in a partner?" he asks, his fingertips gently drawing a trail of goosebumps down the pale inside of my acquiescent arm.

We are sprawled on Dexter's couch, candles flickering around us, our legs entwined. *Double Indemnity* plays on the television, although neither of us is watching.

"Honesty," I proclaim unhesitatingly.

I watch his pupils dilate, like a cat homing in on a toy. Dexter gives me a curious look, as if with that single word, *honesty*, I've handed him the key to my heart's door.

SLOW BURN

With his halfhearted interest at last turning in my direction, my unpracticed seduction continues, conveniently becoming available for his every request, sitting cow-eyed and giggling at his stories, making out while watching old black-and-white films in his apartment, stealing furtive minutes after movies once our unsuspecting friends have driven home. For the next three months, this Eton mess of stolen moments becomes our habit. I'm not so naive as to label these snippets of time "dating." We hang out, occasionally make out, yet never take our covert cuddling any further. We are getting to know each other, with a tacit agreement to keep our canoodling under wraps, keep it away from the gang's prying eyes and opinions. At least, I believe that's why we continue to pretend we are just friends when in others' presence, until the afternoon he gives me a big smooch…in front of his friend.

I try to play it off as no big deal, but his gesture catches me off guard. This has to mean he wants to take things further.

Finally, I silently sigh.

THE ESCAPE

Wrong again.

Less than a week after his sole attempt at PDA, I receive Dexter's email. He is putting a kibosh on our pseudo-romance. A wry smile plays across my lips as I read his explanation: so little time, so many complications vying for his attention—and no room to add me to the list.

"Three months. For three months I've wasted my time," I grumble. While I am aware of one or two of his complications, there must be even deeper, darker secrets he's kept hidden, lurking beyond the depths of our concealed relationship. What else could warrant his full and complete retreat?

I sigh and roll my eyes. Yes, I am disappointed, but my ego takes the real pummeling, staggering back to the corner of the ring to regain its composure.

Dexter says he still hopes he'll see me at group outings, but I imagine my discomfort in his orbit, my bruised ego and unfulfilled desires overcompensating in ridiculous ways. I take a step back from Dexter, from the group, to lick my wounds and write positive affirmations on my bathroom mirror—"So fabulous at singlehood, I deserve my own theme song."

For two weeks I remain MIA, nothing but the sound of crickets when my name is mentioned. Once I deem it safe to return to group adventures, Dexter isn't permitted to hug me in greeting. When he tries to wrap his arm around me for a selfie, I instinctively recoil, my hand pushing him resolutely away. I watch his shocked expression like a dog encountering an invisible fence for the first time. No Dexters allowed past this point. I keep my distance, sneaking away early to avoid awkward goodbyes—the nights we stayed late chatting and kissing still on my mind. This isn't some attempt to torture him into reconsidering, simply my master plan for moving on.

SECRETS

What's a work wife? I wonder.

A month ago, before his break-up email and before my retreat, Dexter casually mentioned he wrote a book. Starry-eyed and impressed he produced a finished manuscript, I made a mental note: perform subsequent literary sleuthing to uncover the details.

I search online today for his work—to see if it's published or at least mentioned. I may be keeping my physical distance, but my retreat doesn't mean I can't Google his name plus "author." Instead of finding *A Heartbreaking Work of Staggering Genius*, I stumble upon the grim depths of the "Manosphere," pages of Dexter's internet comments denigrating women and misogynistic videos he has saved and shared. Words like "Alpha Male," "MGTOW," and "Red Pill" hit me like a sucker punch to the gut.

Heartbreaking, in a very different sense.

His unmistakable avatar stares back at me, alongside his first, middle, and last name, confirming these words are his. I Google MGTOW and am shocked by the Wikipedia page:

"Men Going Their Own Way (MGTOW) is an anti-feminist, misogynistic, mostly online community advocating for men to separate themselves from women and society, which they believe has been corrupted by feminism…the Southern Poverty Law Center categorizes MGTOW as a part of the male supremacist ideology."

The words from our first group dinner, "At least he's past his woman-hating phase," echo in my now-confused mind.

As I scroll through the comments, I can feel my hands become clammy, each new revelation making my stomach churn. I come upon an online post written by Dexter two years ago, in 2017, mentioning his work wife. My understanding is that work spouses are close platonic working relationships, but Dexter is bragging about the amount of sex she is giving him, so often it's distracting him from other interests.

Who is *this man?*

The more I read, the more nauseated I become. I hit the close button on my computer and shakily stand up, pushing my chair back so forcefully, it nearly topples over. I need to escape for a lunchtime walk to make sense of what I have just read.

Walking alongside the dry Santa Ana River Channel in the noonday sun, I struggle to reconcile the witty, lighthearted Dexter I know with this troubling ideology.

I vow to cut all ties, our current platonic situation or otherwise, but something in my brain seems to be at odds with what my roiling gut is insisting I do. The axiom "actions speak louder than words" echoes through my brain. The behavior I have witnessed doesn't align with his online persona. I surmise Dexter has penned these denigrations in a moment of post-breakup pain after other women, those ugly, heartbreaking kind of breakups. I assure my skeptical gut these comments are indeed a phase he has moved past. I accept Dexter's actions at face value. And in these early days, he is funny, amusing, kind. I decide to give Dexter a cautious hall pass—unless I experience his misogyny firsthand (actions), I refuse to give any weight to his online comments (words), a wafer-thin sliver of hope he'll change his mind about us tipping the scales in his favor.

Besides, I convince myself, *the women described in these Manosphere groups don't apply to me.* Even if he honestly subscribes to the misogynistic statements he has written,

I rationalize, he will see I am different—strong, self-reliant, and no desire for marriage or babies, so very different.

I keep my new internet discovery quiet from everyone and push it out of my own thoughts as well. I don't want to stir the pot. Who would believe me, anyway? Maybe I don't know the whole story. I consider broaching the Manosphere subject with him, but I convince myself there never seems to be a reason. Dexter has a few odd gender role quirks, like needing to walk closest to the street to protect me, in case an errant car comes barreling onto the sidewalk, as if his skinny whiff of a body would stop its trajectory. However, I find these antiquated ideas endearing rather than worrisome, so I keep his secret.

AN UNINTENTIONAL RECIPE

I glance at Dexter's text, *"Are we still on for my BBQ Birthday dinner this Sunday?"*

I erased that preplanned activity from my calendar weeks ago, a casualty of his "We're done" email, opting instead to present him with a certificate for a homemade *German Chocolate Cake* at his birthday party. He made it clear that Dexter-Julie time was off the table when he sent that email, and I'm not prepared for one-on-one time yet, even platonically. How cheeky of him to expect cake and dinner.

My Sunday evening remains open, but hesitation grips me. My head rationalizes, *It's just dinner.* But I know better. The mere touch of Dexter's hand can cause my blood to effervesce, reminding me of our tangled and complicated history over these last few months. Alone with him in close proximity—I am not ready for the sparks that still linger.

"Let me think about it," I text back.

An hour later, navigating through the narrow aisles of Trader Joe's, like a moving meditation, gives me a moment to contemplate the situation. By the time I reach the freezer aisle, I text, *"Let's do it. We're both adults and can manage to keep our hands off each other."*

Following our platonic birthday dinner, Dexter's persistent hints to return to his apartment become unmistakable. For what reason? To retrieve my favorite throat lozenges, to give me a back rub, to drop off some breakfast buns I had made earlier in the day and brought with me.

On our way back to his place, he unexpectedly kisses me.

Unintentional Recipe for Inadvertent Coupling – Serves 2

<u>Ingredients</u>

- One email expressing a desire for mere friendship after months of sending mixed signals
- One humbling, yet determined, retreat
- One promise of a German chocolate cake
- One heartfelt, sincerely written platonic birthday note
- One BBQ birthday dinner

<u>Directions</u>

1. Open and read email from Dexter that clearly measures out, no matter what he led you to believe, that you will not be sautéing up romance.
2. Accept terms and allow this doughy decision to rest and ferment for two weeks. See him at group outings, yet keep physical distance. Coolly avoid flirting or touching. Roll and cut out clear boundaries that disorient him.
3. Attend his birthday party. As a gift, add a "certificate" for your rich version of German chocolate cake, his favorite, and fold in a note.
4. Uphold your invitation for a subsequent birthday BBQ dinner after mutually acknowledging you're adults capable of platonic interactions.
5. After dinner, notice he is purposefully, and not subtly, leading you back to his apartment.
6. End up in his bed.

It's a sneak attack, and I am unprepared, clad in decidedly unsexy everyday cotton panties and sporting five o'clock shadow leg stubble. I'm not displeased by this turn of events, just in disbelief. The entire time we are having sex, I keep thinking, *When did "absolutely not" become "hell yes"?*

"What changed in less than a month?" I ask him. My brow would be furrowed in confusion, if not for the Botox. Dexter's response is a tangled mess of evasions, serving me a word salad that provides no clarity about why his mind changed. And, because I am exactly where I want to be, naked in his arms, I don't press.

HAPPY NEW YEAR

Although my cats, and his neighbors, are well aware we are sleeping together, Dexter seems determined to keep our situation on the down-low from our friends.

No touching or sitting near each other anywhere they might be lurking. I call them "our" friends, but most are his longtime acquaintances. I am new on the scene. Dexter not-so-subtly hints that a handful of the women are on the prowl for some Dex-sex, one of them verging on stalking, according to him. With this information, I'm tempted to lift my tail and spray on his leg, like a cat marking its territory—he's mine, ladies, move on. Instead, I keep my distance from my new friends, dutifully keeping our rendezvous quiet, as Dexter prefers.

But soon enough, our proverbial feline will be out of the bag. We are invited to stay at a friend's house for New Year's Eve weekend, and the bedroom situation forces our hand: five bedrooms with three times as many invitees.

"We can share," Dexter tells them.

"We can share," I follow up, unaware he's already made arrangements.

At the party, we smooch and play footsies, even sneaking off a few times for a very adult version of hide-and-seek, yet no one remarks on this new development. We ring in the new year lip to lip, and our friends play along as if nothing has changed. We are in the first blushes of romance, our friends now in the know, it is official—we are an item.

DIMINISHING

On the second weekend in January, a mere two months after becoming intimate and only a week after coming out to our friends, I glimpse a hairline crack in Dexter's lighthearted, charismatic façade. Before my screen door bangs closed, I can sense the heavy air swirling around him, noxious and sooty.

"Hi, sweetheart, what's wrong?" I ask.

"Nothing."

"It seems like you're upset."

"I'm fine," he responds, looking away at the wall.

"Are you sure?"

"Yeah."

"Something's up. Tell me what's wrong."

"Well..."

The night prior, I had suggested Dexter come over early so we could have sex before we went out for the day with our friends. In the morning, he assumed I'd reconfirm. When I failed to do so, rather than remind me of our plans himself or reconfirm for himself, he seizes this opportunity to feel slighted.

I take a deep breath and pull out two dining chairs to face each other. I sit down in one, beckoning him to sit in the other across from me. I take his hands in mine. I apologize, in a soothing and measured tone, like when I accidentally step on my black cat's paw in the middle of the night when I need to pee, "I'm sorry, I'm so sorry, oh poor baby, Mama loves you."

Attempting to pacify Dexter, I accept full responsibility for the error, even though blame could be evenly meted out. I say the newness of our romance assures miscommunications will surface from time to time. I will do better next time, I promise. We sit knee-to-knee for twenty minutes, as I smooth his raised hackles until each hair sits glossy and back in place. I pat myself on my back for my adeptness at managing our first misunderstanding. I am channeling Brené Brown, relationship-ing like an adult. For the remainder of the day, although he assures me all is forgiven, I am left with a gauzy unsteadiness, as if the molecules that make up "Julie" have moved a fraction farther away from each other.

Our second disagreement arises on Valentine's Day, one short month later. Dexter has arranged a dinner this night…no, no, not a romantic gesture for just the two of us. What a silly thought. He has arranged a group celebration for twenty people and, had I not RSVPed, I'm convinced we would have spent the evening in separate celebration. There is no mention of his plans before or after the invitation arrives in my inbox. Valentine's Day has always remained low on my roster of holidays. I much prefer receiving little moments and kindnesses throughout the year than some grand, mandated, overly priced, and underwhelming fancy dinner, so while I feel a moment's neglect when I'm not considered in his plans, my irritation is slight and, besides, we have only been sleeping together for three months, not including the prior three months of his ambiguity and ambivalence.

When I arrive, Dexter is scratching out names on a piece of paper, appearing flustered and concerned by the number of last-minute cancellations. The restaurant is near Todd's house, so, I mention I know someone local who can be invited in a pinch. It's as if a proscenium curtain has fallen between us—end of Act I. Dexter promptly releases my hand, turns his body away from me so I am now facing his back, and refuses to acknowledge my presence. It isn't crimson, long-stem roses I receive on Valentine's, but rather the cold-blue haze of Dexter's silent treatment. He is aware Todd and I had dated, for a month, a bazillion years ago.

Rather than expressing his uneasiness with my suggestion, "Hey, I'm not comfortable with Todd being here, especially on Valentine's Day," Dexter sulks, disengages, and alienates me.

Determined not to spend the evening in icy silence, I once again apply my previously successful approach. I gently pull him away from the group into the cool night air, implore him to tell me why the idea is so offensive, and take full responsibility for my supposed utter lack of sensitivity. He can invite an assortment of friends to this dinner, some, I later learn, who had their own dalliances with him, yet my invitation to Todd is verboten.

The two of us drive south to San Diego the next day, Saturday, for a brief Valentine's getaway. Another argument ensues this evening, the first time his tone and manner cause tears to roll down my cheeks. This time, our voices are strident, the words uglier. I half expect hotel security to arrive at our door any minute. I accept his condemnation, although, on this occasion, reluctantly. We don't leave the hotel room this night, both drained and bruised from a succession of quarrels. Rather, we hunker down in the bed, ordering room service burgers and a movie.

Sunday, we wander around Balboa Park. I conclude it's prudent not to disclose my feet long ago often navigated each bend of these meandering walkways.

I feel vaporous, floating about the botanical garden like a dragonfly, diaphanous wisps of gossamer carrying me from plant to plant. The residue from the last two days remains lodged inside my deepest marrow, turning both bone and skin into delicate rice paper. We snap a photo that day, smiling and wrapped within each other's arms, but when I examine my image closely, the cheerful face staring back is wan and subdued, fragments of me scattered about like startled sparrows... or water ripples, spreading out across an otherwise placid scene.

RISK VS. REWARD

I thought I had pulled off a coup, because out of the bevy of babes Dexter assures me he could have chosen, he chose me. With our shared history of rocky romances and similarity in age, I was convinced we could make a good match. And besides, he is a writer and former artist—the former artist currently known as Dexter—just up my alley.

Now, doubts creep in, the first inklings that perhaps I have miscalculated, that my man-picker has failed me yet again.

I begin weighing the risk versus reward of sticking around. On the plus side, I enumerate the reasons to stay: Dexter brings a playfulness to my life that has been missing, the sex is good and plentiful, and I have invested too much effort catching him to release him back into the wild so soon. On the downside, we are embroiled in these ridiculous clashes—three in less than two months—and, in the heat of these rows, his behavior reminds me of a petulant child. The memory of his accusations and sulking after our last disagreement creates a not-unfamiliar hollowness in the pit of my stomach.

Then there are what I call the "outside concerns." I have met an interesting, exciting new group of friends. Leaving Dexter means losing them too. Plus, I have just asked my CEO if I can invite Dexter to an upcoming work trip in March—a huge step for me since I haven't invited anyone along in about fifteen years. Admitting to my CEO or anyone who knows about us that I've failed after a mere few months makes me hang my head with humiliation—unlovable Julie strikes again.

But the biggest reason I decide to stay is that I care for Dexter, deeply, even with his faults. If I scrape away the gunk of these fights, I am head over heels for the man I believe I detect hiding underneath.

MORNING SUNSHINE WITH CHANCE OF AFTERNOON CLOUDS

Dexter loosely grips the steering wheel with one hand; the other nestles along my left thigh. The dappled sunlight warms our scalps, unimpeded by a convertible roof tucked away in the trunk. My hair restrained by a scarf à la Tippi Hedren, I catch his eye and grin, content and ready for another adventure.

The Southern California weather has been uncommonly hot for early spring. I have missed our road trips over the last few weeks, during these initial days of COVID warnings and self-isolation mandates. All locations now shuttered, our lives seemingly on pause, I remind myself the journey often outshines the final destination. So, I suggest a road trip where the final stop becomes secondary, where we needn't leave the safety of my convertible.

The first weekend, we head northeast to the mountain destinations of Arrowhead and Big Bear, offering patches of slushy snow and the fresh, cool air we desperately crave. Our picnic by Big Bear Lake, Dexter's doing, is a tranquil bonus.

We're hooked on our quarantine-approved road trips, savoring these sweet escapes from the stifling isolation and simmering terror of this "new normal," and relishing the fleeting slivers of freedom they offer.

The next weekend, we drive two hours south to Julian, a town known for its freshly baked apple pies. Not only do we snag a still-warm apple crumble pie—the outside "to go" window still open—but we also pull off at a dusty roadside fruit stand for blood oranges, avocados, and organic honey. For the following weekend, we have planned our longest adventure yet, north along the coast to Solvang, an enclave famous for *aebleskiver* and Danish kitsch.

We spend countless quarantine nights spooning on his couch, watching Netflix. Dexter stocks the side table with our supplies: his weed, my Sauvignon Blanc, crinkly bags of snacks for both of us, and the bed mere steps away.

Dexter opens the medicine cabinet to show me he's cleared a shelf for me, making a cozy home for my toothbrush and saline solution. He performs sweet boyfriend-y acts like stocking his fridge with my favorite foods, making my morning coffee, and buying me flowers, albeit from the grocery store.

There are sun-soaked weekends in Palm Springs, one amorous visit for the two of us, another with his family, and a weekend tucked away in blissful romantic reverie within a serene Idyllwild cabin. While I whip up *Chocolate Chip Pancakes with Macerated Strawberries*, toasted pecans, and clouds of freshly whipped cream in the cabin's kitchen, I spy Dexter lounging on the deck, a look of pure contentment on his face as he soaks in the fresh scent of pine trees.

But the storm clouds always return, clashes and misunderstandings that ruin our sunnier moments, like my dream of an *aebleskiver* weekend. That trip never materializes. As the months tick by, our skies darken from dove to coal, the torrents arrive without warning, and these tempests linger longer. I wonder if we are intrinsically incompatible. Our fights become habit rather than exception, spectacular affairs that can never be labeled lovers' petty or trivial bickering. Our spats last days, sometimes weeks. Every damn time, I choose to apologize first, repeatedly, like a Catholic grandmother clicking her rosary, just to end these unwinnable battles.

Dexter recounts my transgressions, his voice cutting through any chance of reasonable discussion, questioning my character, accusing me of irrationality. I feel myself fading and blurring, like an old Polaroid of Julie, my vibrancy dulling to watery pastel under the searing glare of Dexter's recurring disapproval.

My earlier attempts at soothing de-escalation are no match for his onslaught.

GLUTEN FOR PUNISHMENT

He is a pro: the Roger Federer of arguments (or John McEnroe would be more apt). His bedroom shelves are lined with trophies from prior disagreements fought and won through dogged tenacity to vanquish his "opponent," sans remorse. After one clash, I ask him if he has studied Apologetics because, regardless of how deftly I explain myself, he stands armed and ready with a retort to volley back at me at full force. Set, game, match. In my twenties and early thirties, my romances were sometimes tempestuous, but never with this degree of viciousness.

His outward image being paramount, he demands to know, "What are you going to say to our friends about this?" My response is always the same, "Nothing." This ugly side is no one's concern but ours. Let them see smiling social media posts of kisses and held hands, leaving the reality of me, collapsed on the floor, eyes red and swollen, safely tucked behind our bedroom door.

One night in April, I am crucified for saying, "Mick Jagger looks good for his age. I would sleep with him." Not only don't I want to have sex with Mick, I don't even think he's attractive and, surely, the rock star can do better than little ol' me. It is a morsel of hyperbole, a way to say, "Jagger's still got it for someone in their late seventies." For the next three hours, Dexter remains charming, filled with jokes and puns while surrounded by his friends, yet I can sense the seething behind his façade.

His wrath explodes as soon as we shut the doors to his car. We fight throughout the drive home. Once outside his apartment, I sit in the passenger's seat, door open and body turned away from his unrelenting storm. My feet and legs, firmly planted on the asphalt outside the car, feel strong and solid, ready to extricate me with determined strides across the parking lot to the safety of my waiting car. Yet my body remaining within has wilted into a silvery mist, blown into vapor by the stifling force of his condemnation. Torn in half, I weigh the cool evening air and my liberation against his relentless assault that has reduced me to blurry condensation on the windshield.

We are stuck inside a hamster wheel: My actions or words bruise his ego and spark a diatribe or the silent treatment. My tears soon follow, although I yearn to hold them back, wanting to show, instead, a face of strength and composure. His absurd reaction to trivial incidents awakens my incredulity, the third familiar stage in our inevitable cycle.

Long gone are those days of imploring Dexter to sit near me, catching his hands in mine, attempting to soothe his temper. These conflicts never become physical but, on one occasion, he confesses punching walls during disagreements in years past. I interpret that to mean, "You're lucky I'm not physically attacking you, but I'm capable." Still, even without being assaulted, these rows are a brutal and emotional pummeling that dissolves me into a specter of myself, an afterimage of the woman I used to be before meeting him.

Most people who know Dexter, like our friends, would question the veracity of my story. Outwardly, he is charismatic and magnetic. He'll have puns at the ready, bring a vitality to the chosen outing, and unabashedly flirt. Yet, if allowed behind his curtain, they'll watch these affectations slip away.

Whether through Dexter's manipulation or my own self-flagellation, I blame myself for this bewildering alteration of his persona. Dexter deftly scatters seeds of self-doubt within me: I drink too much, I am a "showboat," I'm gaslighting him, my deficient behavior and character are in want of molding. I become convinced a toxic cancer within me is the catalyst for his contemptuous reactions. All the while, although I don't comprehend it at the time, the malignancy is rooted inside him—merely metastasizing within me.

Psyche eventually begins her tardy crooning in my ear. Maybe she has been singing all along, but the first time I notice is the afternoon Dexter maneuvers into my driveway, flings a half-filled plastic bag on the ground, and drives off, the product of another multiday conflict. He doesn't see me standing at my dining room window. By now, no more than a warm breath on a cold spring morning, I am a shadow of myself, a smudge upon the glass if he glances up.

I stare at that bundle lying on the concrete for a few minutes, hesitant to leave the safety of my home. The content waits for me inside its plastic wrapping. From my vantage point, it appears the size of a sack lunch, yet can just as easily be a pile of dog shit.

I unlock the front door and inch like a tentative deer toward the package, glancing down the street, anxious this is a trap. I exhale. It's neither a trap, lunch, nor shit, just my toiletries, swept from the bathroom shelf and deposited on my driveway. I look down at my tabby cat and dryly joke, "I guess he cleared the shelf twice for me."

Throughout the remainder of the afternoon, Psyche continues her melody in my ear, repeating the chorus like a mantra, that catchy '80s hymn about an emotionally manipulated woman pressured to conform to her partner's expectations: "Voices Carry."

Despite the pain, I remain tethered to him like an unwitting masochist, shoving Psyche out of earshot. I text him, apologizing for transgressions that never were, even as I slip further into a shadow of who I once was.

SEE ME—A MESSAGE TO DEXTER

The woman you seek does not exist, but someone more profound and exquisite (and real) would willingly stand beside you, holding your unsure hand. Place aside your impossible ideals of chaste Madonna by sunlight and sinful whore at nightfall and truly see me. I am angel and devil in equal measure and cannot hide one trait away depending on your desires or the time of day. Sometimes my licentious tongue yearns for daylight. Sometimes my crooked halo still hovers above me in the night.

My femininity is not defined by my willingness to compromise my light and dark selves for your sake. My facets are more complex and surprising than you could ever conceive. See me for who I am, adore me for this dichotomy, and I will shower you with myriad delights.

Watch me dance naked in your moonlight. Trust me to cradle you and gather your flood of tears. I will fill your belly with devilishly divine delicacies, and I will love you, blind to your tapestry of damage and scars.

KNEADING SOLACE

The coup de grâce to the slow death of Dexter and Julie isn't louder or longer or angrier than any other clash, just an anticlimactic repeat of the same, like a rerun in a never-ending series. Even after Dexter delivers the final blow—my fault again, always my fault—I find myself inexplicably reaching out. I try winning him back with a heartfelt note, one of the ingredients that began this romance-turned-horror-story. As I hit send, I can't ignore the gnawing feeling that I have gone insane, especially after what I have endured these last few months, but this cycle of conflict feels familiar, somehow.

I implore Dexter to reconsider, convincing myself our difficulties are due to pandemic stress and not some systemic glitch in our relationship. Thankfully, my pleas go unheard. He has moved on to someone else. How do I know? I saw the signs I had been replaced, just a week later, with my own eyes—or perhaps she was already there while I still shared his bed.

Yet, still, I mourn.

In the aftermath of our breakup, I seek comfort in my kitchen—the feel of dough beneath my hands, the rhythmic push and pull, become my therapy. With my five-pound bag of yeast, a purchase from a restaurant struggling to survive the pandemic, I bake bread and breakfast buns, filling my house with the homey scent of fresh, yeasty goodness. Each warm and comforting creation becomes a labor of love, a reminder I can still create something nourishing, beautiful, satisfying, and good.

GREY

I examine images of his face now, looking deeply in eyes both right and left, trying to fathom how I was fooled.

Dexter once claimed his eyes were hazel, but I disagree. Dexter is slightly color-blind, so he has never looked in a mirror and contemplated the nuances of his irises. He relies on others' interpretations. I am reminded of that parable about the three blind men and an elephant. At one specific moment, on a particular day, his eyes possibly appeared hazel, but they are not so easily described. Hazel is a catch-all category, for those lacking the vocabulary to describe an iris's shade in more… colorful terms. Hazel eyes, by definition, are a combination of green, brown, and golden hues, decidedly not the shade of Dexter's. I am the one with eyes of hazel, a drab olive green with rays of russet brown and a few flecks of ocher. When asked, I liken their unremarkable color to dirty pond water.

Dexter's eyes are grey, a light bluish slate. He dismissed my assessment, assuring me his driver's license states differently and also insisted I am the only person who has ever mentioned the smoke-hued mirrors beneath his lashes.

Has anyone else bothered to examine them closely, I wonder? Their shade ripples, mutable, depending on his clothes or the light, shifting from pale sky to the faintest sage. I am sure the silver from his hair holds sway over these misty specters as well.

When in the throes of passion or paroxysms of anger—states I've witnessed in equal measure—these portholes to his psyche grew graphite dark, like storm clouds just before the deluge. When our romance still blossomed, this kaleidoscope of shifting greys and blues and greens transfixed me, the emerging of a yet-unobserved color arresting me midsentence with their beauty. However, once his kindness drained away, replaced by indifference and contempt, I was met with windows of the bleakest winter, two gravestones, hard, cold, and unyielding as he seethed and accused.

Today, as I look upon his photo, only flat, blank, detached emptiness stares back at me from above his harlequin's smile.

IT JUST TAKES TIME

They said mothers forget how much labor and childbirth hurts, although I'd heard this is a myth. These pundits claim this forgetting is the body's attempt to ensure additional offspring. If the agony is remembered, perhaps the act would not be duplicated. The same appears to hold true for a battered heart.

It's been some time since I've allowed my heart access outside of its protective cage and, had I remembered the sensation of a heart pummeling, I would have chosen a safer path. Yet, I find myself here again. Everyone has advice and comments on how to find my groove again, from "Get back on the horse as soon as possible" to "We never liked Dexter anyway." Most advice remains unhelpful. However, I've managed to cobble together the following steps which have helped me, if not heal my heart completely, patch it up enough to fight another day.

Treat yourself as if you are sick. Heartache is a sickness. If you had a fever, you'd treat yourself with kindness: stay home for a few days, lie on the couch in your jammies, binge on Netflix. You wouldn't beat yourself up for not being "over" your fever. You'd veg on the couch for a few days to get over the worst of it and then slowly start doing things to make yourself feel better: getting plenty of rest, eating well, building up your strength again. After a breakup, allow yourself three days of jammies and Netflix and then, with the kindness a sick person deserves, gently start your journey back. If you have a relapse, nurse yourself lovingly, get a good night's sleep, and begin again the next morning.

Pamper yourself. Do a little something for yourself that says "I love you" every day. Think of all the little things you did for your ex to let him know he was special. You deserve the same. I bought myself fresh flowers (not Dexter's grocery store variety this time), deep conditioned my hair, picked up a new scented candle, bought a sexy new matching set of lingerie, steeped a cup of Earl Grey with honey and a splash of milk, and painted my nails bright red with a new polish.

Move each day. Exercise is known to increase serotonin and dopamine, mood-altering, feel-good brain chemicals. It doesn't matter what you choose: go for a walk with a friend, ride a bike, practice yoga, dance in your living room, whatever gets your heart racing. However, try to avoid spending too much time on activities that allow you to think alone or you'll end up ruminating about him. If you go for a walk, listen to a podcast on empowered women or an audiobook with a strong heroine to keep your mind on something other than your bruised heart.

Talk him up to others. Whether you like it or not, your friends and family (and coworkers, acquaintances, and the dry cleaner) are going to give you their condolences and ask you about why the romance ended. By taking the high road, instead of playing the victim, you take the power back. Tell them about the bits of him that made you smile (if you can't recall any, make something up) and keep the rest to yourself. (Do as I say, not as I do, considering I'm laying bare lurid details of our coupling. At the time, however, I spewed out some positive, quasi-pro-Dexter nonsense).

Don't prod the relationship wound. Just as heartache is a sickness, the relationship is probably feeling like a tender, unhealed, open wound. When you are injured, sometimes the best treatment is to leave it alone. Poking and prodding at the sore just makes it bleed and get infected. Don't moon over pictures of the two of you in happier times, don't open the folder where his emails are kept, don't visit the places where you had your fondest memories. Let the wound scab over and heal. There may always be a scar, but scars don't hurt, do they?

And slowly, very slowly, you will recover.

Just remember, it takes time.

TRUTH

Two months after Dexter and I break up, we are still fighting via text and I continue to grieve. I try to be kind, to de-escalate, but the wrong word sets off his hair-trigger anger, and we once again tumble from this razor's edge balancing game.

Nadine, initially one of Dexter's friends, has been beside me these last few months, helping me heal. She shares her own unfathomable stories of his unrelenting anger, when she became ensnared in his reproach, even as just his friend. She is another unlucky soul caught up in his barrage of texts. Hearing her tales of venturing behind his fun-loving, good-guy curtain provides the validation I need. I am not to blame. I am not crazy.

One night, Nadine places a heavy wooden box on the table in front of me. "Here," she says, "I've hesitated sharing this with you, but since we've grown closer, I can't keep what's inside from you anymore. What you do with it is up to you." In her right palm, she holds out a small, incandescent object—a key. "It's your decision to open it."

A few days prior, I innocuously share a secret with Nadine—a recent HPV-related cervical cancer diagnosis. I am confused by the doctor's findings. In my thirty-five years of sexual activity, I have never contracted an STI. Yet months after getting dumped by Dexter, I am suddenly diagnosed with cervical cancer. The OB/GYN can't tell me who, when, or how this happened, and I am shocked by the diagnosis, feeling dirty. I comment to Nadine, "Knowing my sexual history and Dexter's sexual history he shared with me, how could this have happened?"

Nadine sits in silence. She blinks a few times, her eyelash extensions fluttering like the wings of a startled bird. Her mouth, usually soft and quick to respond, is pressed into a thin line. She glances away, her eyes darting to the window, then to her crimson, manicured fingernails resting in her lap. She asks about my prognosis.

"All good," I respond, "an outpatient procedure. Nothing to worry about," trying to minimize my situation. Our conversation moves to other things, but I can sense something's bothering Nadine. She knows a secret she isn't sharing.

The box Nadine hands me a few days later is about the size of a laptop, but deeper—slightly smaller than a breadbox, to use the familiar idiom. The wood grain feels smooth, worn, like it has passed through many hands. Two metal hinges run along the top, and I draw my thumb across the lock along the front. A few looping vine-like carvings decorate the box, and the word "TRUTH" has been chiseled on the lid.

I hesitate. My head and gut encourage me to reveal what's inside. My heart, on the other hand, cautions me to keep the box firmly locked, aware the contents will likely pain me.

Call me Pandora. I place the glowing key in the lock and turn it. The lid springs open. Nadine sits down, and I believe I catch a tear in her eye, as if to say, "I'm sorry."

The inside reeks of dead things, dank and moldy. A blue envelope rests on top. My name, scrawled across the front, is written in Nadine's familiar script. The envelope isn't sealed. Inside, pages of her notes recount stories Dexter shared with her. Along with knowing of dalliances before and while I was in his bed, Nadine knows details about my private encounters with Dexter only *he* could have told her, bolstering the validity of her other claims. After reading these pages, I understand the secret Nadine has kept. The sexual history Dexter told me is a fabrication—a lie.

Dexter knowingly robbed me of my informed consent and potentially placed my health at risk. With this first envelope, my trust in him crumbles.

I return Nadine's envelope to the top of the pile and take the box home. Once alone, I methodically inspect its contents, layer by layer, like an archeologist. I find a collection of letters and notes, plus a few observations scribbled on cocktail napkins and receipts. The box is filled with details from mostly women, but also a few men, his friends I've grown to know well but also mere acquaintances. The envelope from Nadine is only the first. I practically retch when I come upon an erotic photo Dexter sent to a woman who he swore was "just a friend," and I read about their phone sex. I recognize the bulge in front of me, straining to break free from his underwear. I shudder in disgust. This particular tale's veracity is bolstered when I come across the intimate item he requested and accepted from this woman. Just a friend, indeed. I know his fetishes. I know exactly how he used her "gift." I remove the photo from the stack and place it in a drawer, inside my own folder I label "Vile." It's the only photo I keep of him, lest sentimentality ever soften me.

I pull a sympathy card from the box. "When did you become exclusive?" it reads, before enlightening me on his behavior while I was vacationing in London, missing him terribly. "I thought a month before that," I whisper to myself, astonished I remained ignorant of his actions all these months. Our flirting from those early days, I come to understand, is his standard operating procedure for most women in his world.

Each note is like the bloody and lifeless mice my cats sometimes leave me as presents—gifts I would rather not receive.

Dexter jokes about his female neighbor who glares at him for some unknown reason. I search for a note from her, imagining what she must witness, unwillingly complicit in his deceptions. Rather than a glare, she should hang a banner over her deck railing—"Enter that apartment at your peril, ladies."

"You dodged a bullet," a few friends comment.

I glance down to my gut and watch my commitment, my trust, my humiliation oozing from the crater there. "I dodged nothing," I remark to myself.

I spy a large manila folder near the bottom, with "WORK WIFE" neatly typed across the left corner. Recalling his online post I had read months ago, I remove a stack of documents. On the top is the printout of the original post bragging about the amount of sex he was getting from her. With my new perspective, the pieces click into place. "Oh, of course," I mutter into the silence of my living room. His work wife is a workplace fuck-buddy. How could I have been so stupid? Below his post, his friends share stories confirming this coupling lasted years, continued during the first months we were together, and was still going strong weeks after we broke up. A wry laugh escapes my lips. That would add up to about five years with her, longer than most of his couplings. Was I an intermission for them, I wonder, or did they continue on, uninterrupted, while we were together? Across an index card is the statement, "She's like catnip," supposedly something he says about her. Another note, with a hand-drawn map, explains the logistics. Dexter apparently sneaks over to this colleague's place after work, keeping their assignations secret by texting our friends, *"taking a quick nap,"* before meeting up later for a movie or dinner. Upon reading this particular trick, I recall the evenings I'd prepare for our dates—shaving my legs, painting my nails, spritzing on perfume—and I'd hear his text ping, *"Gonna take a quick nap."* He overslept once. Was he truly napping? Was he with her? I'll never know for sure—and, truthfully, I don't want to.

I slam the box's lid shut, turn the lock, and throw the key across the room, nearly hitting my cat sprawled across the floor. "Enough" escapes through my gritted teeth. Who, exactly, is this man who held my heart? I shared with him, more than once, honesty's paramount importance to me, and he deceived me from our very first interactions. I opened my head, my legs, and my heart to a liar—and a stranger.

My lingering grief morphs into a white-hot anger. I confront him, serving up a venomous email cocktail of fury at being played, disbelief that our time together was all lies, and disgust that I allowed this wolf inside of me. In an attempt to protect his accusers, I reproach him without using names or specifics.

In response, he demands to know which lies I am referring to.

Which. Lies. Which Lies?

All of them.

I purchase a security camera, change the locks on my doors, order a new credit card, and change my ATM PIN, realizing I have yet to understand the limits of his deceit. Have I watched too many true crime shows? Most definitely. Am I overreacting? Probably, but the extent of his lies appears ripped from an episode of *Dateline:* "The Clark Rockefeller of Orange County." Dexter has mutated into a complete stranger.

I am now faced with the knowledge that the man I initially adored never truly existed. What I deemed a foundation of trust reveals itself to be, on the contrary, a house of cards built on deceit. My world has tilted ninety degrees on its axis.

The fights, the misogyny, and now the lies. After decades of dating, this is my first foray into what I would label a genuinely toxic relationship, the first time I've been ensnared by a creature such as him. My world view that people are intrinsically honest and good has been cast into doubt.

I lament this calamity couldn't have occurred earlier in my dating history, that I couldn't have learned this regretful lesson while I was still young, still resilient. In those years, I safely hid my heart from all.

At forty-four, I elected to lay bare these inner fears and defenses holding me back. At that time, I pointed both peep-toe pumps toward Brett, exposing myself to the inevitable heartache that lay before me. That first relationship with Brett, when it ended, was astonishingly painful, but I believe, however inartfully Brett handled the breakup, his motive wasn't to hurt me. He just wanted someone different from what I offered.

This time, Dexter's damage seems predatory, remorseless, and cold-blooded, shrewdly playing out his emotional con on me and leaving anger, pain, and disbelief in his wake. By consciously changing my behavior, opening myself up and pushing my defenses aside, I have allowed this wolf to devour me. How could this happen, I wonder, in my fifties and with a partner who promised me a foundation of trust? It is simple, really. I remained blind to Dexter's secrets and lies.

My friends reproach me, insisting I am not to blame for this outcome.

Todd says, "This is not your fault. You trusted and loved someone who betrayed both. Loving him required trust as well as exposing your vulnerability. To do that is difficult, especially if you've been hurt before. It's a special thing to be loved and trusted. It's shitty as hell to betray that."

Those words are balm to my wounded heart, a tonic to my incredulity that I didn't catch on sooner. Still, I can't claim complete innocence in this toxic farce. I fabricated mutual feelings Dexter at no time possessed. There is a disconnect between the love I was feeling, what glinted under Dexter's façade, and the truth. I never looked too closely during the eight months we were a couple. I didn't question how "we" used up a bottle of lube in just a week or asked why he kept our relationship secret for an additional two months after I thought we were exclusive, later finding out we were not. I never pressed him on the sex toys he swore he bought for me but were presented, out of the plastic, arranged on a towel, and with an aura of prior use. I didn't ask what kind of man would eschew make-up sex, claiming a messy apartment as his excuse—one who is hiding something in said apartment, that's who.

I'm changed, sadly regressing to the untrusting, closed-off woman I used to be. Under no circumstances will I again allow my perceived compatibility, my one-sided chemistry, to blind me to the man in front of me. I will meet men after Dexter and think, *He's cute,* but I must stop myself and retort, *but is he safe?*

I was nothing special to Dexter. From the first halcyon days of November until the dark storms of late June, I was one of his sex toys, his arm candy, his plus-one, his caretaker, with the bonus of being his personal pastry chef, and nothing more. Once Dexter used me up, he discarded me, moving on to the understudies waiting in the wings. He was likely grooming them while he still called me his girlfriend— like he did with me and others while Brigitte Bardot was draped across his arm. Had I wanted to, I could have caught his duplicity early, long before I even considered offering him my heart. I chose ignorance instead.

Keeping quiet about his behavior, not sharing my situation with my new friends, not verifying his words cost me dearly. Dexter deftly triangulated me against these women, so I remained closed off. Had I examined his words and actions closer, had I shared more, this box of Truth would have been in my hands sooner. A number of his friends were quite aware of his damage and sexual escapades, while I remained blissfully oblivious.

Dexter claims his last serious relationship before me ended because her friends convinced her of his supposed infidelity. He swore he never cheated. I believed poor, falsely accused Dexter back then. I doubt his every word now. I can only imagine what her box contained.

ARMCHAIR DIAGNOSIS

Narcissist.

After our relationship ends, Todd tosses around that label to describe Dexter, and I initially discount it.

It's a term seen everywhere these days, and when I think of the embodiment of a narcissist, I envision flashy cars, thick gold chains, expensive watches, and puffed-out chests. The term has become an overused descriptor for any individual who displays a hint of self-worth. It's a spectrum, and we all possess a touch of narcissism—look no further than social media, or someone writing a memoir about their dating exploits. I don't use the term lightly.

Dexter doesn't exhibit any of those stereotypical vain characteristics. His actions, however, perplex me, and while researching his specific behaviors, I stumble upon information describing a form of narcissism known as "covert" or "vulnerable." I delve deeper into this variety, utilizing various sources. This research solidifies my initial recognition and my personal experience. I am not a psychotherapist. I have no formal training and am not diagnosing him as a covert narcissist. To my knowledge, Dexter has never been professionally diagnosed with this personality disorder, but the listed "red flags" feel like Jane Goodall has been watching our every interaction from behind a potted plant: gaslighting, triangulation, anger, blame, shaming, feigned victimhood, cognitive dissonance. The puzzle pieces lock into place.

Going into this relationship, I knew he was damaged, deficient in something essential. Early on, he confessed to having "demons." He admits he was an addict, booze and tobacco in his younger life, weed and possibly sex now, although I'm doubtful he'd ever admit to those last two. Signs of OCD surfaced, like his counting quirks and meticulously kept gas logs hidden in his glove compartment. I didn't set out to rescue him; I knew that approach seldom works. Instead, I believed in my capability to unconditionally accept him, his addictions and disorders, his darker facets together with the light. At the time, I found his eccentricities endearing, but is it any wonder when characteristics of a personality disorder began bubbling up? After it was over, I reminded myself: when a man tells you he has demons, believe him.

I vacillate between labeling Dexter a vile, manipulative creature and recognizing his behavior, his addictions, his disorders likely stem from unconscious coping mechanisms developed in his formative years. This is when most dark personality disorders take root. Our failure had nothing to do with the two people involved, everything to do with the limitations a personality disorder places on any couple. I harbor a healthy dose of vitriol for the mental and emotional abuse I suffered at his hands, yet I also feel compassion and empathy for him as a human being. I see a damaged man in profound pain, coping the only way he knows how. It is difficult to imagine living in a world devoid of true emotional connection, a world that would compel me to pacify myself through various addictions, lies, and socially unacceptable behaviors.

Sadly, narcissists will do anything to protect their exceptionally fragile egos, so most will continue to live in their toxic world, mask firmly in place, rather than attempt to change. My deepest hope for Dexter—when my baser instincts aren't imagining brewing him a pot of oleander and castor bean tea—is that he faces his damage and seeks help. But most experts agree that neither medical nor psychological intervention is likely to succeed, leaving his long-term prognosis for change rather bleak.

REVISITING MGTOW

Behind the supposed safety of our breakup, I finally broach the Manosphere topic. Although we are no longer together, we share friends, and I've been trying to sand down the rougher edges of our interactions, knowing I will run into him again. And although it's unhinged, I also miss him. I'm an undiagnosed junkie, jonesing for a drug that's slowly destroying me.

These intermittent, often contentious texts typically end with his exceptionally cutting responses that leave me dumbstruck, admonishing myself for even trying to create cordiality. During our last text spat, after giving up on de-escalation, I ask whether his adherence to MGTOW could be a factor in our past—and ongoing—issues. He, in turn, accuses me of stalking him, denies posting anything for years, and dismisses his online comments, trying to make the fault mine for discovering them.

Am I misremembering what I read? Now aware of his master gaslighting skills, I type in his name and "author" again—and try new combinations as well. I've never witnessed someone erase their digital footprint, and so quickly. By the time I scour the internet again, posts have vanished, videos no longer contain his comments, other videos are hidden so they aren't so easily found by a simple Google search. Despite this, I find a dozen or so comments, including newer ones I haven't seen before. A dark smile plays across my lips—this wasn't a phase. He remained active on these sites, contributing as recently as a month before we slept together.

I check again a week later, to capture screenshots as tangible proof that I'm not fabricating what I saw. More of his sickening comments have been scrubbed clean. A quote or two lingers, but regardless of what he wiped from the internet, I suspect these antifeminist beliefs are, and will always be, embedded deep within him, just no longer online where others can find them.

BREAKING FREE

First it hurts, then it changes you.
—Unknown

I am trapped by a compulsion to absorb every ounce of knowledge about covert narcissism and its aftermath. While still ensnared within this disorder's lair, I'm digging my way out, using every tool at my disposal. I seek a glimmer of validation that what I have endured is real and not my imaginings, assurances that my suffering would make any woman yelp in pain. I am searching for a toehold to view this landscape of our past from higher ground, making sense of the rough terrain, the hairpin turns, the jagged corners. How did I miss the caution signs placed along these treacherous roads? I yearn to place my magnifying glass above this deformed, hairy, tumorous affliction called narcissism and decode it.

As I dive into my research with a scientist's dispassion, the words "emotional abuse" and "victim" trip me up. Those twin words gut-punch and knock the wind out of me. When I first read the V-word, my blood freezes in my veins. The tough, female warrior inside me yearns to scream in disbelief, *That's not* me. *I am no one's victim.* Yet, that word that unjustly reeks of weakness and shame clings to me, like the sour smell of booze after a night of too much drinking.

When I hear "victim," I envision physical abuse and rape, a broken woman, helpless and damaged. No one wants to claim that label, but that's what I am. I unwittingly gave myself to a conman, who never cared, and only saw me for what he could get. Each of these creatures grabs at any attention they can get their hands on. They gorge themselves on the available buffet of sources like me to feed the ravenous ego lurking in the inky darkness inside of them. I'll never fully comprehend what he specifically sought from me.

Yet still, I can't utter those words, "I am a victim. He emotionally abused me." I am afraid no one will believe me. I am frightened of their questions:

"Was it really that bad?"

"Maybe you're the one with the problem?"

"What did you do to make him react that way?"

"Then why did you stick around?"

These are the same questions I ask myself.

I learn that what I am doing, endlessly researching what I endured, is a crucial step in healing. I devour YouTube videos, books, podcasts, join Facebook support groups, even speak with a therapist who specializes in narcissistic dynamics. As I learn more, I begin hearing the word "survivor." "Survivor" sounds strong and invincible. Being labeled a survivor provides hope. At first, I believe it's just a dolled-up euphemism for "victim," that shameful stench that still swirls about me.

So, am I his victim or a survivor?

I am both.

The language I choose to use impacts not only how I view myself but also how the world sees me. "Victim" focuses on what has been done *to* me and, in the beginning, that is unfortunately where I need to live. I have been damaged and mistreated, initially defining myself by the pain Dexter has heaped on me. My strength and resilience have been assaulted and feel, at times, nonexistent. As a victim, I am divorced from my power.

On the other side of that trauma is the realm of the survivors—and I eventually make it to the other side. Survivors acknowledge the abuser for who they are. I process the hurt, the anger, the realization that people like him exist. I recognize Dexter's incapacity for feeling loving emotions and I acknowledge that, despite my savvy, I fell for his artifice.

As a survivor, I move forward, stronger, taller, sharing my human traits of empathy and caring with those who deserve it—traits men like Dexter can only fake. As a survivor, I reclaim my power, restore my self-worth, and watch my tormentor shrivel into nothing.

THE AFTERMATH 101

Welcome to Surviving Abuse 101, chapter 5. So, you've managed to survive a toxic partnership and its related cognitive dissonance. You are probably beating yourself up for remaining entangled within what you now recognize was an unhealthy, manipulative dynamic. You may ponder how a world-wise, intelligent person like yourself could remain in a situation where not only were your emotional needs disregarded, but you also suffered from an onslaught of mental, emotional, and perhaps physical abuse. Today, we discuss trauma bonding.

ooo

I learned a new term today, although I wish I didn't need it. Trauma bonding is a form of "Stockholm syndrome," a concept I learned in my high school psychology class. The term was coined after a 1973 bank robbery in Sweden where hostages developed inexplicable attachments to their captors, even defending the perpetrators after they were released. *Who would do that?* know-it-all high school Julie scoffed. Now, I understand—anyone caught in a trauma bond.

Trauma bonding is an insidious phenomenon where a strong bond develops between the abuser and the abused. It's a twisted mix of love and dependency toward the offender, coupled with fear and anxiety from the harm being perpetrated. This bond often occurs in intense scenarios of prolonged, repeated mistreatment, like hostage situations or cults.

It can also manifest in relationships with emotionally manipulative partners, through a cycle of reward and punishment, with the perpetrator providing moments of kindness, support, or respite, mixed with explosive anger, abuse, or neglect. These cycles are also called love bombing and devaluation. This intermittent play of positive and negative interactions first creates and then strengthens the trauma bond as the suffering partner remains invested in the relationship, hoping for a return to the sunny days of early courtship. For me, this dynamic played itself out with a week of Dexter's sweet side to keep me hooked, followed by two weeks of angry outbursts or the silent treatment. That constant admixture of highs and lows kept me tethered to him, while I hoped that each following week would be better, recalling our early November and December love-bombing days.

These ongoing cycles of love/reward and anger/withdrawal/punishment created a powerful brain cocktail that resulted in my "addiction" to the wolf's toxicity, despite the glaringly negative aspects of the relationship—the reason I stuck around when any rational person would have left after the "Valentine's Day Massacre."

It was a drug addiction. When we chugged along swimmingly, I was getting high on pleasure chemicals like oxytocin, dopamine, and serotonin. Dexter would then lash out or pull away seemingly for no justifiable reason, leaving me empty, depleted, and jonesing for another hit of the good stuff.

Welcome to Brain Chemicals Anonymous.

"Hi, my name is Julie and I'm an addict."

"Hi, Julie."

Typically, in the beginning of toxic love, there are long stretches of affection/sex/reward sprinkled with small doses of anger and pulling away. As the relationship continues, the punishments and withdrawals outnumber any positive encounters, resulting in a roller coaster of psychological turmoil perhaps unmatched by any previous relationship.

When Dexter emailed me a year later in feigned contrition, I responded, labeling our time together a *"toxic mind-fuck like nothing I've ever experienced in my dating history."* That was not hyperbole. Rather than feeling horrified, Dexter probably wore that label like a badge of honor: "I am the crème de la crème at fucking and then fucking up women."

Those who have grown up within a challenging family environment, like I did, are even more susceptible to trauma bonding, where unhealthy dynamics feel like a normal part of any relationship. It felt all too familiar—each argument with Dexter flashing me back to the near-nightly family tension around the dinner table.

Like many in my situation, I blamed myself, taking Dexter's criticisms to heart—was my character in need of molding? I hid the truth from others, clinging to the hope that things would return to the "normal" of those early months. They never did. Finally telling everyone who would listen about my experience was the step I needed toward moving on.

A MESSAGE TO HIS NEXT PARTNER

Please don't hesitate to IM me.

I'll be there for you after your first disagreement, when he seems overly sensitive to a minor misunderstanding. Or after the next few, when he's unjustifiably upset and leaves you wondering what happened to your perfect relationship and near-perfect boyfriend. Or after the next wave, when he begins gaslighting you, making you feel crazy, and he questions *your* character. When these arguments last for days—or even weeks—and he throws everything you ever did or said back in your face, unwilling to listen to reason and bringing you to tears. When you have to be the first to apologize just to end the battles, and you justify staying because you've convinced yourself the good times outweigh the bad on this roller coaster of emotion.

Please don't hesitate to IM me once you notice he's detached about things going on in your life that aren't about him. After you discover he lied—about everything, including his feelings for you. When you're crushed by an account of his behavior while your head was turned the other way and when you hear rumors that he's already lining up his next partners, some of them possibly rumpling his sheets while you still share his bed. Once you learn about the one he calls his "work wife" and the purpose of his "naps." When you finally comprehend why the neighbor above glares at him and what she's witnessed.

Please don't hesitate to IM me when you wonder where that cute, charismatic, sensitive, boyish partner has gone. When friends warn you he's a narcissist and you protest, "Impossible. Every woman claims their ex has a personality disorder and, besides, men like that are flashy, strutting peacocks and, if I know one thing, he is not that." And then you Google something called "covert narcissism" and the description stops your heart; when you read words like "victim" and "emotional abuse" and you understand.

IM me—or call me, because I've been there, and I can help you heal.

PARASITE

It's easy to label Dexter a predator, file him under that classification, and move on. I use "wolf" to describe him because his behavior seems predatory. Does he not select his prey, groom them, lure them into his lair, consume their energy, and discard their emotional carcass, thoughtlessly moving to the next source with lupine disregard? Recently, though, I've begun envisioning Dexter less as a wily predator and more like an insentient parasite—a simple organism reliant on another being to make him feel whole. His ability to trick me stemmed partly from my lack of prior experience with such a self-serving, almost inhuman presence.

I notice, thanks to Google analytics, the parasite, or someone in his cadre, has been perusing my blog during a recent "boys' weekend," specifically the posts where I chronicle my discovery of the depth of his dishonesty. By "the depth of his dishonesty," I mean its unfathomableness. I only know the tip of the iceberg, and even that is a Mount Everest compared to an average person's molehill of deceits. I have no desire to uncover what lurks below the water line.

He must have pored over the words on my blog, prepping for his self-serving email that soon follows. Thoughts of me, of my blog, don't cross his mind unless there's an egocentric reason. From his first line of his transparent email, I surmise he wants something. I recognize the lurking of ulterior motives when I'm not annihilated for laying bare his shortcomings in a public forum. This is the same creature who lambasted me for forty-eight hours over texting him just nine words during a particularly hectic day. Instead of showing concern for my quietness with a simple, *"Is something wrong? Are you doing okay?"* he countered with his faithful friend—the silent treatment—and ground me down for the next two days until my fingers cramped from repeatedly texting, *"I'm sorry."*

He considered my posts and then wrote, parroting back what I said about him, or at least the morsels he could swallow.

"I know I'm not your favorite person. My flaws abound and I have issues, but I come in peace."

What do you want?

"I'm sorry for the harm my actions caused you. The things you heard would have caused anyone distress."

Bullshit, your smokescreen of feigned regret no longer blinds me to your manipulations.

"I wish I'd had the chance to tell you my side before it got filtered."

Filtered, my ass. If you had been honest from the start, there would be no need to tell your side. Own it—you lied from the beginning and you got caught. After I uncovered your first set of lies, I asked for your side, *begged* you even, and you chose to remain mute. I am no longer your fool. This is just a manipulative technique of blatantly denying, even in the face of irrefutable evidence. You just need a Donald Trump swirly-cone hairstyle.

"I had no idea about the impact this would have on you, and for that I'm sorry too."

Sorry isn't in your emotional repertoire, unless it's for yourself. Enough already—what do you want? Just get to the point.

"I've told [our friends] and others that I'll be accepting future party invites. Perhaps you and I can pause or end our cold war between now and then. If you'd rather not interact and would prefer to leave things as is, I'll understand. Thank you, Julie. I hope this finds you well."

Ah-ha, there it is…five sentences in. You've got FOMO, after declining party invitations in an effort to avoid me. I'm not going anywhere, so you're forced to make nice.

"Dex,

Thank you for reaching out. We agree on this. I don't wish to cause [our friends] consternation regarding who accepts their invitations. Parties should be celebrations, not complications. We share friends. If you and I attend a party, my hope is that we interact in a manner that makes everyone present comfortable.

For me, there is no cold war to end…"

My concession purely for the sake of our friends.

HOOVER

Hoover: A manipulative behavior aimed at drawing someone back into one's life—not necessarily romantically—often after a period of distance.

The inevitable hoover. Why did I convince myself this part of the process would bypass me? Is it hubris, thinking I have the psychology figured out, that I've implemented all necessary foils to ensure the hoover will never breach my ramparts? Or a miniscule flicker of hope I am wrong in my armchair diagnosis— that I survived something else entirely? Could it be my belief I am not empathetic enough to warrant a hoover or not worthy of one, fueled by my constant self-doubt of my own value? How ridiculous is that magical thinking? It isn't about special- ness. It is simply about a dose of energy, positive or negative, substantial or slight, continuous or a one-time top-up, from anyone or anything within reach. These creatures don't discriminate.

If they are genuinely unaware of what they are and what they do, how do they instinctively know the well-documented phases of Idealize, Devalue, Discard, Hoover? At the moment their dark personality begins to take shape, is this behav- ior downloaded into their brains like Neo in *The Matrix*? Phrases such as "I have changed," "I have demons," and "It's not my fault, but yours, that I behaved that way" trip effortlessly off their tongues.

That first message from Dexter, which arrived just shy of a year after our breakup, is benign, couched in remorseful words that held no actual regret, informing me of his future attendance at mutual friends' parties. I reply with my newly learned "grey-rock" approach: a reply so uninteresting that it warrants, I hope, no follow-up from him, ending further discussion.

Three weeks pass before the next message appears. This time, inquiring about my previous cancer diagnosis—a subject seeming of zero interest to him at the time, now suddenly it has *"Been on my mind since you shared the hard news long ago."* I know the rules; I shouldn't engage. But knowing the rules and following them are two different things. I offer another grey-rock response and should leave it alone right there.

Leave it alone. Leave it alone. Leave it alone, my gut croons.

Instead, I'm emboldened to speak frankly to Dexter, about his qualities both good and bad and the futility of contacting me under the guise of friendship. A niggling humiliation has rested within my gut all these months…of my gullibility and blindness. Although scared of his potential reaction to my words, this is my chance to reclaim another sliver of power by saying, "I see you. I see you more clearly than you will ever see yourself."

"This note is written with both warmth and kindness, but above all, honesty, and I hope you hear it that way. I, too, come in peace. I meant what I said about there being no cold war. You have some great characteristics—you're charming, charismatic, and you have a good sense of humor. And, although I'm not an expert, I also think you have a personality disorder, as you know. These recent emails are good examples of textbook definitions, only solidifying my belief. We all have coping mechanisms and, regrettably, I'm fairly certain you developed a severe one that damages people around you, especially women.

Those with this disorder are known to do whatever is necessary to get what they want: lie, cheat, as well as fake emotions they are incapable of feeling. Some will do much worse and most cannot admit they even have a problem. Another tragic aspect of this disorder is that there is no known treatment—drugs and therapy do not work, and people usually get worse, rather than better, as they age. I have compassion for your situation; you've been dealt a shitty hand and, yet, I have greater compassion for myself and the others who got close enough to suffer by knowing you.

Add your adherence to the misogynistic ideologies of MGTOW/Red Pill/Alpha Males and I am acutely aware that your recent words of contrition and healing amount to nothing. If allowed, you will cause further damage. I told you in the beginning that honesty was the most important thing to me and, accordingly, I have no room for your duplicity. So, it's in my interest to keep you relegated to a tangential acquaintance based on shared friendships. Whether you believe what I wrote above or not, contact with me is futile. I've heard too much, I've seen too much, I know too much to ever be swayed.

We'll likely cross paths at parties and, at that time, I plan on being cordial as we discussed. Take care, Dex
—Julie"

His response is classic Dexter: guilt-tripping, triangulation with people both specific, like Nadine, and vague, implying mutual friends are talking trash about me, using the third person, *"people say"* and *"people have told me,"* but he still sees the *"good"* in me.

He patronizes and minimizes his culpability, labeling my belief that he exhibits signs of a personality disorder as just *"venting hurt feelings"* and declaring, *"I understand the difference and don't fault you."* Dexter includes veiled threats about lawsuits for what I've written. *"It's also been suggested by more than one person that I read the blog and keep screenshots in case I need to take legal action, but I trust we won't go down that road."* I've cherry-picked these comments, but the tree hangs heavy with juicy fruit, ripe for harvesting.

Pop Quiz: List the manipulation techniques[1] employed by Dexter in each of the following sentences (ten points each):

1. *"I send these remarks in a hopeful spirit you'll listen, though it currently seems you're beyond hearing me."* Answer: <u>Gaslighting, Blaming</u>

2. *"I understand this version of me does not fit your narrative, and as such you're unlikely to change your view. I hear what you've said here and can appreciate how it*

---

[1]Answers provided by ChatGPT

relates to you, but it's fair to say your experience with me is in the minority. Just as most people who meet you find you delightful, whimsical, and free-spirited, some of us have experienced other sides. I still see the good in you, regardless of your actions since our split." Answer: <u>Projection, Gaslighting, Minimization, Flattery</u>

3. *"Your words are hard to read, hard in the sense that you seem unable or unwilling to acknowledge people do change. As I said, this version of me doesn't fit your narrative so I understand your reluctance."* Answer: <u>Blaming, Gaslighting, Minimization</u>

4. *"It's a strange scorecard you keep in how you forgive, Julie."* Answer: <u>Guilt-Tripping</u>

5. *"Unfortunately, if we'd cleared up the timeline of what happened it could have saved some headache, but your knee-jerk reaction to side with her made it impossible to get my day in court."* Answer: <u>Blaming, Guilt-Tripping, Victimhood</u>

I recognize I'm getting caught up again in his manipulations, feeding Dexter the energy he seeks. I attempt to end it here, nipping the conversation in the bud, convincing him I want to take one step at a time. I tell him that if I'm comfortable with the emotional progress he professes and if I believe a renewed friendship will be beneficial, I'll reach out to discuss next steps. He agrees wholeheartedly, responding, *"That's fair and agreeable, and I honor your role in that decision."*

Score—I have won at his game for once, affording myself a reprieve of six months, if not a year or, dare I say, indefinitely. Yet, a handful of days later, he emails again. An expert in narcissistic behavior has noted the laziness of this breed and how they tend to recycle the same text or email to various targets. Right from the playbook, Dexter sends the same email to two people—Nadine, the friend he triangulated me against, but who became my close friend, and yours truly. We're like one of those Hollywood couples getting their own portmanteau like Bennifer or Brangelina. Just call us Judine. More realistically, Dexter likely views us as interchangeable pawns in his game—Julie's thoughts are Nadine's and vice versa. To him, women are probably all the same…Charm one into forgiveness and the other will follow.

This message appears to express what sounds like genuine remorse and earnest desire for reconciliation. But I know better. Just six days earlier, Dexter had labeled Nadine as *"mean, inconsiderate, and dishonest."* Now he is asking for healing and reconnection? Comparing his two messages, I am immediately transported out of The Dexter Zone and back into reality.

If Dexter can effortlessly move from calling Nadine those slurs from the left side of his mouth while asking her for reconciliation from his right, I can only imagine how he paints me to his friends while simultaneously trying to convince me he's changed.

He hasn't changed, not one bloody bit.

LINE IN THE SAND

Insanity is doing the same thing over and over and expecting different results.
—Albert Einstein

It takes this sham of a relationship, my most recent chronologically, and the guidance of a therapist to finally stretch my hand out, grab the brass ring, and hop off the relentless carousel of dating insanity. After a particularly illuminating session, I race home and feverishly type up my "Line in the Sand" requirements for my next healthy relationship. Each of us is responsible for drawing our own line, but it is crucial to have one and stick to it, no matter how charming the man in front of us may seem.

I Deserve:

- A loving partner who provides encouragement, comfort, safety, and makes me feel cherished and valued
- Someone who is whole, not damaged or broken. I'm not here to fix anyone smashed in a million pieces
- A man who doesn't set off my "Spidey-sense"
- A truthful boyfriend whose words hold up under scrutiny
- A companion who is loyal to me and our relationship
- A partner who does not play childish games
- Someone with an overall positive outlook on life
- A person free from disorders and serious past or present addictions (aka the Dexter bullet)

I deserve to no longer be distracted by something shiny or entangled in old patterns that don't work—have never worked—for me.

DEXTER

the recipes

5-MINUTE PEANUT BUTTER MOUSSE

Yield: 2 servings

This is another one of my "Down and Dirty" recipes. I'm not above scooping a large blob of peanut butter from the jar and licking it directly off the spoon, but this is even better. This fluffy peanut butter mousse can be whipped up in a flash and will satisfy the biggest peanut butter fan's craving. Full confession: I usually scoop the mousse from the mixing bowl directly into my open maw.

Ingredients
- ½ cup heavy whipping cream
- ¼ cup (generous) peanut butter
- 3 tablespoons confectioners' (powdered) sugar
- Chocolate shavings or flaky sea salt, such as Maldon (optional)

Directions
1. In a medium bowl, using electric beaters, beat heavy whipping cream, peanut butter, and confectioners' sugar until fully combined and the texture of a fluffy mousse. Serve in dessert glasses sprinkled with chocolate shavings or flaky sea salt (optional) or eat directly from the bowl (I won't tell).

COCONUT PECAN BROWNIE BUTTONS

Yield: 16 cookies

Ingredients
- ½ cup sweetened shredded coconut
- 1 cup toasted pecans
- ⅓ cup granulated sugar
- 2 tablespoons cocoa powder
- ⅛ teaspoon kosher salt
- 1 large egg white
- ½ teaspoon vanilla extract

Directions
1. Place shredded coconut in the bowl of a food processor and pulse until finely chopped. Remove coconut and set aside.
2. Place pecans in the bowl and pulse until finely chopped. Add sugar, cocoa powder, and salt. Process until combined. Add egg white and vanilla extract and process until dough comes together. Transfer to a medium bowl, spread into a thin layer, cover, and freeze dough for about 30 minutes for easier handling.
3. Preheat oven to 350°F. Line a baking sheet with parchment paper or a silicone sheet. Roll small teaspoons of the dough into balls (about 14 grams each). Roll each ball in reserved coconut and place on the baking sheet. Bake 12-15 minutes until coconut is lightly toasted and cookies are barely firm to the touch (you want the outside crisp, but the inside fudge-like). Cool 5 minutes on baking sheet then transfer to cooling rack and cool completely. These are best eaten the day they are made.

CHOCOLATE CHIP PANCAKES
WITH MACERATED STRAWBERRIES   *Yield: 4 large or 6 small pancakes*

Ingredients

Macerated Strawberries

- 8 to 10 strawberries, hulled and sliced
- 2 teaspoons granulated sugar
- 1 tablespoon orange liqueur (optional)

Pancakes

- 1 cup all-purpose flour
- 3 tablespoons granulated sugar
- 2 teaspoons baking powder
- ¼ teaspoon kosher salt
- 1 cup milk, milk alternative, or water
- 1 large egg, beaten
- 1 tablespoon canola oil
- ⅓ cup mini chocolate morsels

Topping

- ¼ cup salted or unsalted butter, melted
- Lightly sweetened freshly whipped cream
- ¼ cup chopped, toasted pecans

Directions

1. Macerate strawberries: Combine strawberries, sugar, and orange liqueur (if using) in a small bowl. Set aside for 30 minutes.

2. Make pancakes: In a medium bowl, stir together flour, sugar, baking powder, and salt. In a liquid measuring cup, stir together milk, beaten egg, and oil. Pour liquid ingredients over dry and stir just until combined. It's okay if a few lumps remain. Let rest 5 minutes. You can pour the batter back into the measuring cup for easy pouring onto the griddle.

3. Preheat a griddle or nonstick skillet over medium-high heat. Lightly coat the surface with cooking spray or a small amount of butter.

4. Pour batter on the griddle for each pancake and sprinkle about 1 tablespoon of mini chocolate morsels across the batter. Cook until bubbles form on the surface of the pancake and the edges begin to look set, about 2-3 minutes. Flip the pancake and cook for an additional 1-2 minutes, or until the other side is golden brown. Remove the pancake from the griddle and keep warm. Repeat with the remaining batter.

5. To serve, drizzle with butter, cover with macerated strawberries and accumulated juice. Top with whipped cream and chopped, toasted pecans. To make whipped cream: Beat together 1 cup heavy whipping cream and 2 tablespoons confectioners' sugar until soft peaks form.

THE INFAMOUS
RICH GERMAN CHOCOLATE CAKE

Yield: 12-14 servings

The darkest, richest German Chocolate Cake you'll ever find. This recipe calls for a teaspoon of instant coffee granules. The cake will taste fine without adding, but a hint of coffee amplifies chocolate flavor and adds complexity. Nothing wrong with that. I take some satisfaction in knowing I never made that promised cake for Dexter. Instead, I've saved it for those truly deserving of the love I mix into every bite.

Ingredients
Filling
- 1½ cups pecans, chopped
- 2½ cups sweetened shredded coconut
- ½ cup (1 stick) unsalted butter, cut into pieces
- ½ teaspoon kosher salt
- 1 cup heavy whipping cream
- 1 cup granulated sugar
- 3 large egg yolks

Chocolate Ganache Frosting
- 10 ounces (scant 1¾ cups) semisweet chocolate morsels
- 1 tablespoon light corn syrup
- 1 cup heavy whipping cream

Cake
- 2¼ cups all-purpose flour
- 2 cups granulated sugar
- 1 cup unsweetened cocoa powder
- 1 teaspoon instant coffee granules (optional)
- 2 teaspoons baking soda
- ½ teaspoon kosher salt
- 2 cups cold water
- ⅔ cup canola oil
- 1 tablespoon vanilla extract
- 2 teaspoons white vinegar

Directions

1. Make filling: Toast chopped pecans and coconut in a large skillet over a medium-high heat, stirring constantly, about 8 minutes or until coconut begins to brown and nuts become fragrant. Scrape into a medium bowl to cool.

2. In a large bowl, combine the butter, salt, and cooled toasted pecan-coconut mixture. Set aside.

3. In a medium saucepan, whisk together the heavy whipping cream, sugar, and egg yolks. Heat the cream mixture, stirring constantly, until it begins to thicken and reaches 170°F. Pour cream mixture over the pecans and coconut and stir until butter melts. Cool to room temperature (mixture will thicken as it cools). If the filling is still too runny, place in the refrigerator for about 15 minutes.

4. Make chocolate ganache: Place chocolate, corn syrup, and heavy whipping cream in a medium microwave-safe bowl. Microwave on high for about 90 seconds, stirring every 30 seconds until chocolate is completely smooth. Cool to room temperature.

5. Make cake: While filling and frosting are cooling, preheat oven to 350°F. Line three 8-inch cake pans with parchment paper and lightly grease paper.

6. In a large bowl, sift together flour, sugar, cocoa powder, instant coffee granules (if using), baking soda, and salt. In a liquid measuring cup, combine water, oil, vanilla extract, and vinegar. Slowly whisk wet ingredients into dry ingredients. The batter will appear very wet.

7. Pour the batter into the prepared pans and bake for about 20 minutes or until a tester inserted in the center of the cake comes out clean. Cool in the pans for 15 minutes, then invert onto cooling racks, carefully remove parchment paper, and cool completely.

8. Make frosting: Beat chocolate ganache for about 3 minutes until it's light and of spreading consistency.

9. Place the first cake layer on a cake plate. Spread the top with ⅓ of the pecan-coconut mixture. Continue layering the cake and filling, finishing with a layer of the pecan-coconut mixture on top. Frost the sides of the cake with the chocolate ganache frosting and pipe a decorative border around the pecan-coconut filling on top. Chill. Remove from refrigerator 10 minutes before serving to allow cake and frosting to soften slightly.

CHOCOLATE PEANUT SALTED CARAMEL TART   *Yield: 8-10 servings*

A silky combination of dark chocolate, peanuts, and buttery salted caramel come together in this showstopper of a dessert.

Ingredients
- Easy Shortbread Shell
- 1 cup heavy whipping cream
- 1 cup salted caramel, plus more for garnish (jarred or homemade)
- 4 large egg yolks
- 4 ounces bittersweet chocolate, chopped (at least 60% cocoa)
- ⅓ cup (rounded) creamy peanut butter (not natural style, which will separate)
- ½ cup roasted salted peanuts, chopped, plus more for garnish
- Sweetened freshly whipped cream, for garnish

Directions
1. Make shortbread shell: See Easy Shortbread Shell recipe for directions.
2. Make filling: In a medium saucepan, bring heavy whipping cream and salted caramel to simmer. Don't boil. In a medium bowl, whisk egg yolks and then whisk cream mixture into yolks slowly, whisking constantly to avoid curdling egg yolks. Return mixture to saucepan and cook over medium heat, whisking constantly until temperature registers 170°F or until thickened. Remove from heat and whisk in chocolate and then peanut butter until melted and fully incorporated.
3. Sprinkle cooled shell with roasted salted peanuts. Pour filling through a sieve (to catch any lumps or curdled yolks) over peanuts. Chill, uncovered, until set, at least 2 hours. Garnish with sweetened whipped cream, additional drizzled caramel, and peanuts. To make whipped cream: Beat together 1 cup heavy whipping cream and 2 tablespoons confectioners' sugar until soft peaks form. Keep tart chilled until ready to serve.

eleven

THE ELEPHANT
Present Day

A VISIT

(Forceful knocking at the door)

"Go awaaayyy. I'm busy writing and don't want whatever it is you're selling. Can't you see the blatantly unambiguous handprinted sign, 'Don't knock or ring bell'? Thank yooouuu."

(Insistent tapping at the window)

"What the fu...Dad? Is that you? You've been dead for two decades. This makes no sense. Why are you here?"

"Well, Julie, if you let me in, I'll tell you."

"I can't right now. You need to stay in the background. I'm writing about boyfriends and trying to find a good man, not my childhood boogeymen. You don't belong here. Wait for the next book. You have to stay out."

"God dammit, will you listen to me for a minute, Julie? I'm going to stand here, rapping, tapping, and calling your name until you let me in. You won't have any luck finishing that book until you hear me out."

(Opening door)

"Okay, fine, come on in...What?"

"Do you know why the tower at Pisa leans?"

"Ugh, seriously? What does that have to do with me, my boyfriends, this book? I need to focus on this project. You've held enough space in my head all these years."

"I'll ask you again. Do you know why the tower at Pisa leans?"

"Fine. Yes, I think so. It has something to do with the ground..."

"Exactly. The debacle started with the foundation. The tower's substructure started unevenly settling owing to shifting soil beneath. The Italian builders could already see the lean by the time the third story stood complete. As they constructed the next four stories, the so-called 'chief engineer' attempted to compensate for the tilt by adding extra masonry to the shorter side. Any engineer worth his salt would know the additional weight would cause the building to lean even further—which it did. If I was around, I would have told the idiot his 'solution' would never work. The tower's slant increased over the next seven centuries as the ground underneath continued to sink. Total collapse was on the horizon, and only through modern engineering techniques using extraordinary measures have they managed to stabilize the tower and stop the sinking. Why do I tell you this?"

"I don't know, Dad. Why?"

"Because I'm here to explain why you'll never succeed in constructing a lasting monument to love: you're building on a childhood of quicksand.

"I've never been one to mince words, so listen up. The intrinsically unstable foundation I provided in your youth ensures an irreversible lean to your tower. I'm not to blame. I merely passed on what I endured. Do you think my upbringing was a piece of cake? You have no idea how good you had it. I was born and spent my early years in a hardscrabble one-room shack surrounded by desolate fields outside LA. My strict German father focused on his work and our survival, not on coddling. Your grandmother was forced to continuously abandon me to convalesce after each of her miscarriages…and there were seven or eight miscarriages throughout my childhood. I dearly loved my mother, longing to be near her nurturing. I am an admixture of these spartan beginnings, sprinkled with the order and discipline of military life in later years, the residual effects of fighting and surviving two wars, and, frankly, the niggling doubt you were my biological kid."

"Yeah, Dad, I'm aware."

"My adherence to honor and duty remains unimpeachable. I provided you the essentials any child needs: food, housing, doctors, clothing. Occasionally, I even managed the rare moment of kindness toward you. Not 'fatherly support,' but that was your fault—you just weren't very likeable. Don't you remember the handful of times I took you, age thirteen or so, to explore the local tide pools near Laguna Beach? And four years later, when you were seventeen and not yet driving, didn't I pick you up from your work, like I did with your middle sister?

"Unfortunately for you, the essentials were not enough. If you had a disposition more like your two sisters, I would have striven to provide all you needed.

"You yearned for me to love you. You sought a sense of safety in my presence rather than intimidation. You wanted me to buoy you, as if I was capable of any of that. I watched you flinch and tremble when I loomed over you, my explosive anger bubbling out, spilling down upon your young head. Determined to break you, I never held back, mocking you by calling you 'stupid' and 'ugly.' You were too young, too naive to recognize my subtle eroding with systematic gaslighting, criticizing, judging.

"When our dog would bite you, I'd order you not to cry because it was *your* fault, whether you provoked him or not. Who cares if you were only four or five years old? There's also that time I insisted you were neglecting your pet rat, even though, at twelve, you diligently fed him daily and cleaned his cage weekly, more than most kids your age would do. I told you I was going to kill him by throwing him against the back cinderblock wall and I would have, too, if your mother didn't intervene.

"I taunted you, asserting your older sister deserved a horse, yet I couldn't afford one at the time, and although I could afford one when you asked, you were unworthy of such a gift. If my attention turned to you, it was rarely for praise. I was waiting and watching, gleefully, for opportunities to belittle you. You'd look up while playing with your Barbies or watching TV, taking the temperature of my moods, the fingers of fear tightening around your scrawny little neck when I was near, terrified of the one person who was supposed to be your hero.

"I am a hero in battle. I don't seek a child's idolatry.

"After this twenty-one-year atmosphere of denigration and devaluation, I ensured you'd doubt your worth and shut your heart to cope with my lack of love. Naturally your framework for love is unsound. I wasn't built to show you compassion. I made you strong. I made you independent. I made you self-reliant. You'll need those essential traits because it's doubtful you'll ever possess the 'extraordinary measures' to right your leaning tower.

"Besides, it wasn't all bad. We both softened once you turned about twenty-two, once you became a cog in the wheel of society, with your sensible office job and your first home. Or was the change because I finally escaped that terrible, loveless marriage to your mother I was trapped inside? Coincidentally, that's also about the time your middle sister showed me an old photo of my beloved mother and claimed you resembled her. I was never sure if your sister genuinely saw the likeness or said it to soften the hardness between us. After that, my doubts about your parentage faded. We began talking, showing kindness, exchanging hugs. You and I managed, in the last dozen years of my life, to cobble together a relationship of mutual respect and some pseudo version of familial love.

"Yet, I'm aware the damage remains—the crumbling ground I provided in your formative years ensures any future 'towers' of affection you build remain untenable."

"Okay, hold up, Dad. This doesn't even sound like you. When did you find all this self-awareness?"

"I'm dead. Once you're dead, there's not much else to do in oblivion but think. In the years since, I've watched you blindly cycle through the same types of men, either searching for the polar opposite of me or men too similar to me, neither of whom will provide what you seek. Throughout the process, you feel unworthy of genuine love, choosing dysfunctional options because an unhealthy dynamic feels familiar to you—thanks to me. An unstable foundation built upon unsound ground will ensure every future misaligned relationship, each story in your tower, leans a fraction further from plumb.

"Once you understand how I've affected you, the patterns in your life will make sense, and you can begin to move on."

ooo

In the aftermath of my father's visit, a realization dawns over the undulating landscape of my romantic life. Just like in childhood, I made myself small, devaluing my worth and diminishing myself to fit the ideal of these romantic partners—or who I thought they wanted me to be. But I was never meant to recede. I sensed I was never truly the woman these men sought, but my unease rarely stemmed from their opinion—it was about my own. Precariously balanced on quicksand of self-doubt and unmet needs—a structure destined to lean and falter—I attempted to shrink.

A twig is easier to balance than a tree.

This crumbled base provided by my childhood ensured my attempts at love and connection were doomed to lean further off-kilter—reflecting an inherently flawed design.

Now, I see that I must build my own framework, one that is solid and enduring. I can no longer rely on the "engineers"—those men scaffolded my life temporarily but never provided any true support. Jason wasn't capable, preferring to linger in the plaza, lost in his sonnets to my tower's gracefully arched blind arcades and engaged columns. Brett was ill equipped for the job, his tower leaning at an angle worse than mine, while Edmond, despite his professed desires, hesitated at the sight of a hammer. Dexter, meanwhile, seemed intent to topple my tower and watch the pieces shatter to the ground. I've fired them all from my emotional worksite and taken charge of my own construction. The platform I need is one I must build myself—significant, solid, and enduring, like the Great Pyramid itself.

THE ELEPHANT

family recipes

SALTED CARAMEL BANANA CREAM PIE

Yield: 8-10 servings

Layers of buttery caramel gild the lily on an updated version of my mom's original recipe, my father's favorite.

Ingredients
Crust
- ¼ cup (½ stick) unsalted butter
- ½ cup shortening
- 1 large egg white
- 1 tablespoon cold water
- 1½ teaspoons white vinegar
- 1½ cups all-purpose flour
- ½ teaspoon kosher salt

Filling
- 3 cups whole milk
- ½ cup granulated sugar, divided
- ¾ teaspoon kosher salt
- 3 tablespoons cornstarch
- 3 tablespoons all-purpose flour
- 3 large egg yolks, beaten
- 1½ teaspoons vanilla extract
- ½ cup thick salted caramel sauce (homemade or purchased), plus more for drizzling
- 3-4 ripe bananas, sliced just before using
- 1½ cups heavy whipping cream
- ¼ cup confectioners' (powdered) sugar

Directions
1. Make crust: Chill butter and shortening until very cold by placing both in the freezer for 15 minutes. Beat together egg white, water, and vinegar in a small bowl and set aside. Place flour and salt in the bowl of a food processor. Add chilled butter and shortening to flour and pulse until mixture resembles coarse meal (you can also combine the flour and fats using a pastry blender if you don't want to drag out your processor—more effort, less clean-up). Add egg mixture and pulse just until it begins to clump.

Don't overwork dough. Pat dough into a disk, wrap in cling film, and freeze for about 20 minutes to chill. (If you will not be using the dough within 45 minutes, chill in the refrigerator instead.)

2. Make filling: In a medium saucepan, heat milk, ¼ cup sugar, and salt over medium heat but do not boil. Blend cornstarch, all-purpose flour, and remaining ¼ cup sugar in a bowl. Stir yolks into sugar mixture. Pour hot milk over egg mixture slowly, whisking constantly, to avoid scrambling the eggs. Pour mixture back into saucepan. Cook over medium-low heat until thickened, about 8 minutes. Remove from heat. Stir in vanilla and push through a sieve (to catch any lumps) into a shallow pan. Cover with cling film touching surface of filling and chill.

3. Preheat oven to 350°F. Sprinkle dough with flour and then, between two sheets of parchment or waxed paper, roll out the dough, starting at the center and working your way out into a 11-inch to 12-inch circle. Once the dough is the correct size, peel off the top layer of paper and, using the bottom sheet, transfer the dough to a 9-inch pie dish. Flip the dough over, peel off the bottom sheet, and gently press the dough into the dish. Trim dough so the overhang beyond the pie plate lip is only about ½ inch. Fold edge under and crimp decoratively. If the dough is too soft, pop it back in the freezer for 15 minutes before baking.

4. To bake crust, cover with parchment paper and fill with pie weights, uncooked rice, or granulated sugar. Bake on the bottom rack for about 15 minutes or until crust just begins to color and looks dry. Carefully remove parchment and weights and return crust to oven for about 25 minutes until crust looks fully baked. Place on a cooling rack to cool.

5. Swirl ½ cup salted caramel on the bottom of the fully cooled pie crust. Cover with ⅓ of the filling and then a layer of sliced bananas. Cover bananas with another ⅓ layer of filling and another layer of sliced bananas. Top with the remaining ⅓ of the filling.

6. Beat together heavy whipping cream and confectioners' sugar until soft peaks form. Spread whipped cream over pie. Chill pie at least two hours before serving to allow flavors to meld and filling to fully set. Decorate with additional drizzled salted caramel.

Tip: If you cannot find salted caramel sauce, you can purchase regular caramel and add about ½ teaspoon flaky sea salt, such as Maldon.

MOM'S FRUIT KUCHEN

Yield: 12-16 servings

Kuchen means "cake" in German. I'm unsure where Mom found this recipe. It wasn't a passed-down generational dish, but something she must have discovered in one of her many cookbooks or women's magazines. She would make a fresh fruit kuchen for the family every week throughout summer.

Ingredients
- 2 large egg yolks
- ¼ cup cold water
- 1 cup (2 sticks) salted butter, cut in pieces and very cold
- 3 cups all-purpose flour
- ¼ cup granulated sugar
- Zest from one lemon
- Juice from one lemon
- Fruit filling (see below)

Directions

1. In a small bowl, beat together egg yolks and water. Cut butter into flour with a food processor (or by hand with a pastry blender) by pulsing on and off until butter is about the size of lentils.

2. Add egg mixture, sugar, lemon zest, and lemon juice to flour mixture and combine until it just begins to clump together (avoid overmixing). Evenly sprinkle dough into a jelly roll pan (10-inch by 12-inch or 10-inch by 14-inch) and pat into pan evenly. Chill dough for 30 minutes.

3. Make filling using options below: Preheat oven to 425°F. If you are using plums or peaches, lay sliced fruit in tight rows or, if using blueberries, scatter over dough until completely covered.

4. Beat egg and cream together and drizzle over fruit. Sprinkle with sugar and cinnamon or nutmeg. Bake on the bottom rack of the oven for about 25 minutes then transfer to the middle rack. Bake another 10 minutes until crust is golden brown, fruit is soft, and top is bubbling. Remove from oven and transfer to a cooling rack. Cut into squares once cool.

<u>Fruit Filling Options</u>

Plum (my favorite): 4 cups sliced plums, 2 large eggs, 3 tablespoons heavy whipping cream, 1½ cups granulated sugar, cinnamon.

Blueberry: 4 cups blueberries, 2 large eggs, 3 tablespoons heavy whipping cream, ½ cup granulated sugar, nutmeg.

Peach: 4 cups peeled and sliced peaches, 2 large eggs, 3 tablespoons heavy whipping cream, 1 cup granulated sugar, cinnamon.

twelve

MY FINAL DISH

"ARE YOU A PASTRY CHEF?" people would ask, admiring my professional-looking baked goods. This question always tripped me up, leading to a self-effacing, rambling response.

"No, not really. I make my living as an event manager, although I am, technically, a classically trained, nonpracticing chef…but not a pastry chef. Pastry is my passion, but I've never gone to pastry school, although I'd like to. Baking is a hobby."

Ramble, ramble, ramble. Why was it so difficult for me to acknowledge my merit, embrace my abilities, and answer, "Yes. Yes, I am."?

My siblings were the artists, bakers, musicians, and jewelry makers. I came along too late in our family to claim those titles without unwelcome comparisons. As a youngster, I enjoyed writing poetry, but a sibling or parent would quickly point out a spelling error, a problem with my punctuation, my unreadable left-handed scrawl.

I am not a writer, I decided.

It's difficult to soldier on as a child, especially when faced with criticism or lack of encouragement. In the kitchen, my mother was the cook, my middle sister the baker. They had little time or inclination to invite me to the counter and play teacher. To keep me out from under their feet, I was sometimes allowed to sift the flour. Our ancient sifter proved to be as challenging to maneuver as the hand grippers my brothers used to enhance their sports grip. My small hand would grip the sifter's stiff, spring-loaded handle, and I'd manage to pull it back about five times, but then my palm would turn beet red and my forearm would begin to ache. I'd take a few breaks but then give up.

I don't belong in the kitchen, I convinced myself.

I admired what others in my family created, from a distance. In eighth grade, I found myself in a panic when tasked with presenting a five-minute hands-on demonstration to my classmates. What could I possibly show them? I was accomplished at nothing. I had no talent. In the end, I settled on a tongue-in-cheek demonstration entitled "How to Make a Mud Pie," a playful nod to baking, a passion that still lay dormant within me.

Safer to poke fun at myself than put myself out there, I mused.

I am not a real baker.

Even after accomplishing my dream of culinary school at age forty-two, I still wouldn't call myself a chef, and certainly not a pastry chef. The other kitchen staff at the steakhouse where I worked cowed me, sensing my chef's whites hid my imposter syndrome beneath.

"The cookies need more salt," chef A would comment.

"Those cookies have too much salt," chef B would remark.

"Did you bake those enough?" a third would question.

A bustling kitchen full of testosterone is no place for a lack of confidence. Those who I hoped would be my brethren pounced on my hesitation.

I don't belong here, I told myself.

The artist inside me yearned to create, yet I held myself back, afraid to venture forth. So, is it any wonder I sought out the artists in my dating life? Painters, writers, musicians.

I *dated* artists. I wasn't an artist.

I became an appendage to their creativity, appreciating and nurturing their gifts while simultaneously burying mine even deeper. I "played" in the kitchen. I "fooled around" with words, calling them my pretty playthings. My self-doubt ran through my every corpuscle. I shielded my dreams behind men who weren't afraid to label themselves artists, whether they genuinely were or not.

Baking was a pastime. And writing? I was no writer. Jason, Edmond, Brett, even Dexter—they were the writers. I merely dabbled.

Julia Cameron, author of *The Artist's Way,* calls people like me "Shadow Artists." Inexplicably gravitating toward other creatives, shadow artists are unwilling to explore our own nascent talents due to fear, self-doubt, and outside influences. Yes, I posted on my blog, but most of the men I dated never knew of it or, if they did, I asked them not to read it.

"It's just a silly baking blog," I would demur, deflecting attention.

Then, after the Dexter debacle, something shifted within me. I was fed up with denying myself all that I deserved—and I was worthy of more than this feeble attempt at living a life as a shadow artist.

In the wake of Dexter and these other past experiences, I resolved to no longer remain ensnared in the cycle of self-deprecation and yearning for external validation, from my father, from my lovers. Once I found my footing, a burgeoning confidence began to crack me wide open.

Yet, it was only when I embarked on the task of writing this memoir that I truly felt compelled to step fully out from these shadows of my past. As I worked through each chapter, I began untangling these seemingly disparate relationships and held them up to the light, finally recognizing the patterns that had eluded me the entire time. I had been feeding off these men's creativity while harboring a persistent doubt that they, in turn, were capable of recognizing my worth.

Did *I* even see my true value then?

What a liberating revelation to discover that the creativity, as well as the love, I had been seeking externally were within me all along, waiting patiently for a chance to be born. The doubt that swirled about me was entirely of my own making. I had been living in the shadows of others, allowing my inner critic to sit on my shoulder far too long, dictating my worth and defining my creative journey.

But no more.

With newfound determination, I now embrace the realization that creativity is not limited to those with the confidence to flaunt it. The ability to make art resides within me as strongly as it does within them, chomping at the bit to be unleashed. I will most likely never possess the brash swagger of my fellow chefs and writers, but I refuse to be a shadow artist any longer. I have taken ownership of my passions and talents unapologetically.

Rather than writing an essay or short story, tiptoeing around the edges of creativity, I've plunged headfirst into the depths—a memoir and recipes. No half measures. I've wasted too much time. Of course, I still struggle against the weight of comparison and doubt, lingering remnants of my family dynamic, but I continue to return to the page daily. In the kitchen, I find joy in experimenting and creating sugary masterpieces that reflect my unique culinary voice and vision, evident in my orange-anise *Gibassier Cupcakes*. And with each story written and recipe perfected, I'm claiming my power, my strength, my voice, discovering the potential that has always resided within me, perhaps fully for the first time.

No longer content to be an appendage to anyone else's creativity, or to lean precariously, I'm stepping onto a sturdy stage of my own making, one that supports every facet of my life. I am not solely a writer and a baker—I am a creator, a force to be reckoned with. And from this moment on, I vow to shine brightly and proudly, as the artist of my own life.

GIBASSIER CUPCAKES

Yield: 12 cupcakes

These cupcakes are inspired by one of my favorite breakfast treats, a little-known pastry called Gibassier (pronounced zee-bah-see-ay). Originating from Provence, France, these yeasty little fists of dough are enriched with olive oil, subtly flavored with orange blossom water, and studded with candied orange peel and aniseed. For once, I'm showing restraint. When it comes to frosting, the cupcakes themselves are packed with so much flavor, they only need a light glaze and sprinkling of orange sugar for garnish.

Ingredients

Cupcakes

- 1½ cups all-purpose flour, plus 1 tablespoon for dredging the orange peel
- 1 cup granulated sugar
- ¾ teaspoon baking powder
- ¼ teaspoon baking soda
- ¼ teaspoon kosher salt
- ¾ cup buttermilk
- ¾ cup mild-tasting extra-virgin olive oil
- 2 large eggs, beaten
- 1 tablespoon orange blossom water (available online or at Middle Eastern markets)
- 1 teaspoon vanilla extract
- ½ cup high-quality or homemade candied orange peel, chopped into ¼-inch pieces
- 1½ teaspoons aniseed, toasted in a dry pan until fragrant and then slightly crushed

Orange Sugar and Glaze Topping

- ⅓ cup granulated sugar
- Zest from ½ large orange
- 1¼ cups confectioners'(powdered) sugar
- 1 tablespoon orange juice
- 1½ teaspoons orange blossom water

Directions

1. Preheat oven to 350°F. Line a 12-cup muffin tin with cupcake liners.
2. In a large bowl, whisk together flour, granulated sugar, baking powder, baking soda, and salt.
3. In a medium bowl, combine buttermilk and olive oil. Whisk in eggs, orange blossom water, and vanilla extract until fully combined.
4. Make a well in the center of the dry ingredients and gradually add the wet ingredients, mixing until there are no visible streaks of flour. Lumps are okay as long as they're not floury. Be careful not to overmix.
5. Blot candied orange peel dry with a paper towel and toss the pieces with 1 tablespoon flour. This will help peel remain suspended in the batter. Gently stir in the candied orange peel and aniseed to evenly distribute throughout the batter.
6. Divide the batter evenly among the cupcake liners, filling each about ¾ full. Bake for 20 minutes, or until a toothpick inserted into the center comes out clean. Let the cupcakes cool in the tin for about 5 minutes, then transfer them to a wire rack to cool completely.
7. Make orange sugar: In a small bowl, stir together granulated sugar and orange zest. Set aside.
8. Make glaze: In a medium bowl, combine confectioners' sugar, orange juice, and orange blossom water and stir. Add additional orange juice, if needed, until glaze reaches a thick yet dippable consistency.
9. Dip tops of cupcakes in glaze, then dip in orange sugar. Let glaze dry 20-30 minutes before serving.

Homemade Candied Orange Peel (Optional)

Ingredients
- Peel from 1 very large or 2 medium oranges, including the white pith, cut off in wide strips with a knife
- 1 cup granulated sugar
- ¾ cup water
- ¼ cup light corn syrup

Directions
1. Place peel in a medium pot of cold water, bring to boil, and drain. Repeat this process twice more.
2. After the final drain, combine granulated sugar, water, and corn syrup in the empty pot. Bring to boil. Once the sugar has melted, add drained peel. Reduce to simmer and poach for 1 hour or until the pith is translucent.
3. Cool peel in the sugar syrup. If not using within 24 hours, store peel in syrup in refrigerator.

EPILOGUE:
JASON

July 23, 2010 – *The San Diego Union-Tribune*

MAN DIES AFTER JUMP FROM BALBOA PARK BRIDGE

A man died Friday after he leaped from El Prado [Cabrillo] bridge and plunged to the southbound shoulder of State Route 163, authorities said.

The man's identity was not immediately known.

A witness called 911 shortly after 3 p.m. to report that someone may have jumped midspan from the freeway overcrossing in Balboa Park. Another witness reported seeing someone lying next to the freeway southbound lanes, police Sgt. Ray Battrick said.

Officers found the man's body in the ice plant along the shoulder, Battrick said. The California Highway Patrol blocked the right lane for a short time during the investigation.

RETURN TO SENDER

My Darling Mr. Oxblood,

The email arrived today, like a heavy boot-kick to an already wounded dog. Nathan shared the dreadful news…you died Friday night—underneath the Cabrillo Bridge in Balboa Park. He said they're unsure whether you fell or jumped. My heart, or rather your heart still residing within me, knows it's the latter. First my mother's final breath and now yours. Two deaths in two days.

Did you visit the rose garden first? It's probably exultant this time of year. Did you bury your nose deep within the huge, heady heirlooms? Did you pull handfuls of petals from the blossoms, scattering them about yourself, on the pathway, in the fountain? Did you tuck one in your breast pocket as you did the night of our very first visit? Did they find this ephemeral souvenir when they found your crumpled body below? Was your fateful choice a sudden caprice, a response to a melody, an errant ray of sun, or the wind's whisper in your ear? Could I have stopped you?

My unanswered questions scratch like grit within my throat.

I have no choice but to accept I can never tell you, a million times, "I am sorry." I was never enough for you. I could never nudge you, show you how exquisite you truly were. Shackled by reality, I watched from afar as you floated in your illusory dreamscape. Could you feel the depths of my love? Anything short of carving your name into my very skin and you'd remain unconvinced. If I could but conjure a woman to meet your ideals, to care for you like I never could. (If I could have been that woman), would that have saved you?

It wasn't easy for you here. I wish on a blanket of stars there was some other way. I do, however, understand your choice. The day you jumped, a piece of my heart fell to its death with you.

With My Love,
Miss Prussian Blue

GRIEF

Insidious grief has settled in beside me, snuggled against my body like a cat preparing for a long nap. He skulks over my shoulder, in shadow, just out of sight and grasp. I feel his presence, catching his movements from the corner of my eye. He stares at me across the kitchen table, robbing me of my hunger, as my *Pad Thai* remains untouched. Like a lover, he spoons me in bed at night, loosely draping his arm across my waist and whispering in my ear until well past 2 a.m.

I cannot sleep.

He pokes at me as I attempt to read the novel opened in my lap and waits patiently for me while I distractedly stare at *Chopped* on television. He interrupts when I try to speak, leaving choking words within my throat. He is my passenger on my morning commute and sits across my desk throughout the day, waiting for 5:00 p.m. so he can have me to himself again.

Jealous and possessive and relentless grief.

TEN YEARS LATER: WANDER

I long to wander Balboa Park, alone, and ask this witness of profound affections to teach me what she knows about Love.

I spent time within her bosom just shy of a year ago, wan and unsteady, remnants of a lovers' row with Dexter the night before, a state I would come to know too well. In the Botanical Gardens, I strolled among her exotic foliage, hand in hand with a man who would soon enough misuse my love, although I didn't know it then. The day felt brittle, as if the sky was made of the thinnest glass. Although I paid visits to her often in the past, I didn't divulge to him that this park and I were well acquainted…and she did not betray my secret. With all our shared encounters, she was indifferent toward me that day. She knew this was not Love and, thus, unworthy of her attention.

I long to wander Balboa Park, alone, and ask this sanctuary of romance to teach me what she knows about Love.

I first met her in 1989, as young hearts blossomed among her rose garden: he, Mr. Oxblood, and I, Miss Prussian Blue, two shy paramours meandering along her starlit paths. Without words, we spoke of our implicit Love through scented floral filigree, as he cascaded pink-petaled missives down upon my head and together we tossed waves of scented bliss into the fountain. He tucked a few of these sweet remembrances within his pocket. I was happy then. It was perfect, and she smiled and anointed us.

Did she recognize then this Love would endure almost a decade? Did she see that each would forever keep the other's heart within them, even now?

I long to wander Balboa Park, alone, and ask if she was aware, four years later, that he, brimming with Love, recalled for me, reluctant and unsure, our countless nights spent drifting through her splendor:

Why can't you allow today to be like holding hands in Balboa Park? Park of Spanish Porticos and you, content. We were like the courting frogs in the lily pond by the balustrade next to the Botanical Gardens.

Content. That's all I've ever asked from Love.

I long to wander Balboa Park, alone, pleading with her to share her views on Love. I want her to explain why, on that Friday in July 2010, she released his hand, allowing him to slip from her embrace onto the asphalt below.

The newspaper headline read, "Man dies after jump from Balboa Park Bridge." Stark words to me who required a novel's worth of explanations. I always knew, contrary to his friends' assurances, as only lovers know, this would be his fate. Yet I still have things I yearn to say, of love and encouragement, and atonement for my missteps, if only time were mutable.

No silent grave to visit, I want to wander this "Park of Spanish Porticos," alone, listening for her answer to my question: is True Love eternal? I wrote to him, after I heard the news, of love and regret, days after my own mother's death.

I long to wander Balboa Park, alone, and ask her to remind me that I already know all she could ever teach me about Love.

A PLAYLIST FOR AN OVERDUE VISIT

Jase,

I miss the lost art of the mixtape, don't you? And it was an art, wasn't it? A self-portrait painted with musical notes. These Maxell cassettes proclaimed, "This is who I am. These are my sensibilities, and if you don't enjoy my handcrafted present to you, then other incompatibilities surely exist." These labors of love demanded hours of consideration, combing through music collections, selecting the perfect song to open our compilation, an amuse-bouche to launch the perfect musical meal. We'd shove a pencil in the take-up reel, advancing the leader tape far enough so our first selection would begin straightaway. From there, choosing tracks would progress swimmingly until we approached the end of side A. The ideal piece was either too long for the length of remaining tape, cutting the song off midstream, or too short, leaving a minute of unused blank tape, an equally unforgivable faux pas in the mix-tape-crafting world. We'd have to locate a piece, befitting the tape's mood, which fit within the time remaining. Our final choice often wasn't our first option and, frequently, plan B didn't work either. The track meeting the criteria was often an option we would have otherwise overlooked, a musical concession. Once perfected, we'd snap off the write-protection tabs, lest our labors be overwritten, scribbling a label, an esoteric title like "Music for Moonlight and Red Wine" or, in contrast, a detailed cataloging of song, album, and artist.

If I were to create a mixtape for you today, a playlist for you on this drive, what would I include? The first track I'd select would be fun and playful, something like "Koop Island Blues." "England" by The National would have to make an appearance. The first time I heard that tune, parked in the structure at the Fashion Island Mall, thoughts of you leapt to my mind. Released in America in spring of 2010, you were still with us, but only for a few more months. I wonder if you heard it, if you were moved. I didn't discover its wistful refrain until later, and I remember crouching in my driver's seat, my emotions spilling down my cheeks, recalling sweeter days, a memory of a memory. It's strange, isn't it, that a song we never heard together should evoke remembrances of us. I discovered later that the record label was 4AD. Our beloved label, no wonder the tune conjured thoughts of you. I'd also include another National song, the less familiar, "Exile Vilify," but I wouldn't record the two pieces back-to-back. You'd appreciate the piano, but I'd insist on your patience, requiring a little musical foreplay first.

When the notion of recording you a current mixtape for my visit arose, I started a Spotify playlist I imagined you'd like, songs to accompany The National and Koop. At first, I succeeded in adding a mere handful, but slowly the collection grew. I restrict my quota of melancholy music these days, limiting my possibilities. "Anthem" by Emancipator and its violin made the cut (primarily for a little melody at 3:00 that evokes my wistful smile), and at least one song by Andrew Bird. One of my particular favorites is "Roma Fade," but I'd opt for a more somber piece, the slower version, "Gypsy Moth," with more violin or "Hover I." Actually, I'd include both.

I'm aware you've never heard many of these artists or songs, if any, half of them released after you made your fateful decision. I suppose this is just to say, if I could offer you a piece of myself today, musically speaking, as I take this long-overdue drive to the park to say goodbye, I'd surely include these.

Side A

"Koop Island Blues"	Koop
"Anthem"	Emancipator
"Nuvole Bianche"	Ludovico Einaudi
"Tomorrow"	Daughter
"England"	The National
"Outro"	M83
"Childhood's End"	Majical Cloudz
"Experience"	Ludovico Einaudi
"Gypsy Moth"	Andrew Bird

Side B

"Exile Vilify"	The National
"Breathe Me"	Sia
"Shelter – Loffler Remix"	Sasha
"Switzerland"	Daughter
"Codex"	Radiohead
"Hover 1"	Andrew Bird
"Youth"	Daughter
"Goodbye"	Apparat, Soap & Skin
"When It's Cold I Like to Die"	Moby, Mimi Goese

FAREWELL

I am prepared to walk a while, My Dear, but I arrive at the bridge first. It is a lovely expanse with its seven arches, the snaking asphalt below less so. The first thing I notice are the curved bars twelve feet high and scrollwork along the wall, removing the slightest remaining doubt that day was an accident, regardless of what your friends say. There are a few lover's locks attached to the ironwork; not many. The park workers must remove them at regular intervals. Should I have brought a lock for us, or at least flowers for you?

After lingering on the bridge for a handful of minutes, I continue along the path beneath the Spanish portico to the lily pond. I don't dare venture to the rose garden. The bushes cut back hard for winter, I couldn't endure wandering through the bare cane nubs, the fountain most likely drained. I don't venture within the Botanical Gardens either. I follow the path back along the other side of the bridge, surprised to discover I was steps away during my last visit to the park, standing beneath that Rococo-Spanish-Colonial spire of the museum. It's better this way. You wouldn't have tolerated me bringing another man, especially not one like Dexter. Not believing much in Fate these days (I long believed she was conspiring against us), I've found myself on the bridge at the precise time you decided to leave us. 3:00 p.m. Why did you choose broad daylight when the hours of the moon's interlude have always been your aesthetic? Was the time significant? At this hour, the cars and pedestrians on El Prado are numerous. Why didn't anyone try to stop you? Or perhaps someone did, hastening your decision.

I know it's not healthy for me to remain on this bridge too long. I must pull myself away from this place. Since I was fifteen, I've always been drawn to this beautiful, bittersweet melancholy. While living our history, I couldn't begin to comprehend what I so clearly see now: Our connection was unique, impossible to sustain but gloriously broken and exquisite. I wasn't ready then. I'm certain I wouldn't be ready for you, even now.

I should have been more careful with us. I survive, aware I played a part in your decision to leave us, but never fully knowing my role. I live, burdened by this disastrous folly I must own. I had to cleave a part of my heart to pretend I moved past you. I'm not pining, but I do miss you.

I miss your smile, I miss your sapphire eyes, I miss your hands and those long, beautiful fingers. Aristocratic—that's what your mother called them. It's draining, writing our story, re-reading your words. I'm reminded of Keats's epitaph: "Here lies One Whose Name was Writ in Water." I cannot bear thinking of your name writ in water. I'm trying, Jason…trying to leave a piece of you here.

Jason T. Brown
May 18, 1966 – July 23, 2010

ACKNOWLEDGMENTS

This book owes its existence to the support and contributions of many remarkable individuals. My deepest gratitude to Cherie Kephart, whose expertise and patience helped midwife this story into existence. Thank you for believing in me from the beginning and offering your invaluable guidance as I shaped this book into what you knew it could become.

I am immensely grateful to Sheri Quirt and Joe Pierson for their sharp eyes and attention to detail, and to Sally Rinehart for bringing my cover vision to life. To those who read early drafts and shared your reactions—Chris McNeil, Christina Yother, and members of our writers' group, The Writers' Room—your feedback was a constant source of motivation.

Thank you to friends and family who played a part in this long journey. To Robyn Marquardt and Yvonne Brizula, who set me on this path during that fateful walk, your inspiration means more than you know. And to those friends who journeyed with me, regularly checking in with, "How's the book going," and cheering me on through each twist and turn, I am deeply grateful for your unflagging support.

Finally, to Michael Gamstetter, who reminded me I "knew what I was doing" even when I convinced myself I was flailing—thank you for your unwavering belief in me and my abilities. Reading the messy details of past relationships wasn't easy for you, but your warm heart, moral support, and candid feedback are embedded in every chapter of this book—alongside your illustrations. For all of that, and more, I am endlessly grateful.